ROUTLEDGE LIBRARY EDITIONS:
EDUCATION MANAGEMENT

Volume 4

CREATING AND MANAGING THE DEMOCRATIC SCHOOL

CREATING AND MANAGING THE DEMOCRATIC SCHOOL

Edited by
JUDITH CHAPMAN, ISAK FROUMIN AND
DAVID ASPIN

Routledge
Taylor & Francis Group
LONDON AND NEW YORK

First published in 1995 by Falmer

This edition first published in 2018
by Routledge
2 Park Square, Milton Park, Abingdon, Oxon OX14 4RN

and by Routledge
711 Third Avenue, New York, NY 10017

Routledge is an imprint of the Taylor & Francis Group, an informa business

British Library Cataloguing in Publication Data
A catalogue record for this book is available from the British Library

ISBN: 978-1-138-48720-8 (Set)
ISBN: 978-1-351-04158-4 (Set) (ebk)
ISBN: 978-1-138-48782-6 (Volume 4) (hbk)
ISBN: 978-1-138-54530-4 (Volume 4) (pbk)
ISBN: 978-1-351-04142-3 (Volume 4) (ebk)

Publisher's Note
The publisher has gone to great lengths to ensure the quality of this reprint but points out that some imperfections in the original copies may be apparent.

Disclaimer
The publisher has made every effort to trace copyright holders and would welcome correspondence from those they have been unable to trace.

Creating and Managing the Democratic School

Editors

Judith D. Chapman; Isak D. Froumin; and David N. Aspin

The Falmer Press
(A member of the Taylor & Francis Group)
London • Washington, D.C.

UK The Falmer Press, 4 John Street, London WC1N 2ET
USA The Falmer Press, Taylor & Francis Inc., 1900 Frost Road, Suite 101, Bristol, PA 19007

First published in 1995

A catalogue record for this book is available from the British Library

Library of Congress Cataloging-in-Publication Data are available on request

ISBN 0 7507 0396 2 cased
ISBN 0 7507 0397 0 paper

Jacket design by Caroline Archer

Typeset in 10/12pt Bembo by
Graphicraft Typesetters Ltd., Hong Kong

Printed in Great Britain by Burgess Science Press, Basingstoke on paper which has a specified pH value on final paper manufacture of not less than 7.5 and is therefore 'acid free'.

Dedication

To our children and to all those who choose to work together on the journey to becoming inhabitants of the 'Open Society'.

Contents

Acknowledgments

This book was made possible by the generous assistance, cooperation and support of:

- Australian Commonwealth Government: International Division of DEET
- Callina Mining Company
- Institute of Educational Innovations, Russian Education Academy
- Krasnoyarsk State University
- Monash University
- Russian Ministry of Education
- Russian Association of Heads of Innovative Schools
- The University of Western Australia

Special appreciation is expressed to Per Dalin and staff of IMTEC for facilitating the process of interaction between educators in Russia and the western world; Jane Angus for her copy-editing of the manuscript; Colin Moyle and Tanya Putintseva for their careful review of the contents; and Robyn Wilson for her meticulous preparation of the book for publication.

Epigraph

Man's capacity for justice makes democracy possible, but man's inclination to injustice makes democracy necessary.

Reinhold Niebuhr (1892–1971)
The Children of Light and the Children of Darkness – 1944

Chapter 1

Introduction and Commentary

Judith D. Chapman, Isak D. Froumin, David N. Aspin

Origins of this Book

The origins of this book lie in a conference on 'The Educational Reform Process' held in Sochi, on the Black Sea, in what was then the Soviet Union, three weeks after the *coup d'état* in August 1991, when representatives of the former communist regime attempted, unsuccessfully, to reinstate the authoritarian system that had once governed the country and its satellites. The conference had been called by the Soviet Minister of Education, Dr Edward Dneprov, to address the ways in which an authoritarian and highly centralized educational system could be changed, in line with the spirit of democracy that was beginning to animate and find expression in many of the new forms and institutions in which Russian political and civic life was being reformulated. During the course of the conference, delegates were concerned to explore the ways in which a virtually totalitarian approach to school and system organization, management and pedagogy could be reformed to allow the various stakeholders of the nation's and the community's schools a real voice in the selection and prosecution of goals for education, that would be consonant with the principles of openness, democratization, and humanization.

This was a time of immense excitement. Educators in Russia and other states in the former Soviet Union were beginning to breathe the heady air of freedom for the first time in generations. Many had been involved in the demonstrations on the streets of Moscow and on steps of the White House only days before. Such colleagues had been prepared to sacrifice a great deal to realize the ideal of 'democracy'. In September 1991 many of our Russian colleagues believed that they now lived in an environment in which almost any educational innovation and change was possible. The atmosphere was exhilarating, almost euphoric.

Attending the Sochi Conference were fifty-five educators from western countries, who had been invited to Russia to share their visions and experience of educational reform. Western educators came from Europe (including strong representation from the United Kingdom, the Netherlands, Finland, Sweden, Denmark and Belgium), the United States, Canada and Australia.

The contributions that they all had to make to the work of the conference was positive and supportive. For many of both the western and Soviet delegates, this conference, held at that particular moment, proved to be a catalyst in forcing a fundamental reappraisal of their countries' policies for education and the function and purposes of schooling. Amongst the issues ripe for reconsideration, none, given the political atmosphere of the time and the location in which the conference took place, received more serious attention than the issue of the creation and management of schools in a modern democracy.

One of the interesting features to emerge from the conference was the extent to which there were common concerns between Australian and Russian educators. Australia only became a nation in 1901; yet, from its earliest days of European settlement, Australia was one of the newest and most vigorous proponents of the value of the democratic form of life and of the democratic principle embodied in the establishment and operation of its public and civic institutions. Russian and Australian delegates to the conference found they had much in common, and many matters of shared experience, mutual interest, and common concern to explore.

In the period 1991–4 a definite and committed form of collaboration between Australian and Russian educators was established and extended, and visits, meetings, seminars and workshops were held in Russia and Australia, in which representatives at the highest levels of educational and political life participated. All those who took part in these activities agreed as to the importance of the topics, problems and issues being addressed and the quality and *niveau* of the intellectual challenges and exchanges experienced. Both during and after the sessions in which all these matters were tackled, a determination grew and a consensus emerged that the fruits of our enquiries and explorations into the theme of creating and managing the democratic school should not go unrecorded but should be given expression in a publication addressing the issues that we believed to be of great and abiding concern, not only to our own countries, but also to many others around the world. It is believed that this resultant volume is the first publication to have emerged from the collaboration of Russian and western educators in recent times.

Since 1991, of course, there have been many changes and developments in the political economy and educational climate in both our countries. Some of the innovations that were envisaged in 1991 have been implemented. At the same time, however, colleagues have also become aware that the very radicalness of the changes they were contemplating brought with them such immense problems of implementation and the need for such large-scale injections of physical and financial resources, commitment, vision and personnel that the delivery of the reforms they dreamt of in 1991 would prove to be elusive, protracted, and exhausting.

Nevertheless, this pragmatic realization, though it might have attenuated the energies of some key workers in the field and, to some extent, dimmed the euphoria, has not diminished the enthusiasm for the work involved in transmuting educational systems, institutions and schools along the desired lines. Colleagues continue 'to toil and not to seek for rest, to labour and not to ask for any reward', to strive and not to yield before they see the end of the road on which they have embarked — to realize the vision that is represented by the institution of democracy in and for education.

In any case, as Popper warned, there never will be a time when educators can expect to reach finality on these matters: there will always be fresh challenges to face, new predicaments to encounter and perplexing problems to be solved. For of such dynamic and evolving character are human beings and human society, and so numerous the imperfections of their processes, that anomalies and irregularities are always going to occur, the appearance of which will cause difficulties and present obstacles to normal functioning and progress. It is only in the open society of institutions that rest upon and incorporate democratic principles that we can hope realistically to tackle such problems and proffer tentative solutions to them, not expecting these to hold good for all time, but to serve at least as our best theories of explanation or programmes of action for the present. This means that we must, for the time being, lay aside the fond hopes we may have had once, at a time when 'Twas bliss in that very dawn to be alive', and to forget for ever our aspirations to replace the outmoded models of the past with an instant calling down of the millennium. 'Sufficient unto the day', observes the democrat, 'is the evil thereof'.

Background to Reforms

As a preliminary to the opening of our enquiry into current prospects, possibilities and problems facing the project of democratizing education, we think it may be helpful at this point to give some account of the background and context within which proposals and programmes for the reform now being instituted have arisen. These may help us see how far our countries' education systems have come towards democracy and enable us to estimate perhaps how far they may still have to go.

Russia

At present more than 20,000,000 children aged 6 to 17 attend one of the 65,000 schools in Russia. There are over 1,4000,000 teaching and administrative personnel involved in the provision of educational services of all kinds. Compulsory schooling is from Years 1–9, although in reality most students remain at school until they have completed eleven years of schooling. There are eleven forms in most schools and, unless a family moves locality, children will attend the same district school for all of their school years. Traditionally, the Soviet system of education was highly centralized and unified. The control exercised from the centre over institutions, curriculum and pedagogy was heavily influenced by ideological considerations and forces. Principally, neither school-based personnel (students and teachers), nor stakeholders in the community (including parents) were allowed to express or disseminate any opinion on educational matters different from the position pronounced as official by the government. This resulted in the establishment and perpetuation of an extremely rigid hierarchical administrative structure, ruling out the possibility of the introduction of educational or organizational innovations at any level but that of the Communist Party of the Soviet Union Central Committee. It is true that from time to time individual teachers suggested new methods and techniques, but such initiatives encountered almost insurmountable difficulties. With rigid techniques and centrally dictated and approved content and format of textbooks, it is hardly surprising that teachers were dissatisfied with the perpetuation of this state of affairs. As a result we observe that, in 1985 when the period of *glasnost* and *perestroika* was ushered in, teachers were among the first to exercise and enjoy freedom of speech and public discussion.

In the period immediately after 1985, widespread dissatisfaction with the routine character of teaching practices and with the conservatism and monopolism evident in the pedagogic sciences was powerfully and broadly expressed in the newspaper pages and other media and fora of public discussion. It is interesting to note that the protests were articulated overwhelmingly by teachers rather than by education officials or parents. As a result, criticism and proposals for reform centred mainly on teacher interactions and pedagogy.

As an outcome of such discussions on these key matters there arose a movement concerned to develop a 'manifesto' of innovative pedagogy. A document entitled *The Pedagogy of Cooperation* was produced as the first publication devoted to the introduction of democratic reforms in school (Soviet Union, 1988). The most fundamental and far-reaching of its proposals was that concerned to change the nature and form of the relationship between teachers and students.

In this publication, along with the subsequent publication of their educational 'credos' by a number of well-known pedagogues, the emphasis was laid upon altering and improving the learning and educational process in the classroom in accordance with demands exerted by what were regarded as democratic norms. Unlike Australia, the emphasis in these early stages of the Soviet 'reform movement' was not laid on the need for democratic reforms in the administrative system. It is not wholly coincidental, therefore, that in the title of the second platform document, *Democratization of the Individual* (Soviet Union, 1989), the notion of 'democratization' is closely connected with the notion of the 'individual'. In this way the consensus concerning the immediate necessities for educational reform articulated in and by the public and pedagogic movement in the mid-1980s did not concern itself with the attempt to change the whole organization and administrative system of public education. It aimed rather at the introduction of a stress on establishing democratic relations in a school, a classroom or a teaching group.

It soon became obvious, however, that the new democratic approach to teaching and pedagogy could only be realized in forms of reorganization that necessitated alterations in curriculum, teacher training and the organization and administration of the educational system and the school. It is important to recognize, however, that, while alternative education, school councils, and pedagogic experimentation entailed the granting of increased autonomy to schools and altered administrative functions, such changes in organization and administration were secondary to the renewal of teaching methods and curriculum content.

Concern for, and commitment to, the introduction of reforms in these key areas of student learning and development remained strong throughout the 1980s and the spirit animating innovations in teaching activity and curriculum construction and process continued. These primary concerns were reflected in the proceedings of the All-Union Congress of Educationalists in 1987, where democratization was linked to the humanization of the curriculum. These developments and progressions were set out and summarized in the *The New Pedagogical Thinking* (Petrovosky, 1989).

By the late 1980s in the realm of school organization and management, however, although the institution of the school council was allowed and even encouraged as providing schools with bodies that would function as the basic 'agents for democratization', many school councils failed to take advantage of the opportunities offered them by the new reforms, or gave the impression that they were intending to introduce innovations but did not in fact do so. Moreover, some forms of the experience and practice of educational self-governance, which had been previously offered and made available in the programmes and activities of children's and young people's political organizations, had been quickly laid aside. A more concerted effort to bring about democracy in all aspects of schooling was required.

Against this background, Dr Edward D. Dneprov, who was appointed Soviet Minister of Education in 1990, suggested a more comprehensive and complex approach to the introduction of democratic reforms. He formulated guidelines for, and marks of, the reform of education, based on ten principles. These included concern for: democratization; privatization; regional independence; national and cultural autonomy; openness; alternative forms of education; development education; the introduction of humane values; an emphasis on humanities; and a concern for lifelong learning. Here new directions and guidelines for changes and innovations in organization and administration were linked to new requirements concerning the content and style of education. This link, however, was not to be merely declared; it had to be given a concrete expression in the reforms to be discussed in this volume.

Australia

In Australia schooling is compulsory for all young people aged 6 to 15 years. Constitutionally, State and Territory Ministers for Education have responsibility for all school education in their respective states and territories. However, the Commonwealth of Australia plays an important role in relation to the broad purposes and structure of schooling and in promoting national consistency and coherence in the provision of schooling. In cooperation with the states, the Commonwealth addresses resource, equity and quality issues through its general recurrent capital and specific purpose programmes. In addition it has specific responsibilities for migrants and aboriginal people, the provision of financial assistance to students, and Australia's international relations in education. There are more than 9000 schools attended by over 3,000,000 students in Australia.

Two basic sectors of schooling operate: a government sector, with approximately 72 per cent of all students; and a non-government sector, with about 28 per cent of all students. Within the non-government sector in each state there is usually a Catholic school system, other non-government systems, and independent schools.

In the late nineteenth and early twentieth centuries government schools in Australia were organized in large bureaucratic systems, characterized by a high degree of centralized control and a clearly defined hierarchy of authority, with an extensive set of regulations, designed to ensure fair, equitable and uniform treatment of members of the teaching service and efficient and equitable distribution of resources to schools. The operation of these systems was rarely questioned. School principals, staff, parents and students enjoyed and exercised few degrees of freedom. Structures were in place to enforce compliance in curriculum, personnel, finance, and facilities administration.

Recently however, particularly since the mid-1980s, there has been considerable divergence from this pattern, as school systems, in response to a broad range of social, political, economic and management pressures, have attempted to decentralize administrative arrangements and devolve responsibility for decision-making and the delivery of educational services and programmes to regions and schools. In carrying out these processes, policy makers, system-level administrators, representatives of teachers and parents associations, and school-based personnel, have found it necessary to address the considerable tension between bureaucratic concerns for hierarchy, impersonality, consistency, economy, and maximum efficiency, which characterized 'traditional' practices, and the late twentieth-century concern for democratic decision-making and increased local autonomy in the pluralist society of Australia.

In this reform effort it was believed that a qualitative improvement in education would be a function of improvement in the processes of decision-making at school and system level. This found expression in the creation of school councils and the redistribution of authority from positions residing in the bureaucracy to the authority of the local school community. The fundamental assumption underlying this democratic movement was the view that enhancing the capacities of school-based personnel to participate in decision-making would result in better educational decisions and improvement in the quality of education. It was believed that empowering the local school community to participate more directly in the processes of school management and direction would ensure that all members of the community would feel a sense of ownership in, and responsibility for, increasing the effectiveness and quality of the educational process and provision. But it is important to emphasize that this was a shift of policy within a set of existing and well-supported constitutional and legal arrangements already in place; school reform, conceived along the lines set out above and for the purposes mentioned, did not have to take place in a radically new context of altered political settlements.

The organizational reform, the strengthening of school autonomy and the emphasis on school-based decision-making entailed the modification of curriculum, teaching and learning styles and programmes. On the whole, however, it was organizational and administrative restructuring that was basic to the democratic reform movement in Australia. This provides an interesting contrast with the driving forces behind the democratic reform movement in Russia during a similar time in history. It is these kinds of contrasts and differences, together with the affinities and similarities, that have provided the material for this book.

The Contents of the Book

The Philosophical Underpinnings of Education in and for Democracy

A philosophical justification for the move towards the increase of democracy in education is provided by David Aspin in Chapter 1. Aspin begins our exploration of 'democracy' with a challenge: if we are to accept democracy as the basis for the operation of our schools and school systems, we must be able to show that it offers a way of institutionalizing and organizing our educational arrangements that is demonstrably superior and therefore preferable to any other. In response to this challenge, and after giving some account of the various ways in which democratic institutions and procedures may be characterized, Aspin proceeds to put forward a justification for democracy in education on the following grounds.

First, he provides a moral justification based on the notion of 'mutual beneficence'. He argues that incorporated in the democratic life are those principles that structure and define our relationships with others. In our idealized way of relating to each other these make possible, allow and regulate the interaction of equal, autonomous, moral agents. The moral foundations of democratic interchange are the principles of equality, justice, tolerance, respect for others and personal freedom. The notion of mutual beneficence, he argues, is the chief moral underpinning of the democratic enterprise.

It is reasonable, he concedes, that these moral underpinnings are built upon in different ways: what is in accord with the values, attitudes, beliefs and social practices of the Russian people may be different from what is in accord with those of the Australian people. What is important is that there is sufficient common ground to encourage common dialogue about matters of mutual interest and concern. The concept of dialogue and its attendant requirements for conversation, rationality and the peaceful resolution of problems, he argues, provide the framework to apply to democracy in educational institutions. The only way we can get a grip on the problems of policy and delivery is through debate which is rational and objective. We have to talk to each other, and recognize each other as human beings with similar interests and a shared concern to find common ground for the mutually beneficial resolution of our problems. Our first attack on this is through the democracy of conversation.

Second, Aspin suggests an 'epistemic justification' for democracy. This epistemic argument is derived from the work of the Austrian philosopher Karl Popper. Popper is interested in the ways in which 'open societies' deal with their problems: they do so by employing methods that are characteristic of the realm of science: advancing hypotheses about ways in which problems may best be tackled, and then subjecting those hypotheses to the most rigorous scrutiny and wide-ranging criticism. Hypotheses that resist the effort of falsification are then accepted provisionally as tentative theories or policies to apply to our problem situations, with the acceptance of the possibility that even these tentative solutions may have to be modified or abandoned as new difficulties or criticisms appear.

Consistent with Popper's notion of science and his approach to the solution of problems, in which 'truth' functions as a 'regulative principle', we may also classify democracy as one of those 'open societies' which is characterized by its willingness to expose itself and the procedures by which it operates to criticism and refutation. This kind of transcendental justification, Aspin argues, is the special virtue of the democratic form of life. He does not find this capacity and preparedness to tolerate, welcome and indeed seek criticism and refutation in forms of government or systems of organization that are tyrannical, autocratic, oligarchical or plutocratic. What education, democracy and morality are about is finding solutions to practical problems; this involves the production, proving and checking of policies, which in turn necessitates the pursuit of truth in its various forms. And the key part of that search is the concern for the criticism, correction and replacement of the theories with which we operate in addressing our problems and perplexities. This is the special virtue of democracy, which is not evident in other forms of political arrangement. Regrettably the pursuit of truth in all its forms has not been evident in all educating institutions either.

Too often in educating institutions we have been dealing with a 'bestowal' or 'gift' notion of knowledge — the notion of autocratic transmission, the handing over of knowledge to students by the teacher. But the prime function of schools is not the transmission to the student of a body of 'received' knowledge, Aspin argues; it is the initiation of the student into a set of tentative and objective theories about the world and of critical knowledge procedures, in which nothing is fixed, or absolute. In the 'open society' of the democracy of 'knowledge' everything is open to question.

If then we approach curriculum as giving students an *entrée* into these sets of tentative theories, cognitive and critical procedures, and this 'open society' of the learning community, we realize we are all equal participants and there is no autocracy or pedagogic hierarchy of subordinate–super-ordinate relations existing between 'student' and 'teacher'. If we adopt this approach to learning, we can readily see the implications for the social and political forms of organization that are thereby automatically entailed for adoption in both school and society. Schools as centres of learning and knowing would become agents for democratic being and acting. Induction into the world of knowing thus becomes an induction into the democratic form of life. This justification for democracy is a function of, and tightly tied to, the concept of knowledge; it connects both the epistemological and the axiological concerns of educating institutions. This justification is put forward as a way for examining democracy in schools and school systems in Australia, Russia and around the world.

The Political, Legal and Constitutional Context of Reform

In Chapter 1, then, Aspin has provided us with the philosophical framework within which the rest of this book's attack on the problem of creating and managing a democratic school may be shaped and articulated. But an equally necessary precursor to that attack is sufficient reference to, and analysis of, the political, legal and cultural conditions and context in which recent reform efforts in both Russia and Australia have originated and been essayed. An overview of these developments is presented in Chapters 2, 3, and 4.

In Chapter 2, the former Minister of Education of the Russian Republic, Edward Dneprov, takes the reader into an examination of the social, political and economic context within which current educational reforms have been taking place in Russia. Nearly every institution in Russia is, he maintains, in a state of flux. Russia is moving from 'a totalitarian regime to a civil society, from slavery economics to the market, from spiritual Gulag and the standardization of the personality to freedom and individuality'. The school, he concludes, 'is in the epicentre of a political whirlwind'.

In response to, and as a reflection of, these changes in the broader socio-political context, Dneprov identifies major changes taking place in educational philosophy, pedagogy, and the economics and financing of education. The chief principles underpinning changes in each of the areas of educational reform are democratization, pluralism, regionalization, openness and respect for national identity. The approach preferred in Russia for the application of these principles in institutionalized and organizational forms is seen to necessitate realism and independence in policy formulation, a dynamic, accelerated course for educational development, and an outcomes-oriented basis for quality control. In Russia, Dneprov contends, 'a new society cannot be built on the foundation of an old school . . . the major tasks of reform are to change the system of values, to promote decision making and self-dependence, to awaken active forces within the human soul, to change the mentality of society, and to do away with totalitarianism, communist and social ideology.'

Bringing about fundamental changes in education based on, and governed by, adherence to the foregoing principles will be difficult if not impossible to achieve within any society, without there being parallel and correlative changes in the legislative basis of education. Clearly therefore we need to examine the extent to which the constitutional, political and legal frameworks for education in our countries, Russia and Australia, provide a context conducive to the institution and exercise of democracy in our schools and education systems.

In Chapter 3 Yevgenii Tkachenko, the current Minister for Education, discusses the new 'Law on Education' in the Russian Federation. This law sets down the main priorities of education and lays the basis for state policy. The law is based on the principles outlined by Dneprov in Chapter 2 and provides for: the depoliticization of education; increasing autonomy for the regions; the democratization of education; differentiation and an individual approach to student learning. Tkachenko points out that of special pride to educational democrats in Russia is the fact that the law begins with the Article that 'The Russian Federation gives priority to the education sector'. Tkachenko maintains that the new Law on Education in Russia combines both individual freedom and general order — a conjunction of the autonomy of separate institutions and federal educational policy. This 'lays the foundations for the development of educational policy in Russia, and for the development of democratic consciousness in Russian society'.

The importance of the process involved in the enactment of this new Law on Education in Russia — its conception, promulgation, criticism and refinement, justification and defence, and the determination to see it through on to the Statute Book — cannot be overemphasized. It is one of the most far-reaching laws on education to have been developed in recent times. What is remarkable about it is that it provides the opportunity for a 'law' on education to be developed in the context of dramatically altered new circumstances of a state transmuting its entire political institutions and processes and economic policies, away from the totalitarianism of an autocratic state and a command economy to one of democratic freedom and the economy of the open market. As part of this restructuring politicians and the public see that one of the most crucial elements for reformation is to be found in education. In Russia therefore there is now a profound concentration on the legal reorganization of education in line with modern notions of the relationship between education and the democratic state.

In contrast, the broadly based constitutional and legal framework for education in democracies such as Australia have now been in existence for a century or more. In Australia, Birch argues in Chapter 4, there is a sense in which it is assumed that the legal and constitutional context of education is one in which democratic values will obtain and prevail. Notwithstanding this assumption, however, 'whatever democratic ideals may be attributed to ideas about the Australian way of life', these are not very apparent in the laws arranging for, and securing, the provision of educational services. Pedagogical concerns and the interests of those for whom primary and secondary schooling is provided — children and their parents — are of secondary importance in Australian educational law, Birch maintains. Instead, in the law on education as currently enacted and maintained in Australia and its states, it seems to be the case that 'the maintenance of the bureaucracy is pre-eminent and democracy and justice in the educational context are wanting'. If principles such as the interests of the child or the participation of parents were really central to education as provided in Australia, Birch concludes, much of the present legislation would require extensive review and replacement.

Democratic Values, Government Policy and System-wide Reform

Having established the conceptual, constitutional and legal bases for the idea of education and democracy, and creating and managing the democratic school, we now proceed to explore ways in which democratic values and principles may be embodied in government policy towards education and given expression in system-wide structural reforms. What emerges strongly from this examination is that different aspects of our understanding of democracy issue in different forms of institutional realization, and that these forms are very much conditioned and affected by the circumstances and contexts in which they arise. We conclude from this that no particular form of realization and application of the democratic ideal is necessarily superior to any other. As far as differences between preferred forms and versions of democracy go, what one has at any one time and in any one country is a situation in which governments are attempting to achieve a balance between different priorities, working in response to different pressures from the external environments and internal circumstances. Thus in Russia, for example, what emerges in the current reform of education and society is a concentration on two key concepts — those of democracy and humanism; in Australia, by contrast, the principal issue has been the tension between democracy, conceived in terms of participation in decision-making, and bureaucracy. These different preoccupations and concerns will obviously result in different types of policies and different forms of system, structure and school curriculum and organization.

In Chapter 5, Yelena Lenskaya begins this examination of government policy and system-wide reform by pointing to the major platform upon which the Russian government has attempted to build system-wide reformation and democratization. Fundamental to the educational reform process in Russia at the present time is the claim that a democratic society grows from the roots provided by a democratic school system: 'if a society wants to make itself free it gives more freedom to schools'. Russia's 'new society' 'could not be built on the foundation of the old school', claims Lenskaya. 'Every society that wants to become democratic starts with democratizing schools.'

Yet, she argues, there is a danger that some versions of democracy can lead to the total disintegration of a state system of educational provision. Democracy requires that people learn to be responsible for freedom, to accept that democracy is only possible when there is a mutuality of benefit and concern, and where rights and obligations for education are shared by all members of the community. This has implications for system-wide policy and provision in areas such as the curriculum, the financing of education, accountability mechanisms, the provision of parental choice and the existence and availability of alternative or independent schools. The main responsibility of the State and the major task of administrative bodies of education, Lenskaya argues, is to protect the rights of the child for a quality education in whatever conditions provide optimum 'possibilities for individual development'. This is the focus of the development of educational policy in Russia: a concern for the protection and promotion of the rights and freedoms of the individual child.

The challenge facing state systems of education is to achieve the appropriate balance between the promotion of the individual's autonomy and ability to participate in a free and democratic society, achieved as an outcome of education in a democratic school, *and* the responsibility of governments to ensure that priorities, agreed upon by the community and designed to protect the democratic rights of all citizens to equal access to, and participation in, education, are both in place and in effective operation.

Achieving the balance between individual and state rights and responsibilities has also constituted a major task in educational reform efforts in Australia. In Australia, however, less emphasis has been placed on the rights of the individual child in his or her growth towards autonomy. Rather more emphasis has been given to the rights of adult members of the educational community, particularly parents and teachers, to become involved in educational decision-making at the school site. This seems to have been the way in which democracy has been conceived in the development of recent educational policy and in system-wide reform in Australia. Thus, in Chapter 6, Jeffrey Dunstan describes the administrative structures that have been put into place in the state system of education in Victoria in the attempt to address the imperatives for change flowing from the particular conception of the democratization of education as community participation outlined above. He draws particular attention to the tension that may be observed to exist between demands for participation in decision-making at the local school level, which many people in recent times have taken to be the paradigm version of democracy, and the insistence of government and system officials that theirs is the responsibility for administering the system efficiently and effectively from the centre. In so doing they claim they are exercising the right held by elected governments in democracies to intervene, make and dictate decisions from the centre, on what they see as the peoples' behalf and for the welfare of all members of the community on an equitable basis, justified by their position in the central bureaucracy.

Dunstan examines the way in which resource allocation, review and accountability procedures, governance practices and curriculum and student-welfare provision have been altered in light of the recent focus on rights of the members of the school community to exercise their democratic prerogative and participate in decision-making. Alongside the democratic right of members of the community to participate in school decision making, Dunstan highlights the responsibility of the 'system' to ensure equity in provision of educational services and resources.

In Chapter 7 however, Brian Spicer claims that the real issue in the so-called democratization of Australian schooling in recent times has been one of 'power', rather than democratic rights. In this chapter he confronts the dilemma posed for governments facing the challenge of 'balance' by contraposition of 'the individual' and the 'collectivity'. Spicer urges that, in the pursuit of democratization in education, there should be a far greater mixture of both elements — of the individual freedom of the child to develop in ways that will address their particular needs and interests, and of the need for the whole community, at state and local level, to become equal partners in the shaping of the goals and future direction for its educating agencies.

Reform at the Level of the School

The form that increased democratization can take at the local level, with particular stress on the opportunities offered by school-based reform, is addressed in Chapters 8, 9 and 10. In Chapter 8, Alexander Adamsky argues that democracy is only possible when education is built on democratic values such as free choice, self-determination and the sovereignty of the individual personality. He maintains that these values, in contrast to totalitarian ones, are impossible to impose: they are born of themselves at schools from concentration upon educational practices and experiences that are rooted in the democratic impulse. Adamsky offers an account and provides an analysis of what he sees as the main innovative tendencies in Russian education from the 1950s onwards. He identifies three sources of democratic education in Russia: the Moscow methodologic circle; the Leningrad Frunze commune; and the 'teacher innovator' classes. Adamsky points to the ways in which the values embodied in the work of these reform movements became integrated into the 'brief renaissance of public education' which occurred during that time when Edward Dneprov was Minister of Education.

It is with considerable regret that Adamsky highlights the difficulties encountered by the major reformers associated with this 'renaissance'. He suggests that these difficulties were inevitable in the activity and experience of people working in any public organizations committed to reform, in a system of education that had its genesis and gained its motivating spirit in a totalitarian regime. He tells us how the reformers 'irritated officials, deputies, the population and they were banished with infamy from the Ministry . . . the official system of education is closed for development'. The only way forward for Russian education now, he contends, is through school-based change inspired by innovative communities of alternative educators in schools and universities everywhere.

Among the front rank of those who have pioneered a school-based approach to educational reform in Russia has been Oleg Gazman. In Chapter 9, Gazman presents an examination of school-based management in Russia, with particular reference to the development of schemes for student self-management. In this connection it is interesting to note the substantial commitment to making and sustaining an advance in student self-management in Russia, in comparison with schemes of student involvement in countries such as Australia, which have been much less clearly conceptualized, instituted or sustained.

Gazman sees the process of democratic reform in Russia as continuing to be fraught with difficulty. He identifies the deteriorating economic circumstances and growing poverty in Russia as major barriers to school renewal, not only in respect of the provision of material resources to schools, but, perhaps more importantly, in respect of the impact they have on the provision and availability of professional development that is so vital a part of reform and so necessary to retrain the existing teaching and administrative workforce and to educate parents into a new way of viewing education. As Gazman argues, the fundamental psychological shifts necessary to bring about democracy in education and in society depend very largely on the possibility of qualitative changes taking place in the social and economic life of the country.

Limited resources for education in Russia are also being used as excuses to justify the creation of large schools. Schools in which 2000–3000 students are being educated create, according to Gazman, problems of resource provision and management of such magnitude that principals have little time for educational and other organizational concerns. As a result there is a deficit of creative solutions to educational problems.

Despite problems such as these, Gazman is optimistic. He refers approvingly to the increasing importance attached to 'cooperative learning' and the creation of a number of pilot schools and experimental sites where school staff have devised their own curricular and distinctive organizational image and avers that these developments give good grounds for optimism. Increasing progress in the democratization of education Gazman sees as being made possible through the emergence of new types of schools, which will stimulate independence and the creative activity of school principals, teachers and pupils.

Such qualities are seen as fundamental to the creation of effective schools, whether they be in Australia or Russia. In Chapter 10, Clive Dimmock shows, with reference to the school-effectiveness research, how many of the core values associated with democracy, such as tolerance and respect for others, concern for equity and equality, and the ability to make judgments and choices promoting individual satisfaction and community welfare, can be developed and nurtured in effective schools. Effective schools above all promote a learner- and learning-centred culture and these are indispensable prerequisites for any forum in which the lessons arising from the democracy of knowledge-getting are going to be given greatest point of purchase in the development of citizens ready to serve and function in a participative democracy.

Democratization, School Reform and the Life of the Child

The implications of democratization for the life of the child in the school are discussed in Chapters 11, 12 and 13. In Chapter 11, Michael Herriman begins by concentrating on what he sees as the chief value and principal requirement in any form of life claiming to be democratic — that of personal freedom. He shows that this freedom is founded upon the arguments advanced by Locke and Mill that set up individual autonomy as the bulwark of the morality that is supposed to be confirmed by its delivery in the modern democratic state. The continuation of that emphasis, argues Herriman, requires a minimum of government interference in direction and control of individual citizens' lives; and the problem is that there are powerful arguments for emphasizing the necessity of the individual's being subjected to the larger interests, claims and representations of the State. This leads to a situation in which, by the ways in which it chooses to establish and exercise its supposed commitment to open institutions and procedures, the State can end up being profoundly anti-democratic. And if this danger exists with respect to relations between the individual and the State, then how much more must they exist with respect to the role and functioning of the school.

Herriman sees the form in which modern schools are controlled and administered as being bureaucratic, authoritarian and fundamentally conservative. He points out that the modes of teaching, the relations between teacher and taught, and the hierarchic forms of organization and administration all militate against the main value of democracy: personal freedom. From this perspective, there is a real risk that, without profound and fundamental change in the conception of educational institutions, the relations between teachers and students in them, and, above all, in the ways that such institutions are organized and managed, a real democracy will never be achieved. Herriman therefore concludes by arguing forcefully that 'democratic values can only be achieved when the total structure of education is democratic'. Herriman sets out some of the ways and means in which effective conditions of, and for, the increase of democracy may be insisted upon and implemented in the reform of school structures, styles of management, and curriculum. He echoes Aspin's point about the implications arising for education in democracy from its epistemic commitments by adding that, 'This condition includes the need for democratic methods of enquiry and teaching styles.'

The practical implications of this position are discussed in Chapter 12 by Alexander Tubelsky, a principal of one of Russia's most innovative schools. In the attempt to help children to develop the capacity for self-determination — one of the prime prerequisites for the development of a democratic spirit — the school of which Tubelsky is principal is attempting to establish an account of the pedagogical conditions under which both children and teachers are able to acquire and reflect on the experience of democratic behaviour. Tubelsky reports that teachers, parents and students in the school are especially attentive to two guiding principles: first, that all students and teachers are to realize that they are all equally involved in the generation and adoption of the norms and rules of school life; and second, that the laws of the school should be developed gradually as the school community confronts its emerging problems. In Tubelsky's school, problems are to be resolved only by democratic means.

It is interesting to note Tubelsky's observation that in such a school context the children acquire and accumulate the experience of democratic behaviour faster and more effectively than teachers. The reason, he suggests, lies in the stereotypical thinking of adults who have spent all their lives under the conditions of the totalitarian system; to this extent children and young people come to the enterprise of democratic education with visions and preconceptions more untrammelled by the coercive imperatives of the past and with their spirits more ready for the freer opportunities offered by the present. As against the positive effects of this set of starting conditions Tubelsky notes that a further disadvantage arising from the previous stereotypical thinking of the teaching force, brought about by conformity to the norms and standards of a totalitarian state, is found in the pedagogical approach of many Russian teachers 'in which [he or] she transmits knowledge rather than organizes the process of acquiring living knowledge'. As a result of teachers holding this particular view of their pedagogical function, many tend to assume an authoritarian approach in their interpersonal conduct towards the students.

Tubelsky calls for greater cooperation between teachers and academics in order to bring about change in the content of curriculum and the methods and procedures of teaching and learning. In Tubelsky's school we see put into action a philosophy of knowledge in accordance with which the teacher relinquishes claims to absolute truth and in so doing adopts a teaching style which is far more democratic. In this example of institutional pedagogic reappraisal and reorientation we see the practical application of the philosophical underpinnings of the ideals of democratic education, as articulated by Aspin in Chapter 1, and advocated by Herriman for a democratic school.

The volume ends with Chapter 13 in which Froumin considers the child's growth towards becoming a responsible and free member of a democratic society. He maintains that this is not merely a process of socialization concerned with the acquisition of social norms, but a whole pattern of organic development and growth, one which, informed by the work of key theorists such as Dewey, Gessen, Vygotsky and Mead, incorporates democratic values into deliberate and self-conscious forms of special pedagogical expertise and classroom procedures deployed and in operation at every stage of development towards maturity.

Discussion: A Comparative Analysis of Educational Reforms in Russia and Australia

The Value of East–West Comparisons

A popular quotation from Leo Tolstoy's novel *Anna Karenina* says, 'All happy families are alike, every unhappy family is unhappy in its peculiar way'. There are few models of educational reform which are happy and successful in all respects but there are many troublesome and dramatic ones. And each of them is troublesome in its own way. This analysis of educational reform in Russia and Australia was embarked upon for a number of reasons. The democratic reforms in Russia in the late 1980s, and in Australia from the mid-1980s onwards, appeared to be inspired by a similar concern for democracy and its increase in the educational setting. Educationalists in both countries, working independently on the democratization of their schools and education systems, developed interesting approaches and ideas, that we deemed to be suitable and fruitful for cross-cultural exploration.

A cross-cultural analysis applied to the study of democratization in education has the potential to be illuminating, helpful and fecund, inasmuch as the problems and difficulties of democratization in education are broad, diverse and complex. Only by viewing the whole range of problems and difficulties from different angles and perspectives can one possibly hope to achieve a more fully informed, heterogenous and yet comprehensive understanding. In this way we may be better placed to study the problems, frame hypotheses and generate theories with which to tackle the particular difficulties we encounter in our own systems' and institutions' attempts to create and manage democratic schools.

There is another reason, which makes the comparative analysis important. Some Russian and western policy makers and educationalists suppose that the problem of democratization in western educational systems has been practically solved, and that Russia should merely copy one of the western systems already in place. In recent times, however, some western reforms have been much criticized. A number of problems, which seemed to have been solved, have reappeared and the results of the reforms did not meet the expectations according to which they were instituted. From the perspective of Russian policy makers and educationalists, a study of the western experience of reforming education is invaluable, but it does not present models for replication.

From the perspective of Russian educationalists it was deemed of much greater utility and value to compare their own approaches to democratization with those of a western country, equally concerned with democratization, and to observe the achievements and failures of systems, institutions and schools in that country, before embarking upon the large-scale educational reform process in Russia.

The democratic reforms in Russia also provide an interesting focus for western study, for Russia is a country in which it could be argued that the gradual, steady and cumulative evolution and development of 'democracy' was interrupted. The democratic reforms in schooling currently under way in Russia are not supported by a lived experience of the democratic mentality in application among the public at large, or by the existence and practices of democratic institutions of popular authority and power in the broader social context. The democratic reforms, which are taking place in education, are perceived to be, and to furnish, the basis upon which it is hoped that democracy will grow and flourish in Russian society at large.

The experiment in which Russian education is engaged is almost 'pure' in the sense that the innovations conceived and implemented to bring about democracy in schools are starting from what is virtually a 'blank sheet' and, from the political/ideological point of view, are unconstrained by the pressures of the existing political norms and conventions, with which institutional change in the West is so often beset.

Similarities and Differences Between Australian and Russian Experiences of Reform

An examination of reform efforts in Australia and Russia highlights some important differences in the nature of the reforms, the reasons for their introduction, and the ways in which that introduction has proceeded:

- Australian reforms were both 'top down' and 'bottom up'; they were initiated from 'the top', and were driven forward and supported by powerful interest groups in the education service, the community and the public at large. Russian reforms were initiated from 'the bottom' by teachers and the teaching profession.
- The primary target of Australian reforms was the democratization of administration and the development of school-based management, in the belief that the empowerment of teachers and parents for participation in decision-making at the school site would in time enhance the quality of education provided for children in the classroom. In Russia the primary target was democratization of the teacher–pupil relationship.
- Russian reforms developed at a time and under circumstances in which there was still total state control of schools. In Australia state schools were already in competition with independent schools, in which over 25 per cent of all pupils were enrolled.

- Australian schools were enjoying the increasing degrees of autonomy that had been granted since the 1960s and 1970s. Russian schools were subject to a rigidly centralized direction and control, and had been so for decades.
- Australian teachers were working primarily for what they believed would be the improvement of their schools and their students. Their Russian colleagues had an ambition to reconstruct their entire society in the democratic vein.
- The drive for the democratization of education took its impetus amongst Russian pedagogues as a reflection of the general exultation over the possibility of political reform leading to democracy. In Australia democratic values were considered to have been embedded in society and its institutions from the beginning.

On the other hand, the following beliefs may be observed to have been held in common by reformers in both countries and may therefore be seen to have been shared as joint starting points for processes of the Russian and Australian reforms:

- a dual interest in offering choice to individuals and to increasing social justice; and
- the impulse to tackle and turn round parents' conservative attitudes towards innovations in school.

Moreover in the reform process the following steps seem to have been taken in both countries:

- the formation of school councils;
- the formation of 'councils for education' or boards at different levels of administration;
- a strengthening of the emphasis on the necessity of diversification in the teaching of gifted and handicapped children;
- the decentralization of the decision-making systems; and
- a strengthening of the independence of the school and individual teachers.

Naturally, however, given the different circumstances, causal background and reasons for the impulse towards education innovation and reform in our two countries, there existed considerable differences in the ways and means by which those reforms were introduced and the procedures and progress of those reforms in practice. Notably:

- The Russian reform makers emphasized the character and style of the changes in teaching methods and programmes. The Australian reformers stressed organizational and administrative restructuring.

- In Russia the movement for the introduction of democracy in education was intended primarily for the work of pupils and teachers in classrooms and schools. In Australia it extended to, and included, parents and the general public. In Russia, therefore, it was new forms of self-government in school councils that were most attractive for pupils. In Australia there was less pupil involvement but far more involvement by parents in the control and management of schools.
- Relative to each other, Australian educationalists were more concerned with the evolution of the 'traditional' system and its improvement. Russian educators expected a revolution in their schools, and saw as indicators and features of the revolutionary move towards democracy in education an emergence of alternative schools and new pedagogic approaches in the classroom.
- Along the road towards, and in the process of, democratization, many Australian schools employed practical improvements and single techniques in classroom curriculum and teaching method. In Russia teachers have attempted to introduce a whole set of, and approaches to, educational-reform measures based on, and incorporating, entire integrated pedagogic systems (such as those of Steiner, Montessori, A.S. Neill etc.).
- The broad thrust of Australian reform was meant for the development of the general public school. The direction democratic reform took in Russia favoured the setting up of, and recourse to, a broad 'alternative' schooling sector.

Notwithstanding these differences in form, process and orientation, however, it is worthwhile noting that the reform strategies and approaches put into effect in both countries encountered difficulties that were very much alike. Mention should first be made of the difficulties encountered in the introduction of participative decision-making into the management of classrooms and schools. For one thing, both in Russia and Australia many teachers were unprepared for the new range, modes and styles of interaction with their students; for another many members of the new schools' councils lacked competence in those areas in which they were now required to be capable of functioning. As a further difficulty, many school-council members lacked qualifications, experience and even the taste for the now necessary participation in decision-making on such difficult, complex and demanding matters as resource distribution, staff selection and the development of teaching programmes. Moreover the facilities and resources of the pre-service and retraining systems available were simply not capable of meeting the demands of reform and the needs of the teachers in developing the ability to respond to them.

Secondly, the increasing independence granted to, and enjoyed by, the school has inevitably heralded the start of a process of disintegration of the united educational system and of the stress on centrally dictated and unified teaching programmes and requirements. In the eyes of some, this development carries with it the danger of lowering educational standards, of countering the otherwise sound arguments for the movement towards, or continuation of, a 'national curriculum', and of diminishing the possibility of achieving national goals for education.

Thirdly, the relaxation of some traditional requirements for, and marks of, discipline in schools and classrooms has resulted in some members of the community perceiving a growth among young people of school age in what they see as antisocial behaviour, and, along with and as result of that, a certain neglect for the system of values established and held by adults and the community.

We conclude that a number of negative features, difficulties and problems in the introduction and implementation of innovation and reform arising from the impulse towards increasing the democratization of educational institutions, systems and schools can be perceived to be common both for Russia and Australia. Among these may be included:

- the absence of a well-developed theory of the democratization of education;
- the lack of coordination at various levels of the educational system; and
- the lack of resources, programmes and efforts that are required to increase and expand the range and level of the necessary competences that should be expected of all participants in the educational process.

It seems to us in consequence that few positive and constructive lessons regarding the optimum conditions under which there can be effective implementation of educational innovation and reform appear to have been learnt by those trying to overcome the difficulties inherent in, and thrown up by, the reform effort. Both in Russia and Australia attempts are being made to reinforce the integrity of the educational systems by recourse to the imposition of a set of centrally dictated uniform educational standards. Unfortunately, most of the steps in this process are not based on a comprehensive and theoretically integrated analysis of the need for a fundamental and thorough-going restructuring of education, in all its forms and agencies, entailed by the move towards democratization, viewed as both process and outcome. We believe an analysis of this kind to be necessary for giving contemporary educators, determined to introduce and increase democracy in education, the prerequisite insights and solid foundations called for in the planning of new advances in the reform of education.

Problems and Challenges in the Conceptualization and Process of Democratic Reform

Among some of the thornier issues and problems to be faced in creating and managing a democratic school, we have been able to identify the following:

education, democracy and social change; democracy and the market economy; democracy and the life of the child in school; and democracy, the school and the system.

Education, Democracy and Social Change

Issues for consideration:

- Should we endeavour to prepare children in school to live in a democracy which takes the form of the contemporary society in which they live or should we provide them with an experience of democracy in school life, which they can use to develop a better form of that society in the future? What should be done when the experience of democracy in the school actually precedes the democratic experience in society itself?
- How does a community develop an education system when it finds itself facing the larger challenge of responding to changes in the form, structure and direction of society — a society which is not yet sure what form its future identity and preferred direction is going to take?
- Is it right to subject the child to experiments in social and political institutions that are concomitant parts of the school's endeavour to adjust to the organic and dynamic changes in the nature and form of the society of which it is an educating agency?

Democracy and the Market Economy

Issues for consideration:

There are different conceptions of democracy and an open society. Some believe that the democratic state has the right to intervene in its citizens' lives so as to shape them for the best interests of community welfare including individual autonomy; others hold that 'individual autonomy' comes before every other value and that, for that reason, the State has minimal rights to intervention in the private lives of individual free agents, who may use their own powers and resources to secure access to the 'goods' they want.

For the first group, education, health and social-welfare benefits are seen as necessary services which the State should provide in common for all as a public entitlement; for the second group, such 'services' are facilities or utilities which individuals should be able to purchase as though they were 'commodities' on the open market. Both interpretations are effects of the working of powerful ideologies in the current debate about the nature and work of those agencies and institutions we should establish or employ in pursuit of the freedom all might enjoy in a democracy.

But the question may be asked as to whether the ideology and language of the market can be validly employed and appropriately realized in the education field. Given the moral character of education's work as an agency operating ultimately for community benefit and improvement, we may ask whether it is proper to create competition between schools and try to create a real 'market' for educational goods. And in such a case, how does one provide equitable opportunity and real choice for all parents and children? What are the implications for democracy in the delivery of education and for the management of schools and school systems, when education moves from being seen less as a public good and more as a commodity subject to the pressures of the market-place?

Democracy and the Life of the Child in School

Issues for consideration:

- What form shall be taken by the work and experiences in the life of the child in a school which values democracy? Are democratic values and principles the same for adult society and for the society of children? If they are, how shall they be best given institutional realization? If they are not, how shall the school best prepare the student for life as a citizen in the adult form of democracy?
- In all community debates concerning the optimum form and mode of organization of its educating institutions, does democracy demand the question be raised as to who shall have the overriding right to speak on behalf of the child? Shall the child be seen as having rights, and if so, how far shall they extend? How shall the community confer rights on the child and what form and content shall they be given? When do the child's rights emerge and in conformity with what stages of development do they expand until the full range of rights is granted? How shall this be measured? Who plays a role in conferring the rights? What are the correlative obligations that come with the rights and how shall children and young people be taught and expected to exercise them?
- This leads to the larger and more general question of the best form of organization for students in our schools. Where, for example, on the spectrum of control, do we think institutional arrangements for democratic and effective organization and administration to secure quality in education is best placed? With respect to the involvement of students in running schools' internal organization, for example, we might counterpose:
    - (a) the 'traditional' system in which senior students are appointed by the principal and staff to exercise delegated power to organize the behaviour of students (sometimes involving the

use of punitive sanctions of various sorts serving as public marks of their designated authority), such appointments generally being made on the presumption of such students having special wisdom or capacity to conform to what principal and staff perceive or desire to be the dominant culture and ethos of the school;

(b) a system in which all students have equal rights, where each is free to speak and where each student has authority to require of everyone else acceptance of, and conformity to, a set of rules to regulate the effective behaviour, learning and interaction of all members of the school community.

Democracy, the School and the System

Issues for consideration:

- How is it possible to develop and sustain alternative 'systems' of education at the same time as ensuring respect for equity, social justice, access and inclusivity rather than exclusivity, and preferential treatment for a favoured few? How does one provide access to, and enjoyment of, the opportunities offered by a high-class and empowering curriculum to all students (whether male or female, of a majority or minority ethnic linguistic group, disadvantaged or talented, urban or rural), in such a way that all of them emerge with life chances significantly expanded and enhanced as a result of their experiences and achievements within the school?
- How does a government, in its provision of a national system of education, deal with the dual challenge of granting to schools the powers of managing their own affairs and promoting and providing for an increased sense of self-consciousness and self-determination among school-based personnel without letting the system become so diversified that it may lose all internal coherence, consistency and sense of direction, and without compromising, limiting or abolishing other structures, procedures, or goals, that have national relevance, importance and utility?
- How might a school develop a positive sense of community within itself and, in pursuit of its goals, involve itself with members, agencies and representatives of the community more broadly?
- How do we learn to teach, develop and measure the complex and sophisticated abilities and competences presupposed by, and necessary for, a sense of involvement in the community and a commitment to democratic processes and forms of life?
- How do we achieve a consensus on the values a community might require of and expect to see reflected in the operations of its educating

agencies? How might schools work together with the wider community to prepare students for those times and occasions when a national or regional government proposes to introduce changes, some of which may well be alien or even antithetical to those values or structures espoused and cherished by a particular element of that larger society — even to the level of the individual school?

'Touchstones' for Use in Formulating and Implementing Educational Innovation and Reform

In our deliberation on these issues, a number of areas of common agreement and shared understanding have emerged. For example, we are certain that:

- The school should have a clear commitment to the values and principles embodied in a philosophy of democracy as well as to its practices and procedures.
- The pursuit and dissemination of knowledge and understanding are the principal preoccupations of all institutions in a democratic society. This implies that the teacher, the student and other members of the school community are all bearers of knowledge in the learning community, that all have an interest in its transmission and questioning, and are all, in their own ways, contributors to, and responsible for, its claiming, promulgation, extension, refinement, assessment, certification, correction and continuing communication.
- The extension, communication and evaluation of public knowledge, and a commitment to the increase of community welfare and of individual and social justice, are the prime values in education and democracy.
- For these reasons schools need to be aware of their dual function in respect to education for democracy: they need to teach children about democracy and to get them to practise it. In both school and society we have to secure acceptance of the virtues of intellectual uncertainty and tolerance as the prime principles through which the realm of knowledge and the realm of values combine and coalesce. The enterprise of immersion in democratic procedures and contexts needs to be tempered with the realization that we are helping children to deal with human imperfections, on a rational and humane basis.
- In education for democracy we need to balance the competing demands of duty and inclination; internal choice and external force, realizing that we might never see all our students motivated in all their doings by internal choice and inclination.
- Individual liberty is promoted by a commitment to intellectual freedom based on and incorporating the public, objective and impartial character of knowledge and understanding. Associated with this is an

awareness of, and a determination that, the outcome of one's education shall have point and purpose, that it will affect our lives as autonomous individuals and increase our capacity to make a contribution to the welfare of the community. In this way both parts of one's life as a citizen are involved in realizing that one can be effective in one's life in society. Thus there is a need for both an intellectual and a practical evaluation of democratic values and institutions.

- Contemporary educational systems and institutions, if they are to be democratic, need to undertake an appraisal of the granting, suitable ordering and orientation of the rights of children and their parents, and the responsibilities expected of them, and of the ways in which this will impinge on priorities for school reform. These will then provide schools, students, parents and the community with knowledge of the preconditions for the implementation of democracy in educating institutions.
- The State has an important role to play as a guarantor of schools', students', and parents' rights against local pressures, and should provide strong leadership in helping all educational institutions and stakeholders take the question of rights seriously.
- A commitment to the discovery and institution of soundly based approaches to the democratization of education will mean that one cannot democratize just one part of the education system: one must look overall at the content, administrative structures, modes of delivery and means of evaluation, in the whole and in parts, of the system, the curriculum, and the values expressed in the educational programme. Such things need to be interconnected. If one wishes to achieve an integration between all elements and aspects of the democratic process in education, one must have a democratic system, a democratic school and a democratic classroom.
- If we are sincere in our desire to create a democratic atmosphere in a school, we should appreciate the point that part of democratic procedures is a requirement that power should be widely distributed. In a school, this means that thought will have to be given to ways in which it is desirable and possible to distribute powers of decision-making and action.

  Furthermore it will be necessary to provide an arena in which students are given the opportunity to think about change, and be responsible for its implementation and evaluation. If students are not involved in decision-making, there is a danger that they will develop a diminished sense of efficacy and their capacity to be responsible for change, with the consequent risk of their transferring this assumption to their role in the wider society. Just as a person who has played a part in developing a law is likely to have a stronger commitment to the implementation of that law, so a citizen who has come equipped ready, willing and able to take an active part in the governance and service of the community, and has come to understand the rights and responsibilities of citizenship in a democracy, as a result of being informed, shaped and prepared by previous experience in an educating institution, will be less likely to let others take power and exercise control in their name and on their behalf.

This means that students must be prepared for the exercise of autonomous political judgment and community action by immersion and engagement in a programme of activities, both formal and informal, in school, that enshrines the values, principles and practices of democracy. Thus in all the endeavours of a school that would be truly democratic, the commitment to openness and participation in the acceptance of responsibility and the exercise of distributed power must be real, and not merely token.

- Education should prepare us to cope with the psychological, moral and economic challenges and threats that we may have to face in modern life in a democracy, by equipping us with both the knowledge requisite to meeting those challenges successfully and the competences of a critical intelligence and the skills of practical wisdom (what Aristotle called 'phronesis'). We need to equip students with a brave mind and a brave heart to accept differences, stand up to and be able to deploy criticism without fear, and accept that there are many good ways of doing things and of effecting change in our educating and social institutions.
- We would do well to take, as our motto and our watchword, acceptance of the premise that democracy is both a goal and a means of education.

Some Paradoxes

Arising from our deliberations on such matters, we have come to be aware, amongst the problems and issues to be tackled in this exploration of democracy and education, of the point (raised explicitly in Chapter 1) that paradoxes, both theoretical and practical, remain in the concept of democracy in and for education. These include at least the following:

- In the name of freedom as a part of, and condition for, democracy, some citizens may have to be forced to do certain things or follow certain norms that they would not willingly choose for themselves. This is especially so with the institution of education, where, in the name of democracy, we require compulsory school attendance for all children at school. This raises the question of how one may use compulsion and justify the use of force in helping children to become free.
- Freedom may be a value but it does not guarantee happiness. The sense and functioning of being a citizen in a modern 'free' society

presents us with an agonizing dilemma of existentialist proportions — the awareness that being free in today's society may pose many challenges, threats and even dangers to our psychological and moral well-being.

- Democracy implies the right of the majority to make a decision but the majority may not always be 'right'. One example generally relates to the fact that a majority of voters in some countries continues to demand the reintroduction of capital punishment, yet this is a proposal that their parliament has consistently rejected. As far as education is concerned, we may point to the example that in the USSR in the past women could not be denied the right to an education, whereas in the allegedly more 'democratic' Turkestan of today, female children may be denied the right to attend school. It is certainly paradoxical that, in what was regarded previously as a totalitarian state the 'right' to full female educational emancipation was secured and guaranteed.
- It could be argued that what some people regard as one of the most undemocratic institutions in Australia, the High Court, has played a more determinative role in the democratization of Australian education than many other, more democratic institutions. If this is true, it is certainly paradoxical.
- When we think of the experiences of many members of the community in pre-1989 Russia and other former Communist states — some academics and members of religious orders, for example — we realize that, notwithstanding the constraints of autocracy, authoritarianism and totalitarianism, a person can develop a heightened predilection for, and a commitment to, the values of the democratic form of life 'outside' and indeed far removed from the presence or availability of democratic procedures. Some children in schools may actually develop as passionate democrats in spite of the authoritarian atmosphere that rules their institutions.

Conclusion

It is to the study and attempted resolution of some of these difficult and complex problems, issues and paradoxes that we address the attention of readers of this volume. Certainly the time to do so is never more felicitous than now, when the opportunities for democratic advance are being opened up and expanded, not only in Russia and Australia, but widely across the world. It is even more vital at this time, when the risks and dangers to democracy and openness — from the corporate State, from multinational corporations, from forms of extreme nationalism and religious fundamentalism, from political correctness and fierce ideological convictions of all kinds — in all our societies seem almost daily to be increasing.

As educators we shall do well to remember the aphorism that 'The price of liberty is eternal vigilance.' It is our view that the impetus towards giving expression to the emphasis a democracy must lay upon the development and deployment of all the various forms of knowledge and skill needed to combat the risks and dangers mentioned in the foregoing paragraph can be nowhere better brought out and deployed than in the endeavour of creating and managing the democratic school. For, as we seek to show, that educational enterprise is vital and indispensable to securing the future of any democracy.

References

PETROVOSKY, A.V. (1989) *The New Pedagogical Thinking*, Moscow, Pedagogika.

SOVIET EDUCATION (1988) *The Pedagogy of Co-operation*, Report of the First Meeting of Innovative Teachers, 30, 56, pp. 30–45.

SOVIET EDUCATION (1989) *Democratization of the Individual*, Report of the Second Meeting of Innovative Teachers, 31, 5, pp. 80–95.

Chapter 2

The Conception of Democracy: A Philosophy for Democratic Education[1]

David N. Aspin

Introduction

Throughout the world education systems have recently been moving towards forms of provision, devolution and organization that are claimed to be based upon a principle, that, it is argued, is increasingly necessary in the control, direction and management of our educational institutions: the principle of democratization.

Various means and forms of arrangement have been employed to put in place structures of school management that will give most of the power to those whose interests are most directly affected by the presence and working of schools in particular localities — parents, students, employers and employee associations, cultural agencies, minority groups, political parties and other community institutions. To such constituencies has been delegated an increased degree of responsibility for such vital matters as the educational direction, financial control, and administrative arrangements, so as to enable the school to function as a centre of learning and preparation for community living.

This increased responsibility has led to a number of types and styles of innovation in educational administration — delegation, decentralization, devolution, local school management, and so on — though all of these forms and styles seem to have one thing in common: they reflect a general impulse to give power to the people who will most benefit from the school's work and presence among them.

During the 1980s and 1990s this impulse has been much in evidence in the education systems of Australia and Russia, too. But when politicians, legislators, policy makers, education bureaucrats and administrators, along with members of the broader educational community, use the rhetoric of democratization as a self-evident warrant by which they can claim authority for their proposals and plans, it is not always clear whether they all mean the same thing; indeed it is not always clear whether they mean anything much more than simply achieving the result they desire by using the language of currently fashionable slogans to secure assent to, and support for the particular changes in the education policies or schemes they are proposing or administering. They may claim that nothing in present times could be more important than for a community to create and then manage a democratic school, but we need to be reasonably clear, before we accept their proposals or vote for their policies, about what might be meant by their talk linking 'democracy' and 'education'.

In this chapter therefore I propose to look at the concepts of democracy, democratization and education, and explore some of the philosophical issues of meaning, intelligibility and justification that emerge. In particular, I wish to put forward a justification for democracy in learning institutions which is based upon the concept of knowledge and, as such, is able to transcend any particular local issues, sectional concerns, political agenda or national interests. I want to argue that, of all forms of educational management and political arrangement, the democratic principles inherent in the extension, transmission and acquisition of knowledge provide us with the best guarantee of an open society that offers greatest opportunities for personal growth and all-round community welfare.

Political Authority, Power and Democratic Values

I want to begin with the claim that democracy is first and foremost about the exercise of power by a group of people and the gaining or granting of the legitimate authority to do so. In the political realm there is a straightforward connection between having authority and exercising power, and it is the political context that formalizes this relationship and vindicates the exercise of sovereignty in matters of the decision-making, the implementation of policy, and the taking of responsibility for power exercised in that way. For it is the concept of sovereignty that justifies the exercise of power on the part of certain kinds of rulers acting as authorities. They derive the justification for their decisions and actions from some source of legitimacy external to them.

These conceptions may still be seen exhibited in the terms we employ for various forms of government involving 'power'. We talk about, and distinguish between, different forms of political direction and control such as are embodied in the various ways by which that power and rule has come to be exercised. We distinguish between:

- *aristocracy*, the rule of the best people, where best usually refers to membership of an upper class of some kind;
- *monarchy*, the rule of just one person, the concept of which is sometimes associated with 'aristocracy';
- *oligarchy*, the rule of a few;
- *plutocracy*, the rule of the wealthy;

- *gerontocracy*, the rule of the old men;
- *patriarchy*, the rule of the fathers ('males'), a special form of which is often 'gerontocracy';
- *ochlocracy*, the rule of the mass; and
- *democracy*, the rule of the people.

We contrast these kinds of government with such arbitrary and non-publicly justified patterns of power as are exercised by a 'tyrant' or an 'autocrat' (someone who rules by him or herself simply on the authority of his or her own say-so). It is clear that nowadays democracy ('government of the people by the people for the people') is the form of government most societies prefer. For this reason we must ask what sense can be made of the idea of democracy — of the rule 'of the people' — and what there is about democracy that makes it especially important to them. An answer to such questions is crucial if we are to go on to elucidate what we might mean by the idea of 'education for democracy'.

Nature of Democratic Values

Democratic values seem to me to include a number of different elements — the social, political, economic and technical *inter alia* — but to be primarily 'moral' in nature. I characterize the main features of democratic values, thinking, choice and action as follows.

The actions that we as democrats engage in will spring from a free choice on our part, as bearers and agents of democratic values, and these will be based upon our ability to give reasons for them that are relevant and appropriate, capable, in principle, at all events, of being judged such by people generally. This means that the decisions or actions undertaken by democrats, and the reasons they give for them, will be seen as *generalizable*: objective, impartial and equally binding on all those who regard such acts as intending to promote human welfare.

The latter consideration will mean that the grounds we advance for our actions as democrats will not be trivial but will really count for something — will have 'a certain magnitude'. Our beliefs and values about such matters will be held sincerely and applied and exercised with consistency. And, after their implementation, the success or failure of policies or practices, and the reasons given for them, will be subject to the demand for accountability: they will be open to inspection, evaluation and the bestowal of approval or disapproval, praise or blame, even, in the final analysis, reward or punishment. For the justification of the actions we engage in as democrats requires us willingly to take responsibility for them and willingly to accept the consequences flowing from them.

I take the view that democracy, as a species of morality, is about adopting, justifying, analysing, applying and evaluating policies, programmes or plans in interpersonal affairs in the social world, and that all those people whose interests are likely to be affected by the implementation of those plans or policies have the right to be consulted about them and to have an equal say in their adoption, amendment or rejection. Implicit in these requirements is the presumption that our actions and decisions in such matters are governed by principles that are public, objective, generalizable, commendatory, other-regarding, action-guiding, primarily related to the promotion of human welfare and the avoidance of human harm, and *accountable*. These principles are valued and adopted in those various forms of freely chosen self-governance that people call 'democracy', and they are made normative for the purposes that democracy has. Among these are the rights of individual citizens to develop their own preferred lifestyles in an atmosphere of minimum interference, tolerance of others' rights to do the same, and care for the avoidance of public harm, and for the promotion of social harmony, peace and justice, which seem to be the ends at which institutions of democracy aim.

Characteristic Features of Democratic Institutions and Practices

On the basis of the above elucidation of the public and interpersonal characteristics of democracy as a moral concept, we can, I believe, construct a list of criteria that would probably be regarded as illustrations of the principles typifying and encountered in democratic institutions. These would include the following:

- that policies and actions will be based on decisions and not arbitrary or autocratic acts of will;
- that decisions will be arrived at by rational discourse and on the grounds of the objective and convincing character of the arguments advanced to support them;
- that in general the suffrage shall be universally extended and full powers and rights made available to all people in the state, subject to limitations of age or other such qualifications as render the citizen incapable of making their vote (e.g., prisoners, mental incapacity, etc.);
- that all citizens shall vote, decide and act freely according to their conscience, and without being subject to duress;
- that in general the will of the majority shall prevail;
- that in general the rights of minorities shall be preserved, respected, allowed full and proper hearing and given due consideration;
- that regular periodic review shall be had of policies and practices;
- that the principle of reversibility shall obtain;
- that all citizens shall be guaranteed rights of access, equity and participation (direct, wherever possible) to and in the political process and institutions;

- that those responsible for the implementation of policies shall be accountable to the whole of the body politic for their conduct;
- that all shall count equally for one and none for more than one, in matters of voting, decision-making and accountability;
- that powers shall be separated and distributed equitably between and among government, executive and judiciary;
- that there shall be a system of checks and balances to ensure that no part of the system can gain pre-eminence and overriding control;
- that the arrangements shall be socially and politically operative and not mere rhetoric: in other words, that social justice shall obtain.

Along with such criteria by which we might hope to recognize democracy in the operation of any organization or institution, we also need a clear sense of the defining limits of the group of those to whom the rights implicit in these principles shall be extended, and in accordance with the qualifications for admission to it. We must therefore try to answer the question, who *are* 'the people' who shall have legitimate access to power; who shall be the citizens of a democracy?

The Concepts of 'The People' and 'Democracy'

By and large we tend these days to recognize as citizens of a state all persons in that state above a certain age and with the desire and appropriate qualifications to be placed on the roll of electors. But the extent of the franchise has not always been so wide: in Athens suffrage was restricted to male adults who had Attic forbears over three generations; while in many countries it was not until this century that women were given the right to vote. Also in the past some countries have refused to enfranchise particular sections of the population, on grounds that others regard as illegitimate or immoral: examples would be Germany in the 1930s, some American states before the late 1960s, and South Africa until 1994. In the United Kingdom at the present time full suffrage is extended to any person over the age of 18 years and with appropriate genealogical antecedents, with the exception of the peerage and the nobility, criminals, and those suffering from psychotic disabilities in mental hospitals.

It seems clear then that suffrage is not automatically regarded as 'universal', but that it is only granted to those who fall within certain restricted categories and that it can be withheld, and people excluded from it, on legitimate grounds. This explains why those in prison or in mental hospitals are regarded as falling, for the time being, outside the class of those who may properly be granted access to political power in a democracy. In such cases the presumption is against those who are unable for the moment to measure up to the demands of rationality, autonomy, goodwill and commitment to social order — the basic preconditions of democratic rights and the freedom to vote.

Normally speaking, the suffrage can only be returned to such people when they show that they are able to operate as autonomous individuals, with sufficient intelligence and benevolence to understand, evaluate and decide upon political issues for themselves.

Democracy: A Set of Valued Procedures and Principles

The indispensability of rationality as a precondition of, and a requirement for, democratic standing and operation is taken further by Peters (1966). He maintains that in a democratic state the public and supposedly rational character of its institutions necessarily commits its citizens to establish and willingly participate in their political arrangements by recourse to rational procedures in which the 'fundamental principles of morality' are implicit.

For Peters, ethical principles are presupposed in our commitment to the democratic form of life: in a democracy we settle our differences on important matters of principle, policy and practice by appeal to rational procedures, in which reason-giving has a public character. The practices and procedures of democratic institutions are exemplifications of large-scale moral principles at work. In Peters' terms, these principles are presuppositions of all democratic forms of life. They include the demand for:

- **Equality.** This is the presumption that in interpersonal transactions there shall be no discrimination between or against one group of people and in favour of another, without good, relevant and socially operative reasons being given. All people and human beings are to be presumed to be equal until grounds are given for treating someone or some group differently.
- **Freedom.** All people shall be presumed to be free agents until good reason can be given for constraints to be applied and freedom to be taken away.
- **Tolerance.** This ensures regard for the expressions of opinion and choices made by other people and for their right to be different and to follow their own path towards the creation and fulfilment of their own life-options.
- **Consideration of other people's interests.** This imposes on us the obligation to do nothing that will cause other people harm but to do everything possible to promote their welfare.
- **Respect for other people.** This reflects our regard for other people as 'ends-in-themselves' equally with us and our concern to preserve and promote our own *and* other people's search for happiness.

In a democracy these presuppositions are embodied and exemplified in particular political procedures and institutions. These function so as to:

- consider the interests of the governed;
- allow the free expression of public opinion;
- guarantee public accountability;
- encourage the emergence of consensus decisions;
- rely on and institutionalize the willingness of the governed to participate; and
- give citizens experience in such democratic institutions.

These are the minimum institutional requirements generated by the moral presuppositions underlying all democratic procedures. In this way they make the justification of democracy synonymous with the justification of morality. But of course that can only be so when the appropriate levels of rational autonomy, knowledge and benevolence have been reached. And, as we saw, this is presumed not to operate in the case of convicted prisoners and inmates of mental hospitals.

A similar presumption usually operates with respect to children and young people. One thing upon which groups and systems seem to agree is that young people below a certain age shall not count as valid persons to be included in the constituency of the 'adult' electorate: that their chronological age below a certain number of years shall be held to count as a sufficient disqualification from the extension of the suffrage to them. One supposes that the reason for this is the feeling that democracy requires its citizens to have arrived at some state of 'readiness' and a necessary degree of appropriate information, for meaningful and effective voting and political action to take place. The normal presumption must be that this state is reached as a result of maturation, education and the development or emergence of a political will.

It is this that must give us pause, however. Is it not odd that in trying to develop and educate our children and young people as future citizens, we do so (a) by means of compulsions of various sorts, and (b) in institutions that are, certainly in practice and maybe also in principle, anything but democratic? What are we then to make of the notions of 'education as a species of democracy' or 'education *for* democracy'? Is there not some paradox in the notion of the development of a predilection for democracy, that is built in and by institutions that seem to thrive on autocracy and compulsion? Can we really 'force people to be free'? Does not the idea of 'educating for democracy' contain a contradiction?

Can We 'Educate' *for* Democracy?

We therefore come to the key question for the undertaking, which this volume represents, of encouraging educators in their attempt to create and manage a democratic school: in what sense, if any, can we properly talk of, and plan for, 'education for democracy'? Does this phrase contain a truism, a contradiction in terms, or simply an unrealizable ideal?

In attempting to answer this question, we should perhaps make one preliminary observation. For we should note with caution that 'education for democracy' is a slogan. And it is important briefly to comment on the logic and function of such slogans. Slogans are, as has been remarked, 'empty of all positive content but rich in emotional appeal'. They provide 'rallying symbols' (Scheffler, 1960) for those committed to particular causes or sets of causes; slogans are usually intended by those who wave the banners containing them to have the same effect as moral imperatives. But slogans can also serve as instruments for the refutation or dispersal of the uncommitted or the positively hostile to those causes. Their utility is that they can mean all things to all people; in other words, there is in the case of such slogans an extent to which we can, like Humpty Dumpty in *Alice Through the Looking Glass*, make such words as 'democracy' and 'education' mean almost anything we like — within reasonable limits. And that is why it behoves us to try to be particularly clear about what we have in mind when we are framing educational proposals, plans and policies predicated on the idea and value of 'education for democracy'.

So much is necessary as a prelude to the discussion of the above question. Our aim will be to argue (a) that the idea contained in the slogan cited above does not contain a contradiction or (b) that definition of its terms will reveal it as either (i) a contradiction or as (ii) a tautology.

We might begin by suggesting a couple of possible meanings for idea of 'education for democracy'. We might, for instance, read it as meaning something along the following lines: 'one can educate for the maintenance of democracy' or (better) 'one should educate to produce democrats'. Now, if we take the slogan as containing a contradiction, then it will mean that either one cannot 'educate' to produce good citizens for a democracy; or that one may do so but the end-product will not be 'democrats'. My own view is that the first of these alternatives is the correct one. The evidence to support this contention arises from an account of 'education'.

'Education' I take to be an activity — deliberate, self-conscious and aimed at achieving some aims that are an improvement upon what has been accepted from the past — because one cannot educate by accident. Expressions like 'the only education I received was on the streets' (which seems to suggest that a society may indeed educate accidentally) take their force from a contrast with education in formal and institutional settings. We should not normally apply the term 'educated' to someone who claimed that those were all the experiences they had that they were prepared to count as 'educational'. Of course, locutions like 'formal education' suggest that there could be such a thing as 'informal education', and this is indeed so. But by the use of the latter term we should merely be implying things about the institutional, pedagogical or methodical aspects of the educational process, not that it was 'unconscious'.

Further evidence that education is an activity is provided by the concepts 'teaching' and 'learning', which are also used as names for particular activities which are seen as essential parts of any process describable as 'education'. 'Learning' is an 'achievement' word (in Ryle's sense [Ryle, 1949]): expressions such as 'I have learnt the names of all the rivers, capes and bays of the United Kingdom, but I can't remember them' might reasonably evoke the response, 'then you haven't really learned them'. And one cannot succeed at or achieve something in learning without meaning to do so. In my view, then, learning is an active endeavour in the sense of being a conscious undertaking to reach a goal by means judged by the actor to be the best (all things considered) for doing so. 'Teaching' is not necessarily an achievement word ('I am teaching English literature to 4C but without much success' seems a reasonable and intelligible remark to make) but to teach is certainly also an activity, for one cannot do it accidentally: one notices and looks for success in it. Given that the main parts of formal education consist as much as anything else in teaching and learning we might therefore reasonably claim that the major parts of education involve conscious and rational activity, aimed at the acquisition of knowledge, beliefs and skills of various kinds. And the achievement of these on the part of the student is a matter of value and importance to the student, the school and the community.

Education is also a process in that it requires at least a learner; it usually requires an educator, some information (or a notion of desired terminal behaviour) and the transmission of that information by morally reputable means, and relates to some wider ends than the mere receipt and reproduction of information. We should not generally regard someone as 'educated' to the extent that they could simply reproduce the information which the educator organized for their consumption as part of the process of making them educated (though it does make sense to say 'I was educated at X High School or Y University'). Statements like 'He's an educated person but that's no reason to expect him to solve a problem he didn't do at school'; or 'He was educated as a historian but he can't tell you anything about the Treaty of Utrecht because that isn't his period'; or 'She was educated at a private school and hasn't ever considered voting anything but Conservative' are therefore educationally odd — indeed, on this analysis, they are (potentially, at any rate) contradictory.

The study of problems in mathematics, history and politics at a school seen as an 'educating institution' (not a spy school, a bridge school or a driving school) is usually part of an effort on the part of a teacher to (a) bring the student to recognize and solve problems of similar structure with different values for the variables, and then (b) to enable the student to select as problematic certain questions which interest or puzzle them, to frame them as clear problems, to recognize what would count as evidence for its solution, to frame an hypothesis as to how it might be solved, to put that hypothesis into effect, and then to evaluate its outcomes — as Dewey (1938, also 1966) says, to 'undergo' its consequences. The aim of all truly educational processes, on this analysis, seems to be the reaching of a kind of autonomy (even if limited) in whatever field is studied. As I see it, education involves acts like judging, questioning, considering, criticizing, doubting and making up one's mind for oneself.

Let us therefore now come closer to the case in point. What might one say about the process that the student in the third example cited above had undergone regarding her political affiliations being decided by her schooling? If that schooling had indeed included political instruction of a conservative character, we might be inclined to say that the student had been indoctrinated rather than educated. Many authors in this field (Snook, 1972) seem to hold the view that to indoctrinate is to inculcate particular kinds of value preferences. I would disagree with this position and contend rather that 'education *for* anything' (where the goal includes elements of value), which would normally tend to predispose the actor to decide how to act in one way rather than another in moral, political, social or religious matters, is indoctrination. Indeed, any attempt to present questions of value as matters of fact, or opinion as established truth, or the requiring of an unquestioning acceptance of certain sets of unexamined propositions for which no, or highly slanted, evidential support is given, is also indoctrination. So part of the definition of indoctrination has to be concerned with the content of acts or beliefs as qualifying them for that label.

Another part of this must also have to do with the ways and 'means' by which such instruction or education is attempted to be imparted. It is entirely possible to use indoctrinatory methods to produce an appearance of open-mindedness and independent thinking, as for instance when one is asked to give reasons for making particular moral judgments or advancing particular religious opinions. One may, of course, have been taught justifications and the ways of making appropriate answers to the various objections one will be likely to encounter in such cases, to a high degree of generality and sophistication. But this is still indoctrination: the essence here is the idea of 'doctrine'. For this reason both content and method are parts of indoctrination, though the former is perhaps more telling. As opposed to this, however, we might say that an essential part of educating a young person to be an 'actor', a 'chooser', indeed a 'person', is helping to develop in him or her the power of 'autonomy' — of having free choice and independence in judgments or conduct, especially in moral or political matters. If one cannot decide moral or political issues 'for oneself' then one cannot be held to have made a free choice, and, for that reason, one cannot be held responsible for the consequences. That would put one on a par with psychotics, animals and babies: the difference between such creatures and adult human beings is that the latter have acquired the power to make decisions and choices autonomously, with full information about, awareness of, and willing acceptance of responsibility for, their likely outcomes, especially as regard their effect on other people.

This is why 'autonomy' in moral or political matters cannot be 'taught' as a series of rules or propositions, or as a recipe set of skills. Even if rules are taught, the ability to operate with them in a skilful manner is 'caught': for example, doing a succession of addition sums, one hopes, will lead to the child's being able to do addition sums they have not seen, to the point at which the child can say 'Now I know how to go on' (Wittgenstein, 1953).

But this cannot be taught, only demonstrated. How much more, then, must not only the ability to operate with rules but to 'choose' between conflicting rules, be a matter of example. Moral or political autonomy therefore depends on the learners observing a moral or political free agent at work and in situations calling for the exercise of independent moral or political judgment. Techniques such as brainwashing or conditioning, the use of force, lying and manipulating, and so on, which are normally associated with indoctrinatory aspirations and intentions, are ruled out, since such immoral behaviour (immoral because they treat students as less than full moral persons in their own right) would be dysfunctional in any attempt to make the student morally autonomous.

As Aristotle points out, the house builder or the harp player becomes good at that skill by being required and shown how to exercise it in appropriate circumstances: they learn how to act in the circumstances calling for it, by watching other practitioners, following the guidelines observable in their behaviour, and then gradually coming to select particular practices and adopt certain guidelines for themselves. Aristotle employs the concepts of justice and temperance to put this in a framework of moral and social values. Virtuous acts are only done when the agent himself is in a certain state of mind when he performs them:

- he must act with knowledge;
- he must deliberately choose the act, and choose it for its own sake; and
- the act must spring from a fixed and permanent disposition of character.

From these the implications for education and democracy flow almost self-evidently: one becomes a morally autonomous person or a good democrat by being exposed to all the practices and institutions of morality and democracy from the very earliest times and, by habituation, imitation and direct personal involvement, one actually acquires their values and grows into the state of being in which one has a settled disposition to adhere to, exemplify and practise them. This growth takes place by a kind of process of osmosis and gradually maturing appreciation of the prime value of those activities, practices and institutions in influencing behaviour, helping to determine human affairs and conducing in that way to the promotion of happiness and welfare and the diminution of harm and suffering. As Peters (1963) put it, 'the Palace of Reason is entered through the Courtyard of Habit and Tradition'.

We may now draw all this together. In one sense the slogan 'education for democracy' does indeed contain something of a contradiction. This is because, as we have seen, any process aiming at the students' taking a particular position on matters of value or opinion is indoctrinatory. Therefore, to try to 'educate' for democracy by teaching or giving instruction in 'democratic' rules and behaviour is, in a quite decided sense, to fail to educate: it is to indoctrinate. If we continue to take the view that there is a contradiction here, then it goes even deeper than that. For to indoctrinate for democracy is to be bound, practically and conceptually speaking, to fail. The citizens of a democracy are ideally as autonomous as it is possible to be, helping in the business of 'government' (at however low or high a level) and making their decisions according to the evidence and their conscience. We have seen that autonomy (like 'criticism' or 'taste') is not so much taught as caught, in the sense that one may, after a series of ostensive definitions and guided attempts of one's own, finally 'see the point'. Therefore to try to 'indoctrinate' our young for democracy is to make them unfit as citizens for a democratic role and indeed, a democratic form of life.

So 'education for democracy', viewed as a contradiction with the emphasis on 'for', is a very deep contradiction indeed and is an undertaking that is bound to fail. This brings me on to my final point, then, which is that, in quite another sense, 'education for democracy' is a 'tautology' — and, as a tautology, it is *bound* to succeed. We can easily see from the foregoing account of democracy and education how this is the case. Education is concerned above all with autonomy. This is learned by example and personal growth in practice and confidence. An autonomous person is automatically and self-evidently a democrat. That is, the definitions offered above of both 'educatedness' and 'democrat' are both based on, and encapsulate, similar notions about the mind and conduct of the person and his or her ability to choose.

My last point therefore is this: where 'education for democracy' is seen as requiring instruction in the 'rules' of being a 'democrat', as if these were not themselves part of the democratic debate, then this is to abandon 'education', to fail to understand 'democracy', and to be seen to be attempting a course of action the contradictory nature of which makes failure certain and leads instead to autocracy, fascism and totalitarianism. On the other hand, where 'education for democracy' means 'promoting mental autonomy by encouraging the predisposition to make informed and rational choices and clearly distinguishing truth (however we define that — though clearly 'objectivity' will be a presupposition of all attempts to elucidate it) from opinion, in order to facilitate the development of a settled disposition towards the making of rational choices in the adult', then we see that the slogan's two terms mean just about the same, and in that sense the slogan is tautologous. In this sense 'education for democracy' simply means 'education': the two concepts are coterminous.

Some Problems with the 'Procedural' View

Peters (1966) takes what we have so far seen as a tautology in a rather different way. His claim is that we can educate for democracy by initiating children into the world of basic moral principles, so making them necessarily democrats. And there is certainly very much to be said for this claim: it means that education is necessarily at one and the same time an induction into the democratic form of life and into moral autonomy itself.

Unfortunately, there are some problems with such a view. For one thing, we might reasonably ask, along with Kleinig (1973), Koerner (1967 and 1973), and Watt (1975), whether Peters' use of transcendental arguments maintaining that the principles of democracy are functions of the fundamental presuppositions of morality is sound. It is one thing to argue that those who question the value of democracy are *ipso facto* committed to the sort of life-form that democracy is; it is quite another to claim that this thereby necessarily commits them to democracy as the best form of government. To argue that is to commit the fallacy of thinking that, if you secure my agreement that clothes are things worth having and wearing, you have automatically thereby secured my commitment to the wearing of particular styles or fashions. Government involving reasoned discourse is one thing; it does not follow from that, that the only form of such government is the democratic (in our sense) nor that, of all forms of government that are called 'democratic', the western model is self-evidently the best and most fully paradigm version of it.

In any case, to claim so much presumes that a clear and unambiguous account of democratic procedures can be given and a universally agreed definition of democracy arrived at. But this presumption is questioned if not rejected by a number of people. Schumpeter (1967), for one, points out that there are at least two concepts of democracy: 'classical democracy', which he calls 'an institutional arrangement for arriving at political decisions which realizes the common good by making the people itself decide issues through the election of individuals who are to assemble in order to carry out its will'; and 'modern democracy' — 'an institutional arrangement for arriving at political decisions in which individuals acquire the power to decide by means of a competitive struggle for the people's vote.' Graham (1976) goes even further and contends that in the modern world 'there is no such thing as democracy'.

To say so much is, however, to be unduly restrictive: we all do use the term 'democracy' and we clearly have something of importance in mind when we use it. The trouble is that, as we are sometimes uncomfortably aware, there is, in public discourse on matters of vital significance involving the use of such terms as 'democracy', often such difference of opinion, interpretation, and intention that the only thing about which we *can* be certain is that people will disagree profoundly on the meaning and content of such terms.

Gallie (1956) believes there is a sound explanation for this phenomenon. Such concepts as 'democracy', 'art', or 'religion' he calls 'essentially contested' inasmuch as, along with other such terms, they give rise to considerable contention in conversation centring on them. While people may think they share a broad understanding of the range and limits of allowable interpersonal usage, in the case of some terms no such broad agreement can be assumed but rather the strong possibility of argument and controversy predicted. This is because there is in fact very wide variation in the range of uses of such terms and consequently very considerable variation in our understanding of the range of meanings we have of them.

Terms like 'art', 'religion' and 'democracy' are somewhat like loose-knitted woollen garments, the texture of which is open because of the size and width of the mesh, the interstices between the very loose strands of the garment. For this reason there may well be little shared agreement on major matters of substance to be packed into those frameworks. Gallie educes from the employment of some key terms in such conversations what he calls seven conditions of 'essential contestedness'. He would argue that the term 'democracy' satisfies these conditions, making it thus an 'essentially contested' concept. As an instance of this, we may note that membership of the United Nations is only allowed to a country if a democratic form of government is in operation, yet great diversity of democratic approaches to government by its members is evident.

Quine and Ullian (1970) employ a similar metaphor, except that their version of it relates not merely to concepts but to the theories of reality and meaning with which we work. For them our theories of the world are like webs of belief in which, like the spider's web, everything coheres in one single system and in which there are tighter enmeshments at the centre, looser ones toward the periphery. 'Democracy' would have a strong place somewhere in our own network of thinking but it would not necessarily be the same as everyone else's; its significance for us would be its place in our overall theory and it would be that overall theory we should be comparing and testing against other people's.

It is as a result of our own theoretic commitments in the matter of 'democracy' that we feel justified in asking whether some modes, forms and institutions of governance that are alleged to be democratic, such as that of a single-party state, for instance, are not really ruled out. Further, while it does not follow from the above analysis that the 'Westminster' system must be the only form which democratic government can take, we may ask, does not its adoption, even in modified form, by very many countries claiming to be democratic suggest that there is something substantial in that kind of *modus operandi* that goes beyond mere forms and procedures and suggests that democracy must be found in a conjunction of particular forms and contents?

Perhaps the wisest course here is to agree that our use of the term 'democratic' of some forms of government is approbationary or prescriptive, and that the best we can do in such cases is to follow Wittgenstein's (1953) advice and 'look and see' what a particular 'democratic' society does in its own particular versions and workings of the social institutions that govern it. All this would pave the way for an acknowledgment on all our parts of the need to seek, from usage, context, interlocutors' intentions, the significance and value placed upon it by the community generally and the customary 'flavour' of the discourse in which such words have their home, an appropriate basis for our use of the term 'democratic', and an appropriate set of forms and procedures in and by which we might maintain democratic principles and institutions are developed and deployed.

This might then provide us with a reasonably objective account of the concept — but it would be an account requiring local adaptation and interpretation, together with an awareness of the need to be alive to the difficulties of translating those interpretations into our own terms; of the need to beware of, and avoid, the constant liability of falling into fallacy when making comparisons of those local variants with our own models of democratic value; and of the need for the making of constant adjustments to our own theories and paradigms, with all the potential problems and dangers to which that exercise could expose them. The Australian form of democracy, we do well to remember, is not the same as that of Russia; and neither is identical to that of the United States. To follow the suggestions arising from the above accounts of meaning is to engage us in a highly complex and sophisticated exercise of political analysis and linguistic and social anthropology — an enterprise rendered even more difficult by our awareness of its shifting, unstable and dynamic character.

Values Informing Democracy and Education: An Alternative View

Rather than engaging in such an undertaking, and as a way of avoiding the difficulties, I want to argue that the prime focus for democratic values in education comes from one of the central concepts in education — that of 'knowledge'. The pursuit of truth in all its various forms, the generation, growth, dissemination, criticism of, and communication about, new knowledge, all involve their own ethical imperatives — and all of them are democratic. I maintain that the ethical/socio-political values that come in democratic education are a function of educating institutions' epistemological preoccupations (other forms of upbringing, training, etc. which are not democratic are authoritarian and based upon the desire to propagate a 'faith' system of belief. Such institutions are in principle totalitarian).

I also want to argue for the inherence of certain democratic principles in speech and discourse generally. I contend that the presumption of equality, toleration, generalizability and prescriptivity is implicit in every occasion of language use and thus human communication more largely. Just as Hare (1964) argues that human discourse is an activity that is the very stuff of morality, so also I claim that the very activity of speaking a language is in some sense a democratic enterprise. It presupposes the same commitment to telling the truth, to treating interlocutors as equals, to allowing freedom of expression, to tolerating what people say and allowing expression to their differing points of view, and respecting their rights to parity of esteem.

This is a point made strongly by Ackerman (1980) in his celebration of 'conversation' and its presuppositions as being an instantiation of the moral/

democratic form of life and an exemplification of liberal education at work. A liberal education not only teaches people to communicate and to converse: it teaches them *eo ipso* to be autonomous moral agents, sensitive, benevolent and considerate human beings — and good democrats.

Implications of Democratic Values for Education

Ackerman (1980) and Powell (1970) have pointed out the presumption that democracy in its turn requires an informed citizen body to exercise its powers and to participate in debate relating to decision-making, the outcomes of which will prove binding on all citizens. This places enormous emphasis on education and the production of a curriculum for democracy. But not only must there be a policy of, programme for, and commitment to, exposing a state's future citizens to the knowledge that is appropriate for the democratic form of life, and helping them acquire it by providing them with, and engaging them in, an appropriate curriculum for that purpose in schools: there must also, according to Powell (1970), be practice in 'activities' appropriate to a democratic form of life and a set of organizational and administrative arrangements that will exemplify democracy. Adoption of these procedures and practices will then function as preparations for the life of the democrat when maturity is reached and the suffrage finally conferred.

The Justification of Compulsory Education in a Democracy

It is in this way that the supposed 'paradox' of democracy and education may be dissolved and the question raised above concerning the justification of compulsory attendance at educational institutions might be answered. We take (and enforce) decisions on our young people's part that they would take for themselves had they the requisite education, information and wisdom to enable them to do so. Proof of this comes from the realization that the end of compulsory schooling is not coterminous with arrival at adulthood. In this way we solve the paradox of education for democracy by compelling attendance at educational institutions, which may *seem* to be autocratic in point of time but should turn out eventually (at least in principle) *not* to be so. Perhaps young peoples' studying at universities and other tertiary educating institutions where attendance is voluntary is the best exemplification of this principle. Armed with these considerations, we may now turn to the attempt to provide some answer to the fundamental question: Is democracy *in* education possible?

The School As a Democratic Institution

In attempting to characterize the notion of a 'democratic' school, we might make a beginning with a quotation from the work of Neill (1968), the late founder and principal of 'Summerhill', the school seen by many as a prime example of real democracy at work in education:

> Th(e) loyalty of Summerhill pupils to their own democracy is amazing. It has no fear in it, and no resentment. I have seen a boy go through a long trial for some anti-social act, and I have seen him sentenced. Often, the boy who has been sentenced is elected chairman for the next meeting . . . The sense of justice that children have never ceases to make me marvel. And their administrative ability is great. As education, self-government is of infinite value . . . (Neill, 1968)

We might perhaps think that Neill's emphasis on trial, sentence and, presumably, some form of punishment, suggests that its institution and use at Summerhill may have been rather more negative and coercive than liberating and positive. We may also wonder whether the successful operation claimed for that school might not have been possible only as a function of the enclosed environment and the very small number of students involved. Yet the contrast between what was claimed to be typical features of the Summerhill school democracy, and the organizing principles of a conventional school, would certainly bear some further reflection.

The two models involved may be thought to be capable of characterization (if not caricature!) something along the following lines:

At Summerhill:

- Students have a major say in running the school.
- There are no authority figures.
- Attendance at lessons is optional.
- There is a relaxed approach towards discipline and punishment.
- There is considerable emphasis on play.
- There is a premium on letting children develop and follow their own interests.
- Nothing is compulsory.

By contrast at a Conventional School:

- Students have little say in the running of school.
- There are strong authority figures.
- Attendance at lessons is compulsory.
- There are strong attitudes towards discipline and punishment.
- There is a greater emphasis on the need to develop skills, and on the importance of hard work at mastering them.
- There is a strong emphasis on getting students to work at learning what is considered by the school authorities to be in their interests to study.

- Most activities and pursuits are compulsory, such as games and physical education, aesthetic, moral and religious values, etc.
- Discipline is externally imposed not internally chosen.

It is, of course, highly questionable whether government schools should seek to emulate Summerhill or other such 'alternative' schools, which in any case are almost always independent, often boarding, sometimes highly selective, and almost always decidedly expensive. Nevertheless, government schools might still learn some very useful lessons in democracy from the approaches of such schools. They would do well to remember, though, that many of the other practices found in or associated with the operation of such schools might only lead to difficulties or even disasters in the conventional sector. Such difficulties might arise not least in those matters concerned with attendance at lessons (compulsory or optional?), participation in curriculum activities (serious or non-serious?) and relations between students and staff.

Not everyone, for example, sees any sense in allowing children and young people to devote much of their time in school to 'play' and other non-serious activities and pursuits. Teaching and learning are necessary if young people are to acquire personally enriching, economically necessary and socially desirable knowledge and skills. Sometimes, for reasons already given, students have to be required to work hard to acquire such knowledge and conform to such norms and conventions of conduct as are called for and appropriate in the hard work of study. Teachers may of course choose to educate by methods and styles of teaching involving activities that are playful, create enjoyment, or are carried out with humour all round; but that should not misrepresent the deeply serious purpose of the actual subjects of study. Furthermore, in laying on their students the obligation to work hard to acquire and then exercise such cognitive skills and repertoires devoted to serious educational aims, one cannot conceive of public institutions operating without sanctions of some sort, whether praise for hard work leading to success or blame for lack of attention or effort required to achieve good learning outcomes.

This holds good, too, with respect to matters of conduct and behaviour generally. Though there is much to be said for involving all a school's students in securing and caring for good order and conditions in which the disciplines involved in learning are more likely to be effective, there is nevertheless every reason to hesitate before handing over powers of counsel, judge and jury in disciplinary matters to those whose maturational growth does not yet enable them to think in the highly multifarious, intricate and sophisticated ways required for the assessment of claims about conduct, the evaluation of evidence, the calculation of consequences, and the matching of appropriate sanctions to particular offences. It would clearly be a difficult business, and one likely to cause problems, to elevate those who have as yet made relatively little progress through the developmental stages along the road towards moral autonomy to positions in which those highly elaborate and refined skills are at a premium. These are matters which many adults find difficult and demanding and in which principals and teachers are constantly aware of their own shortcomings. How much less then should we imagine that persons below the age of maturity or most students at school will be capable of exercising them?

On the matter of curriculum choices, too, though it might be reasonable to give students the opportunity to decide on their options in a range of subjects offered to them in school, it is surely only reasonable to do so when they have some minimal understanding of those cognitive activities and concerns between which they are choosing. I might properly, for example, have some say in deciding whether I should learn Arabic or Zulu, or choose between astronomy and zoology, but the decision that the curriculum of a school should be arranged on the basis of students *having to* learn a foreign language (in addition to English) and science is most properly one for the whole community.

Schools are not apart from the community in this: they cannot teach exactly what they like, nor can the students choose whether to attend or not to attend classes, without their parents and representatives of the wider community wanting to have some further say about that. The body of mature citizens, being well aware of the kinds of knowledge, skills and values required for successfully coping with the demands of life in a modern democracy, may think it perfectly in order to ask whether children and young people are self-evidently the best judges of what they should study and work hard at acquiring, The community, having a legitimate interest in the knowledge and skills to be expected of its future citizens, values the part it plays in determining the content of their education and what factors should be taken into account when schools are framing their curricula, and is willing these days to specify that in some detail.

Then there is the question of the part students should play in the organization and administration of their schooling. It is not unreasonable to expect that, once students have made decisions as to which of the range of subjects on offer they wish to study, they should be able to work out their chosen goals and preferred learning style in discussion with the teachers of those subjects; modern educational technology, computer-assisted learning, individualized instruction and a range of aids and equipment will help them forge their own way forward, with the assistance and under the supervision of the teacher. Between them they will be able to organize and administer times, dates and places, and the necessary amount of time and energy to be devoted to achieving their objectives. The idea of the 'negotiated curriculum' is a good example of this principle being put into practice.

Students can also play a useful part in deciding upon, putting into place and then executing many measures that have to do with classroom and lesson preparation, the cleanliness and neatness of the school environment, and the promotion and preservation of order and discipline — though care needs to be taken with respect to the duty of care properly devolving upon principals and school councils, who are legally required to be accountable in law for the safety, security and welfare of children and young people put into their care by the community for the purposes of education and schooling: obviously students can play no part in that.

Quite apart from the obligations of the legal responsibility, however, there is another idea emanating from the 'Summerhill' tradition and ethos, that needs similar caution. For the idea that students can play a major part in the organization and administration of an institution so complex and multifarious as the modern school is surely to place excessively weighty burdens on shoulders that are as yet ill-equipped and insufficiently strong to carry them. Principals and teachers will speak feelingly about the demands that their engagement in the planning, provision and delivery of the pedagogical imperatives of quality schooling make upon them and for which they need to draw upon all their resources of intellect, understanding and emotional resilience.

Furthermore, the requirements of effective organization and management of the highly complicated and heterogenous institution in these days of local school management — including the responsibility for the appointment of staff, human-resource management, the planning, delivery and assessment of curricula, and the framing, administering and control of budgets involving very large amounts of public money — are so onerous and intricate that they almost always demand special training and qualifications. Decisions relating to all the areas of a school's concerns and the ways in which policies meet to address them can best be framed, articulated and implemented call for mature deliberation and evaluation before they can be put into place, followed by expert ability in evaluation to see how they work. It is hardly likely that young persons below a certain age will have the qualities of maturity, judgment and impartiality called for in such exercises.

Then there is the question of the interpersonal relationships carried on in an educational establishment, both those between staff and students, and those between students. Some government schools clearly have much to learn from Summerhill in this respect: the ease of approach and ready acceptance of individual differences, the use of given names and the acceptance of all as being moral equals worthy of adult address, observed and practised in relations between students and staff at Summerhill might be looked on with envy by students in more conventional schools, where a considerable degree of distance and a sense of superior–inferior relations very often obtains. The style of Summerhill's relations sets a model for, and might well be emulated by, staff in such schools, to the betterment of their students' learning.

Relations among students are, of course, much more difficult to regulate and direct towards positive educational outcomes. But the experiences described in Neill's and others' writings on this subject suggest that, in this area too, many conventional schools have much to learn from Summerhill: current reports regarding the incidence of bullying, intimidation and harassment in government schools do not find any echo in the Summerhill environment, where mutual tolerance and regard seem to be enshrined in students' acceptance of the responsibility they have to creating an effective and mutually supportive learning environment.

All these considerations encourage me to voice a cautionary conclusion. Notwithstanding the interesting experiments carried out in Summerhill and other similar forms of alternative education, government schools might do well to recall that the idea of democracy in a modern school preparing students for citizenship does not demand that students should have a determinative voice in the making of all decisions affecting or concerning them, though they do, of course, have a right to be consulted about those matters held to be in their interest and of which they might be expected to have some degree of knowledge and understanding, together with the readiness to think objectively and give opinions impartially. How many students have such cognitive competences and psychological maturity must be a matter for local assessment and decision.

These reflections on the lessons that can be drawn from the Summerhill model of the democratic school may then encourage us to go forward and make a positive set of suggestions as to ways in which government schools can avoid the pitfalls of a too slavish imitation of such educational innovations, while at the same time profiting from the kind of thinking that animates their establishment and operation. Working on this basis, we may now think it entirely reasonable to require of government schools, insofar as they aspire to function as agents of initiation into the democratic form of life that characterizes the adult society in which they shall operate as citizens, that they should adhere strongly to the principles, if not the letter, of the kind of school *Charter for Democracy* put forward by Knight (1985):

Rights and Responsibilities
of students and teachers in a democratic school

Expressions of Unpopular Opinion:

Rights to freedom of speech (not slander or defamation) and peaceful assembly.

Responsibilities of students to listen and not obstruct the opinions of others; of schools to provide forums for assembly and student press.

Protection of Privacy:

Rights to be protected from the abuser of authority; to be protected from harassment; to be protected from unlawful attacks on honour and reputation.

Responsibilities of students to protect their own and others' property; of the school to provide parents and students with access to student's personal record, test results and evaluations; of the school not to divulge student records without permission of students and/or parent.

Due Process

Rights of access to legal protection under the law;
to be presumed innocent until proven guilty;
to participate in classroom and school decision-making.

Responsibilities of students be *accountable* for personal actions;
of the school to provide forums for students to negotiate grievances;
of the school to issue each student annually a list of their rights and responsibilities.

Freedom of Movement

Rights to be free from subservience to the will of others;
to be free from cruel and unusual punishment;
to be treated with dignity;
to maintain a social identity.

Responsibilities of the school, to create choices in language communication;
of students and teachers not to humiliate, harass or physically maltreat others;
of students not to infringe upon the rights of others.

It is worthwhile comparing these prescriptions with the kinds of rules and disciplinary procedures that generally obtain in many government schools of today. It could be interesting to try to work out what kinds of places schools would be if we legislated for, and enforced, conformity in all our schools to the kind of requirements set out above, that as citizens of democracies we all insist upon and take for granted in our institutionalized forms of democracy. If we were to require the acceptance of the principles implicit in the Knight charter and the setting in train of deliberate moves to implement some such system in our schools tomorrow, we should have to look, first and foremost, to the ways in which school councils, principals and teachers would react to that challenge. For it is among such constituencies that the question of creating and maintaining a democratic school gets its real point of purchase.

The Role of the Principal and School Council in Creating and Managing a Democratic School

Any discussion on democracy in schools must therefore and inevitably involve an appraisal of the role, powers and authority of the principal. We need to consider ways in which principals exercise their authority and practise leadership, for by doing so we might begin to tackle the question of whether their schools can be counted as democratic communities, and if so, in what sense and to what extent.

Democratically minded principals will usually consult the whole of their staff on a wide range of important educational issues. Such principals will hold regular meetings of deputy principals, directors of studies, heads of departments and teachers of subjects to discuss matters that affect the academic and intellectual life of the school. In such discussions principals will also exercise leadership in making proposals regarding matters of principle, policy and delivery, and open their ideas on these matters to appraisal and further elaboration.

Such principals will also constantly communicate with those whose school responsibilities lie in its organization and administration — deputy principals, house directors, year leaders, guidance and counselling staff, and so on — to consult over matters affecting the management and running of the school. At such meetings democratic principals will ensure that all will have a say and none will be counted as more powerful than anyone else. Where necessary, external advisers or interest groups or individuals will be brought in: social case workers, careers advisory officers, welfare agencies, health and social service department officials, representatives of employers, trade unions, parents and religious groups. All have a valid contribution to offer in matters affecting the educational welfare of the school and the various aspects of the development and growth of its students.

Principals will try to shape, direct and monitor the decision-making process; they will ensure that decisions reached are put into effect; and they will take measures to assess and evaluate the effectiveness of decisions that are made. And they will report on, and take responsibility for, these processes to the school council, the appropriate authorities, and the wider school community. The same requirements, *mutatis mutandis*, would operate with respect to the roles and responsibilities delegated to, held by and exercised among other staff colleagues working in the school in the interests of its students and the wider learning community.

Students too can, subject to the cautions expressed above, be involved in the running of their school in a number of ways. One of them is by the class, tutorial group and house system, which offers students good experience of, and training in, democratic procedures. Class, house and group meetings may still operate according to democratic group principles and methods in what may be the wider and more authoritarian structure, and the legal framework, of the school. Occasionally principals may appear to be excessively autocratic, legalistic or managerial, but at least if they are willing to allow class and house meetings, and student involvement in, and responsibility for, some extra-curricular activities, then there will inevitably be some procedures — those of discussion, of respecting and tolerating others' points of view, of voting, of keeping records, of personal participation in decision-making, of being willing to carry responsibility for implementing, monitoring and amending group decisions, being punctual and courteous, and so on — that will count as conforming to the community's expectations that children and young people have some training in democracy and citizenship.

The appointment of school captains or senior students is one further means of getting students involved in the day-to-day running of the school.

In any secondary school, they can play a part in helping to maintain discipline and in the arrangement and completion of certain tasks or duties, though Peters adds an important note of qualification: 'Office holders should be appointed on a purely functional basis for limited periods with defined spheres of competence.' Within such clearly defined guidelines, the advantages of engaging the more mature students in taking a role in the operational functioning of their school and of helping it consolidate and enhance the quality of life and work in it are obvious. The same will be true of the opportunities opened up to students for learning the skills of leadership, democratic participation and personal responsibility that are offered by games, physical pursuits, outdoor activities, various forms of community service, and participating in or running school clubs and societies of all kinds.

The school council, where it includes student representation, is another means of offering students direct experience of democratic principles and procedures, though students will play a relatively restricted role in deliberations and decision-making on some matters. But of course the membership of the school council will comprise more than staff and students; if a school council is to be democratic, it will seek representation from all the constituencies and communities in which the school 'lives and moves and has its being', and in the name, and pursuit, of whose interests it claims to operate.

This will mean that the council of a school that values and promotes democracy in its administrative and operational procedures must have in its composition not only representatives of students and staff: it will need membership from parents, business, industry and commerce, trades unions and professional associations, other educational institutions in the locality, other community and local welfare agencies and organizations, the local Education Ministry or other authority and (where necessary) minority ethnic, cultural, and/or religious groups. Only then will it be able to say that it can guarantee the widest possible consultation of, communication with, and accountability to all its community's interests. And only then will it be able fully to address its principal term of reference — to provide access to and ensure effective participation in a high-quality and empowering programme of educational experiences, and in ways that maximize and make most efficient use of all the various resources (human, capital, material) placed by that community at its service and disposal.

The Curriculum, Teaching and Learning as Exemplifications of Democracy

With the foregoing in mind, then, we might now feel it possible to tease out some general requirements for the hoped-for growth in democratic understanding and practice that will emerge particularly from the work our students do in their work on curriculum activities. Students need to be given experience, practice and maybe even formal training in the running of democratic institutions and they will certainly acquire such practice in some of the ways set out above. But, whether students join clubs, run societies or are appointed as 'senior students' or monitors is often a matter of luck, personal inclination or particular need. With matters of knowledge and curriculum, however, there can be no such fortuitous element. Engaging with the curriculum and acquiring knowledge of various kinds is, after all, why students are there in the first place and their greatest and most numerous opportunities for growth into the democratic mentality will arise from their being exposed to liberal democratic procedures within their classrooms, subjects and lessons, that operate in the public, objective and impartial character of the procedures required for the getting of knowledge.

Democratic teaching and learning will involve having recourse to such strategies as the use of hypothetico-deductive methods, discussion, debate, argument and independent research as to best pedagogic practice in teaching and learning activities, rather than by the teachers simply lecturing, instructing, or employing other such didactic and more formal approaches. In all the preferred ways mentioned, it is possible for students to observe the democracy of knowledge at work, get some understanding of its operating norms and conventions, gain experience in, and in that way to acquire a taste for, the staffing and running of democratic institutions, of which knowledge-getting and assessing is the chief exemplar.

Given the point that in the pursuit, dissemination and gradual mastery of knowledge the principles of objectivity, truth, impartiality and rationality are implicit, then student learning will need to be conducted in ways that manifest the prime requirement that some ways of imparting and acquiring knowledge and some kinds of behaviour on the part of both staff and students — violence, bullying, bribery, cheating, intimidation, harassment, the use of belittling or demeaning language — are out of place in the realm of knowledge and the freedom of the democratic classroom, and will not be accepted. Students will need to be told and shown that a commitment to rational ways of doing things carries as a consequence the promotion of particular desired and valued forms of conduct: telling the truth, not stealing or copying from other people's work, not cheating in tests, not loading the results one comes up with, not manufacturing or distorting evidence, keeping promises, not causing other people unnecessary pain, treating other people equally, allowing other people their own room to have their say and make decisions and choices for themselves, not interfering with their freedom to do as they wish until their choices threaten to interfere with the choosing of others, . . . the list goes on and can be added to, in the light of our own experience or classroom situation.

Perhaps a good place to begin, as Braithwaite (1959) so well perceived and described in *To Sir, with Love*, is with the fundamental demand for courtesy, civility and consideration for others in the classroom. In respect of the minimal demands of politeness and care about other people, as well as all the values and practices set out above, students will need to be shown first, and daily be exposed to, all those forms of interpersonal conduct that civilized people take courtesy and politeness to consist in. Then, as Braithwaite ably showed, students can be helped and encouraged to make a start on learning to act according to the canons and criteria of proper behaviour themselves, in the hope and confident expectation that in time they will come to appreciate the utility and value of doing things in those ways rather than others and choosing some forms of arranging their political and social relations rather than others. When they reach that point we may say they will have learned the lessons intended for them in the creation and implementation of the idea of the democratic school.

The Need for Caution, Effort and Knowledge as a Safeguard of Democracy

However, students need also to come to appreciate that democracy is a way of institutionalizing our political arrangements and our social intercourse that is very difficult to sustain. It requires constant nourishment and the most determined efforts at preservation. Without such care and attention, it is easy to overthrow it and when it is overthrown the cost in human misery and suffering is enormous and takes sustained effort, time and expense to recover from, as peoples of the former eastern Europe, Vietnam and Cambodia are still painfully discovering.

They need also to come to realize that a community's commitment to democracy is expensive. It is expensive of *effort*: democracy requires work and active engagement on the part, not only of those who run it but of those for whom it is run. It is expensive of *time*: the conception, development, establishment and refinement of democratic institutions is not something that can happen overnight, nor, as we shall say below, can a sufficient number of democratically minded citizens, with the considerable repertoires of intelligence, knowledge and competence and the reservoirs of goodwill required for the operation of, or willing compliance with, the norms and demands generated by those institutions, be expected, like Topsy, just to grow up of their own accord. And finally it is expensive of *resources*: it goes without saying that the running of democratic institutions and constant recourse to their various ways of consultation, policy determination and evaluation require the investment of appropriate levels of finance and funding.

Students may also need to be reminded that a commitment to the democratic way of doing things provides the community with no guarantee of infallibility: plans put forward and policies implemented are not always successful. Indeed such is human fallibility, such the resistance to change of existing well-established community institutions and social practices, so great that phenomenon called by existentialists the 'facticity' of external circumstance, that citizens committed to democratic values in all forms of political arrangement, cultural organization and educational establishment will be only too well aware of what efforts and expenditures of time, effort and money, what increments of knowledge and critical awareness, and what measures of patience, benevolence and emotional resilience are called for on the way to achieving their goal.

Education Indispensable to Democracy

Thus only gradually, with immense expenditures of time, effort and resources, will our students begin to understand that democracy requires knowledge about, interest in, an active commitment to participate in the public affairs of, and a widespread and generally accepted willingness to work the various forms and institutions of democracy, on the part of its citizens: that, without continuing succour and sustenance from those springs of life, democracy is a delicate plant that may well wither and die. Its growth and flourishing depends on a number of factors, all of them deployed by those who have come or been brought to the view that it is worth all the trouble.

Citizens of a democracy do not, as Peters intimates, simply arrive at political maturity and stand ready, willing and able to run its institutions. They have to be 'trained'. In a democracy, people must know their rights and be ready to exercise them — and both they and their children must value, appreciate and practise that knowledge and the commitments that go with it. It follows that one cannot achieve a good democracy without a good education, and indeed education in an institutional setting of a particular sort: it will surely be reasonably clear that, if a school is run by autocrats, it will not be likely to produce democrats. Indeed we might say that a school will hardly produce democrats if it is *not* run by people committed to, and living, the principles of the democratic form of life and government.

If then we can encourage our students to play with, and strive to achieve, some understanding of, competence at, and commitment to employing open-ended approaches and principles of critical appraisal in their acquisition of knowledge and the contributions they make to the running of their schools, and if we in our turn can see democracy actually at work in our schools, then we might be reasonably confident that our students will themselves ultimately become democrats in the rest of their lives.

Democratic Principles and the Need for Engagement in Appropriate Activities

At this point, however, the question may well arise: how can we ensure that this criticism, when called for, will be caring not carping, positive not destructive, restorative not detrimental? Above all, how can we ensure that questioning and critical enquiry, while rigorously scrutinizing and assessing policies and practices even at the most fundamental level, do not deny the worth of, or act with the ultimate aim of subverting the whole system and its values, in which such criticism is allowed and has a constructive place?

The work of Karl Popper (1943, 1960), the Austrian philosopher, may help the educator in this context. Popper argues that 'Democracy works best when faced with problems.' When a theoretical solution or proposal is put forward in an open, democratic society, it must be openly tested and criticized. Take any policy proposal — on language teaching, on decreasing gender bias in maths, science and technology, on catering for the educational needs of disadvantaged children or students from minority ethnic groups — and ask simply, will it work? And this means putting it to the test — trying it out and seeing. If it will work and resist for the time being all attempts at criticism and refutation (a central value of open societies and the democratic form of life), it may be accepted as a tentative policy. If it will not work, then either its failure will be manifest or time will allow scrutiny and criticism of it through open democratic structures that will lead to its correction and improvement.

On this basis, those committed to the increase of democracy in education need to be prepared to come up with proposals for developing democratic values, as exemplified in policies for devolution, equity, or giving students the means for enhancing their and their communities' quality of life, in Australian, American or Russian schools and education systems. But they will also need to be ready to subject them to inspection, critical scrutiny and rejection or amendment, or have other people do it. If that assertion is true, then it follows that a major key to the democratization of schools is the democratization of principals and school councils. For they will be the prime agents of the changes necessary to create and manage effectively the transformation of society, from the autocracy, hierarchy and the patriarchy of the present, to the democratic schools and the democratic society of the kind that we might all hope to see in the future.

Conclusion

It was pointed out above that the idea of 'education for democracy' looks very much like a slogan. It can also be said that 'education' and 'democracy' are both 'hurrah' terms (as Ayer, 1971 would call them), and I am uncomfortably aware that all definitions of them — including the ones I have given above — are functions of the definer's most profound metaphysical, ideological and moral preconceptions, beliefs and commitments. To that extent they are, as well as being highly prescriptive, also highly contentious — and completely open to appraisal, critique and the most strenuous efforts at correction and falsification.

What is remarkable is that, of all forms of political ideology or arrangement, the activities of clarification, criticism and correction are perhaps the chief characteristic features of 'democracy' as a form of government that we most commonly seek to identify: its constant concern for, and preoccupation with, self-examination, self-criticism, self-review and self-assessment.

What is special about and saves democrats in my view — and this, I believe, is finally the prime justification for our preferring democracy over every other form of government and the democratic school over any other style of educational administration — is that they follow the Popperian path in accepting and embracing that very attempt at refutation. Democrats place a premium upon exposing even the most cherished of their beliefs, definitions, policies and plans to public scrutiny, review and possible refutation. The very activity of democratic debate is itself a transcendental deduction of its being and value. It is this realization that gives intelligibility and point to the remark of Sir Winston Churchill speaking in the House of Commons in 1947 on 11 November — a significant day, as Australians will testify, for the concepts of accountability, open government and the need for democratic education:

> Many forms of government have been tried, and will be tried in this world of sin and woe. No-one pretends that democracy is perfect or all-wise. Indeed it has been said that democracy is the worst form of government — except all those other forms that have been tried from time to time. (Churchill, 1947)

Note

1 A longer version of the argument contained in this chapter may be found in Chapter 7 of the forthcoming book by David N. Aspin and Judith D. Chapman, with Vernon Wilkinson, *Quality Schooling* published by Cassell (1994), whose permission to publish this shorter version is most gratefully acknowledged.

References

ACKERMAN, B. (1980) *Social Principles and the Liberal State*, New Haven, Conn., Yale University Press.

ARISTOTLE (1934) *Nicomachean Ethics* (trans. H. Rackham), London, Loeb Classical Library, William Heinemann Ltd.

ASPIN, D.N. and CHAPMAN, J.D. (1994) *Quality Schooling: A Pragmatic Approach to Problems, Issues and Trends*, London, Cassell.

AYER, A.J. (1971) *Language, Truth and Logic*, Harmondsworth, Penguin.

BRAITHWAITE, E.R. (1959) *To Sir, with Love*, London, Bodley Head.

DEWEY, J. (1938) *Experience and Education*, New York, Macmillan.

GALLIE, W.B. (1956) 'Essentially contested concepts', *Proceedings of the Aristotelian Society*, LVI, see also Ch. 8 of Gallie, W.B. (1964) *Philosophy and the Historical Understanding*, London, Chatto and Windus.

GRAHAM, K. (1976) 'Democracy, paradox and the real world', *Proceedings of the Aristotelian Society*, LXXVI, pp. 227–45.

GUTTMAN, A. (1987) *Democratic Education*, Princeton, NJ, Princeton University Press.

HARE, R.M. (1964) *The Language of Morals*, 2nd ed. Oxford, Clarendon.
KLEINIG, J. (1973) 'R.S. Peters' use of transcendental arguments', *Proceedings of the Philosophy of Education Society of Great Britain* (PESGB), VII, July.
KNIGHT, T. (1985) 'An apprenticeship in democracy', *The Australian Teacher*, 11 February, pp. 5–7.
KOERNER, S. (1967) 'The impossibility of transcendental deductions', *The Monist*, 51, 3.
KOERNER, S. (1973) 'Rational choice', *Proceedings of the Aristotelian Society*, [Supplementary Volume], XLVII.
NEILL, A.S. (1968) *Summerhill*, Harmondsworth, Penguin.
PETERS, R.S. (1963) 'Reason and habit: The paradox of moral education', in NIBLETT, W.R. (Ed) *Moral Education in a Changing Society*, London, Faber and Faber.
PETERS, R.S. (1966) 'Democracy and education', *Ethics and Education*, London, Allen and Unwin.
POPPER, K.R. (1943) *The Open Society and Its Enemies* (Vol 1, Plato; Vol II, Hegel and Marx), London, Routledge and Kegan Paul.
POPPER, K.R. (1960) *The Poverty of Historicism*, 2nd ed., London, Routledge and Kegan Paul.
POWELL, J.P. (1970) 'On justifying a broad educational curriculum', *Educational Philosophy and Theory*, 2, 2.
QUINE, W.V. and ULLIAN, J.S. (1970) *The Web of Belief*, New York, Random House.
RYLE, G. (1949) *The Concept of Mind*, London, Hutchinson.
SCHEFFLER, I. (1960) *The Language of Education*, Springfield, Illinois, Charles C. Thomas.
SCHILLER, M. (1969) 'On the logic of being a democrat', *Philosophy*.
SCHUMPETER, J. (1967) 'Two concepts of democracy', in QUINTON, A. (Ed) *Political Philosophy*, Oxford, Oxford University Press.
SNOOK, I.A. (1972) (Ed) *Concepts of Indoctrination: Philosophical Essays*, London, Routledge and Kegan Paul.
WATT, A.J. (1975) 'Transcendental arguments and moral principles', *Philosophical Quarterly*, 25.
WITTGENSTEIN, L. (1953) *Philosophical Investigations* [trans. G.E.M. Anscombe] Oxford, Blackwell.

Chapter 3

Background to the Reform and New Policies in Education in Russia

Edward E. Dneprov

Current educational reforms in Russia can be best explained by the major social, economic and political paradigm shifts taking place in our country. Nearly everything is in a state of flux. Russia is moving from a totalitarian regime to a civil society, from slavery economics to market economics, from a spiritual *gulag* with a general standardization of personality to freedom and individuality.

Both the scope and the depth of educational reform can best be described in terms of these changes, as can the difficulties encountered. And it is not purely economic obstacles that block the way of the reform, as is claimed by many people. Major problems have to do with the necessity for changing the mentality of the former Soviet society. These problems are difficult to solve.

The Russian educational system now is at a stage in which there are three distinct shifts: a political, ideological and philosophical shift; a pedagogical shift; and an economic shift. The present ideological breakthrough, or the first paradigm shift, is the most difficult to make because of its revolutionary nature. Soviet education was functioning in the paradigm of a totalitarian society and produced a corresponding type of personality and nation. A democratic civil society requires a quite different type of personality and nation, characterized by personal freedom and democratic rights.

This first political, ideological and philosophical shift predetermines the success of the two other shifts. But one should not be tempted 'to cut corners' in any of these shifts. You can bypass a lot of problems and enter a more or less neutral technological space where many educational processes and technologies are piloted, instructional designs are perfected and possibilities for scientific and technological progress are accumulated. Let's not cut corners, for technological amendments without a total change of the old educational system will serve to stabilize and strengthen the former totalitarian regime.

The dramatic change in the regime makes the ideological, political and social problems of education even more acute. The school is at the epicentre of a political whirlwind. Schools have always been a focus of ideological and spiritual influence in Russia, and they are once again providing an arena for political contention. From the very beginning, revolutionary and revenge-seeking forces have been consolidating and attacking. As the reform goes further and increases its scope, these attacks are becoming more frequent and aggressive and counter-revolutionary attempts more persistent (1991 and 1992 are solid proof of this).

The five basic principles which provide the underpinning to contemporary educational reform are:

- comprehensive democratization of education;
- pluralism (including flexibility in educational financing and multiple sources of financial support), multi-systems of educational finance, diversity and alternative patterns of schooling;
- regionalization;
- national identity development through the system of education; and
- openness of the system.

These principles determine the major axes, vehicles and mechanisms of the most important shifts in the political and philosophical paradigm of civil society.

Five further principles of the reform — humanization, humanitarization of education, differentiation of education, developmental and active character of education, and lifelong learning — set the basis and mechanisms of a pedagogical shift towards a new pedagogical paradigm which has a distinct ideological character, and is a negation of the former totalitarian pedagogy. A breakthrough towards a new economic paradigm is occurring in the context of the transition from state-ownership to a market economy. This shift sets the educational system free in terms of its financial obligation, begins to establish new economic mechanisms for educational development, and influences both the mentality, social psychology and self-esteem of educators and their educational practice. There is a change from a philosophy of consuming to a philosophy of producing.

These and other major changes within educational reform require consistent and often strenuous efforts, and results are not achieved easily. The old traditions have penetrated our blood and soul and have become deeply entrenched in our psyches. However, new market diseases are equally dangerous. They can block the way of educational reform, but not to the extent that it becomes futile and doomed. Sometimes our success is beyond expectations, which means that the educational environment is a healthy one and that the changes are needed and demanded.

I believe that there are two fundamental ideas which have become the basis for educational reform in Russia:

- A new society cannot be built on the foundations of an old school system.
- Education is not only the most important factor in personality and human-resource development (the only resource that is inexhaustable

in Russia and constitutes the nation's treasure), it is also the major factor in the development of society leading to radical changes in all spheres of life.

Both this development and these reforms imply major changes in society itself, in the cornerstones of its beliefs and orientations. Thus the major tasks of reform are to change the system of values, to promote decision-making and independence, to awaken active forces within the human soul, to change the mentality of a society, and to do away with totalitarianism and communist and socialist ideology.

Changes in human thinking are the most difficult to achieve. You cannot stop a society as you can a ship, and put it into dock for repair works. You have to repair it while it's afloat — even in stormy weather. Moreover, you have to change the whole configuration — the engine, the fuel and the steering wheel simultaneously. And, which is even harder, you have to cure the whole crew, since all of them suffer from a common disease — the old mentality. In the same way, you have to reconstruct the system of education, which requires similar comprehensive repair work. And what is more this reconstruction must precede other changes if education is to be of use to the society.

Accelerated development of education is a prerequisite for social development, because it is education that either limits this development or sets new horizons for it. It is education that changes the mentality of a society, destroys old, outdated stereotypes, prepares the way for a new political culture, and changes the very nature of a society from being closed, one-dimensional and unitarian, to being open, multidimensional and pluralistic.

Education is an important instrument in working out and implementing the new social ideology. It can be a powerful catalyst for intellectual and spiritual Russian revival, restoring peasant, entrepreneurial and intellectual communities which were dispersed or destroyed in the Soviet period. It is the major prerequisite of an efficient market economy which must be successfully introduced to solve the problems of unemployment and economic literacy, and to facilitate a market way of thinking and a market culture in the population. Education is a no-less-important prerequisite for agricultural reform, the revival of the countryside and private farming based on a revival of peasant culture and a sense of land ownership, and the development of motivation and skills for managing agricultural production. Finally, education is a major factor in society's stabilization, its commitment to the care and development of children being future-oriented and, what is even more important, a working model of harmony in interethnic relationships leading to the revival and mutual enrichment of national cultures and traditions.

Today we are constructing a bridge from a side-road of civilization — which is in fact a blind alley — towards its main highway. Education is one of the cornerstones of this bridge. And the future of the country to a major extent depends on whether this cornerstone is reliable, whether the system of education can meet the challenges of our time. It is the system of education that sets the framework for what Russia will be like in the twenty-first century, and determines whether Russia will stop 'chasing' economically superior countries and move into the front line, or whether it will remain in the rear.

An understanding of the important role which education plays in the contemporary world and its utmost importance to contemporary Russia has but superficially penetrated government and public consciousness, and it has not yet become an integral part of state policy. The first decree of the President of Russian Federation, though, dated 11 July 1991, confirmed the necessity for changing political strategy in relation to education as well as to changing educational policy. The President confirmed the necessity for stopping the constant adjustment of the educational system to pragmatic needs, and for making the accelerated development of education a major goal.

This goal was the basis for the principles of the new educational policy which resulted from the reform in 1987–8. This policy was regarded not just as a considered statement of economic reform, but as a concentrated embodiment of new social values. It was not considered 'the art of possible' (according to Gorbachev) but rather 'the art of getting what is necessary'.

This new educational policy has proceeded from the assumption that past failures had proven the futility of piecemeal amendments within the system. Such amendments can't resolve major contradictions; however, they can make them more dangerous. Our new policy was meant to depart from collective irresponsibility, and the short-sightedness of former methods of educational reforms that were often based on Napoleon's principle of 'first attack, and then we'll see. . .'. We had to know the route very well before we could turn on the ignition and take the wheel. That is why the development of reform guidelines was a necessary prerequisite of new educational policy implementation.

Major Characteristics of Educational Policy

As a result we have now established the major principles underlying our educational policy:

- The popular 'institutional' approach to education and its provincial decentralization and self-sufficiency should be overcome by involving public mechanisms of educational management.
- The course of educational development should be dynamic, mobile and accelerated. It should eliminate the dogmatism and the double subordination of the former social policy which, firstly, always had to 'interpret party and governmental decisions' and, secondly, always followed social changes sometimes reflecting changes that had already occurred and sometimes contradicting them. This double subordination

lead to a paralysis of policy, which kept schools from advancing for quite some time.

- Educational policy should be realistic and independent, guarding against the former counter-reformist and new reformist myth-making. (As Yuri Levada has stated, 'overcoming our illusions we get rid of nightmares of disillusionment'). Educational policy should use compromise as a possible strategy, but with a clear understanding of its limits, for where compromise ends, double thinking begins. Educational soil is capable of producing quite different plants from those that may have been expected. It is important to understand that one breakthrough does not constitute a reform, although it provides for it; that a reform is not a momentary change but an ongoing process, and a lengthy one at that. English 'democratic' law was cultivated for 300 years to become what it is now. Realism in educational policy indicates not just awareness of the existing educational reality; it indicates also an orientation towards a future reality and the skills that will be required to reach future goals, commencing from accepted points of growth.

  This orientation implies much decision-making with a measure of flexibility consistent with educational policy. It provides for the protection of the educational system from the hardships of a transitory period, and from the rocks of political, economic and social mistakes or misunderstandings.
- There should be an emphasis on pluralism, openness, and truthfulness with just reference to the requirements of educational policy. New policies, unlike the former policies of the State, should (apart from the former policies of the State) be capable of taking into account not only the interests and needs of the State, but also the needs of the different strata of our society. Totalitarianism tried to fool itself, by constructing an ideologically homogeneous society. The normal state of society is heterogeneity. But with respect to this heterogeneity, educational policy should have two dominating tendencies — humanistic and democratic.
- Educational policy should be oriented to the rapid attainment of particular outcomes. Decades of 'bright future' prospects have exhausted the trust of Soviet people. Educational policy must include consistent goals, means, methods and results. The test of any policy is whether it achieves a significant result. This can be its crown or its tombstone.

Conclusion

The former school policy of the Soviet Union consisting of declarations and superficialities is dead and buried. Its tombstone bears an inscription similar to that on the tombstone of our 70-year-old social experiment, an anti-pedagogical axiom: 'Don't follow me!'

Chapter 4

The New Law on Education in the Russian Federation

Yevgenii V. Tkachenko

The democratic reform of education in Russia has required a completely new legislative basis. The reform embodies maximum freedom for all participants in the educational process combined with a high level of social guarantees and cultural awareness.

From 1990 to 1992 officials of the Ministry of Education of Russia, in collaboration with leading experts in education and public policy, worked to develop the new Law on Education. Opportunity was also provided for the public to discuss this law and, to this end, the bills were published twice in various newspapers.

The new conception for the development of education, which is set down in the law, directly reflects a number of radical changes which have recently taken place in the political, economic and the spiritual life of Russian society. This means that the new law of 1992 is not only a breakthrough in the realm of education, but is also one of the first laws in Russia to be based upon the developing principles of democracy.

Main Principles of State Educational Policy

The law sets down the main priorities of education, and lays the basis for state policy. The law is based on the following principles:

- depoliticization of education;
- increased autonomy for the regions of Russia in the domain of education;
- democratization of education;
- an individual approach to students; and
- differentiation of education.

These principles are formulated so that each teacher and principal can use them in practice. Such practice will promote:

- the humanistic character of education, the priority of universal humanitarian values, the life and health of citizens, the free development of personality, the cultivation of civil-mindedness and love for the Motherland;
- unity in the area of federal culture and education, and the safeguarding of national cultures and regional cultural traditions throughout the Russian Federation;
- general accessibility to education, and adaptability of the educational system to the level and specific needs of students;
- the secular character of education in state and municipal educational institutions; and
- freedom and pluralism in education.

The implementation of these principles is provided for in the following documents:

- a federal programme for the development of Russian education up to the year 2000;
- a basic curriculum; and
- Russian Federation educational standards for all subjects within a federal component.

Of special pride to educators is the fact that the law begins with the following Article: 'The Russian Federation gives priority to the educational sector.'

General Provisions of the Law

Part 1 of the law includes the following:

- legislation of the Russian Federation with respect to education;
- objectives of education legislation of the Russian Federation;
- state guarantees for rights of citizens of the Russian Federation in the field of education;
- language(s) of instruction; and
- state educational standards.

The Radical Changes Embodied in the Education Legislation

The Law on Education is to be implemented throughout the entire territory of the Russian Federation. According to the federal power which has been established, the law regulates the relationships between educational structures and is binding on all members of the Federation.

This law constitutes a kind of basic law or framework law on education, and includes general stipulations concerning the activities which fall within the competence of the members of the Federation. The members of the Federation may, according to their status and competence, set up their own legal regulations in the domain of education — they may adopt laws, legal provisions and/or other regulations which are not in conflict with federal educational legislation. Legal provisions and regulations which are adopted by members of the Federation must not limit the natural and legal rights of persons with regard to federal educational legislation.

In this law, the concept of educational standards (study objectives) is introduced for the first time by the State. State educational standards provide a scale against which it is possible to assess the level of training and the qualifications of school-leavers in an objective way. These standards have a federal component and a regional component. The federal component of the study objectives stipulates the compulsory minimum for curricula in the major teaching programmes, the maximum study load in terms of study hours for pupils, and requirements concerning the level to which school leavers are to be educated. These educational standards are to be set down by federal government bodies.

The educational standards are being worked out by various teams of academics that compete against each other on a project basis. Teachers from schools and people from many different sections of society are also involved in this process. The standards will be reviewed by teams at least once every ten years, also on a competitive basis. Educational standards for new teaching programmes will be applied no later than five years after the programmes are introduced. The regulations for working out, ratifying and implementing educational standards are set down by the Government of the Russian Federation. In order to protect national cultures and cultural traditions in the various regions of the Federation, a regional component will also be included in the educational standards. The regions may make their own decisions concerning the content of this component.

Decentralization and Maintenance of the Unity of Education in Russia

Decentralization is one of the key issues of Russian educational reform. How can we provide for autonomy of educational institutions? And how can we maintain the Russian educational system as holistic at the same time?

The educational system of the Russian Federation comprises:

- a system of consecutive study programmes with state educational standards for various levels and disciplines;
- a network of educational institutions of various types which realize these study programmes; and
- a system of agencies of educational administration and subordinate institutions and enterprises.

According to the Law of Education, pupils may follow courses or teaching programmes in different forms, according to their needs and abilities: in daytime education, without having to work at the same time; in evening courses after work; in the form of self-study; and through home schooling.

The law permits citizens of the State not only freely to choose a form of study, but also to choose in which educational establishment to study. Pursuant to the law, educational establishments may form part of the system of state education, municipal education or non-government (independent) education — private schools, schools associated with non-government and religious organizations. By allowing educational establishments of various types and legal forms to exist, the law creates an educational market. In order to create the opportunity for these educational establishments to exist, the law defines only some general requirements with respect to their registration. This sets the tone for the balance between central policy and autonomous implementation.

With the aim of encouraging competition between educational institutions the law defines general requirements with respect to their registration. The details of the registration procedures not covered by the law, are to be specified by the founder of the educational institution. These specifications should be included in an acceptance charter developed by the individual institutions. (Every school now can have a charter — a set of rules/laws. It is a basis for the school's life.)

In municipal non-government educational institutions, the founder defines the registration procedures for general elementary education and general primary education in such a way that admission is ensured for all citizens living within the relevant territory who have a right to general primary education (Article 16).

The following levels of education are provided for citizens of Russia:

- general primary education;
- general secondary (complete) education;
- elementary vocational education;
- secondary vocational education;
- higher vocational education; and
- postgraduate vocational education.

The law provides for the sharing of responsibility for each level among federal, regional and local authorities and citizens.

The jurisdiction of the Russian Federation, represented by the federal agencies of state power and administration, includes the following functions relative to the educational sector:

- development and implementation of the federal policy for education;
- legal regulation of relationships in the educational sector within the boundaries of federal competence; and

- elaboration and implementation of federal and international study programmes for educational development, taking into account socio-economic, demographic and other conditions, including the furthering of education in languages of the Russian Federation in other countries.

According to the law, the educational institution has a great deal of autonomy in its educational, organizational and financial activities. It has the flexibility to fit in with the needs of the individual and society. This is not simply devolution of responsibility from central to regional levels of power, but also a legal guarantee of the independence of an educational institution from the direct control of any educational authorities.

Economy of the Educational System

For the first time, the law includes a section on the economic aspects of education. It sets out certain problems relating to the ownership and financing of educational establishments, and outlines the guarantees for the priority given to education in current state policy. Depending on their structure and legal status, educational establishments are generally exempt from all taxes, including land tax, for the purposes of the non-profit activities which are carried out according to the status of the school. The school has the right to attract extra financial resources, including foreign currency and additional sources of assistance, by providing extra educational or other services for payment, as stipulated by the statutes. Educational establishments can take advantage of new financial opportunities for raising funds through voluntary gifts and sums of money given for specific purposes by bona fide individuals, including gifts from abroad. If extra financial resources are obtained, this does not result in a reduction in the funding provided to the educational establishment by the relevant education authority.

Under this law, educational establishments are for the first time given the right to provide educational services for payment outside the framework of the compulsory curricula and state educational standards. Income from these activities can then be used for the development of the educational establishment itself, including pay increases for the teaching staff.

Education as a Human Right

The humanistic aspect of the law is covered in Part V, 'Social guarantees for the realization of the right to education'. Under article 50 of the law, all school-leavers, regardless of the type and legal status of their school, have an equal right to register in an educational establishment at the next level. However, there is one general condition which has to be fulfilled in order for them to continue studying at a state or municipal educational establishment at the next level: the pupil must be in a possession of a certificate of education, the form of which is prescribed by the State.

The law requires all educational establishments to issue such certificates to their pupils. However, in order to do so, the educational establishment must go through a procedure of accreditation or registration by the State. Proof of accreditation not only gives the educational establishment the right to issue state-approved educational certificates to its pupils, but also, very importantly, the right to receive funding from the central budget. This means that even a non-government educational establishment can enjoy financial support from the State.

Conclusion

The new Law on Education in Russia ensures individual freedom within a state-supported system; and the autonomy of separate institutions is guaranteed within a federal educational policy. The law lays the foundations for the development of education in Russia, and thus for the development of democratic consciousness in Russian society.

Chapter 5

The Constitutional, Political and Legal Frameworks of Australian Schooling

Ian Birch

The purpose of this chapter is to demonstrate the extent to which the constitutional, political and legal frameworks of education in Australia provide a context conducive to the exercise of the concepts of democracy, which others in this volume have already addressed. Whilst there is a sense in which it might be assumed that the context of education in Australia is necessarily one where democratic values will prevail, the thesis underpinning the argument in this chapter is that whatever democratic ideals may be attributed to ideas about the Australian way of life, these are not very apparent in the provision of, and participation in, education in this country. It is proposed to examine the constitutional, political and legal contexts of Australian education and, in a concluding comment, to examine the extent to which the thesis asserted above is tenable. Discussion is directed at the schooling of children, that is, primary and secondary education.

The Constitutional Framework of Australian Schooling

The Commonwealth of Australia came into force in 1901, a clearly recent occurrence in the terms of federations such as those of the USA, Canada and South Africa, but not so new when compared with the former Federal Republic of Germany or the present Republic of Germany or of Russian Federation. But the age of the Australian federal system is not as important as the context in which it emerged. Prior to federation, the Australian colonies (these became states at federation) were jurisdictionally discrete constitutional entities, each with its own constitution and powers. Certain powers, however, such as external affairs, were administered only by the British government.

The colonies which emerged after 1788 (when colonization of what is now Australia by Europeans began) were gradually granted forms of government and constitutions. The latter tended to provide for government by the Crown (the monarch of Britain), and the parliaments established in the colonies slowly emerged as elected bodies, at least in part. Amongst the range of powers they were allowed to exercise was that of education, or more specifically, schooling. At the time of federation in 1901, all the colonies had school systems in place for which their governments were responsible, along with a range of what might be called social services.

The decade of debate which led to the establishment of the Australian federation rarely mentioned education, although democracy was an issue. Given the struggle about power between the stronger and the weaker colonies, it was not surprising to find a national constitution which provided for two Houses of Parliament. One, the House of Representatives, was democratic in the sense that members were elected by the people. As compulsory voting, preferential counting and an unequal distribution of seats per head of population emerged the democratic ideal of one person one vote was lost to the Australian electorate. The second House of Parliament, the Senate, was said to be a House of review, election to which was determined on the basis of an equal number of seats for each state. As is the case with any federation, therefore, political democracy in Australia is a very dynamic and coloured concept.

The movement towards federation and the formation of the Commonwealth of Australia left rights in general, and educational rights in particular, very much in the domain of the newly formed states. The constitutions of these tended to provide the broad power to legislate 'to make laws for the peace, welfare and good government' of the State, to cite the general provision. The breadth of such a provision, despite its not having any reference to education, enabled the states to make laws about education and most other matters.

At the national level, three factors affected a democratic intervention in school education. The first of these has already been touched on and that is the extent to which democracy prevailed in the election of persons to the Australian parliament. Although more democratic in some senses than election to the states' parliaments, only two or three political parties have ever controlled Australian parliaments; Australia has generally known government by party or coalitions of parties, formal or informal.

The second factor was the notable omission in the Australian constitution of any direct reference to education. In historic terms, schooling was clearly perceived to be a very domestic matter to be administered by domestic, i.e., state, governments. Any review of federal systems in western countries would establish an identical outcome — the USA, Canada and Germany being cases in point. Former British 'colonies' which are now federations, India for example, also determined that education was a responsibility of the provinces, although there as elsewhere, the pendulum has shifted a little in recent times (Singhal, 1990).

The third and pivotal factor was the constitutional absence in the Australian constitution of any general reference to civil rights of the sort found in the constitutional amendments to the constitution of the USA, and, more recently, included in the constitutions of Germany, India, Russia and Canada. There are some such rights in the Australian constitution but, symptomatic of the time and the dominance of English common law traditions, personal rights were not an important issue at the formulation of the Australian constitution. At the time of the federation of the six independent colonies as the Commonwealth of Australia, the historical constitutional context was not one to inspire any consideration of a democratic school environment.

Non-democratic institutions have been responsible for democratizing the Australian school system — at least in part. Principal amongst these is the High Court of Australia, an appointed group of judges. This non-democratic institution has been responsible for changing the face of education in Australia through several seminal decisions, some directly related to schooling, some not. These are mentioned briefly to provide a historical context for the present constitutional situation in regard to schooling in Australia.

Section 107 of the Commonwealth constitution provided that:

> Every power of the Parliament of a Colony which has become or becomes a State, shall, unless it is by this Constitution exclusively vested in the Parliament of the Commonwealth or withdrawn from the Parliament of the State, continue as at the establishment of the Commonwealth, or as at the admission or establishment of the State, as the case may be.

Section 109 of the constitution provided that:

> When a law of a State is inconsistent with a law of the Commonwealth, the latter shall prevail, and the former shall, to the extent of the inconsistency, be invalid.

Taken on any plain reading, schooling which was neither included in the Commonwealth constitution nor withdrawn from the states remained a state responsibility. Not necessarily so, said the High Court in a 1920 decision which had no substantive connection with education. But the decision has created the possibility for a reconsideration of the constitutional responsibility for education in Australia. The essence of the decision in the *Amalgamated Society of Engineers Case* (1920) was that the concept of reserved states' powers, which led to the doctrine of an implied Commonwealth prohibition to legislate in certain fields, was not an acceptable constitutional interpretation. Rather the doctrine to be applied was that the national government had plenary power in the areas accorded to it by the Constitution. Further, subject to certain reservations suggested by the High Court, when these powers were appropriately exercised, state law was required to give way to Commonwealth law.

This decision stoked the constitutional furnace, although educational issues did not emerge until considerably later. The Commonwealth government had a range of powers related to defence (s.51 (vi)), communication services (s.51 (v)), immigration (s.51 (xxvii)), and Aboriginal persons (s.51 (xxvi) which was amended in 1967). The *Engineers Case* decision enabled the Commonwealth government to pursue its own policies in each of these areas, which it did, resisting constitutional challenges. To this extent, whilst the Commonwealth government may have subsequently been seen to have been governing in the field of schooling without a formal constitutional mandate, the High Court provided the constitutional means for such governance to be constitutionally pursued.

Three further interventions of this non-democratic body paved the way for a democratic opening of schooling to federal as well as state governments. In historic order they were: a 1926 decision related to funding, a 1945 decision related to social services and a 1982 issue affecting international relations. Continuing in its politically 'non-responsible' way, the High Court addressed the meaning of Section 96 of the constitution in the *Roads Case* (1926). Section 96 of the constitution asserts:

> During a period of ten years after the establishment of the Commonwealth and thereafter until the Parliament otherwise provides, the Parliament may grant financial assistance to any State on such terms and conditions as the Parliament sees fit.

In its decision in 1926 and in a number of subsequent cases the High Court ruled, in the words of one of its Chief Justices, that Section 96 was 'susceptible of a very wide construction in which few if any restrictions can be implied' (*Victoria v. Commonwealth 99*, 1957). Not only did the run of rulings in these cases vary the constitutional balance between the national and state governments in a range of matters, it particularly enabled a broadening of the constitutional responsibility for the funding of education, particularly after the Commonwealth government took over the power to tax incomes in 1942. As I have commented elsewhere:

> The importance of such a judicial ruling lies in that the fact that section 96 has been the constitutional power used by successive national governments from the right and left of politics directly to influence developments in education in the Australian States, so as to give the lie to the assertion that education is a States' right. Such intervention has significantly affected education systemically, as with the maintenance of a private fee paying educational sector, through a range of schemes begun with the introduction of the Science Laboratories Scheme, in 1964. (Birch, 1990)

The second High Court decision was that taken in 1945 in the *Pharmaceutical Benefits Case*, again one not involving schools. In this case, the High Court ruled that a particular social-service provision related to the provision to citizens of pharmaceutical benefits was beyond the power of the

Commonwealth government. The implication drawn by the analysts of this decision was that much of the national social-service legislation might be impeached. The resultant political action — glossing over its fascinating detail — was that the people, acting in accordance with the provisions of the national constitution, voted to amend the constitution by giving the national government power to make laws for the provision of a range of social services, including that of providing 'benefits to students'. Thus a non-democratic body's decision provoked a democratic reaction which in turn resulted in a constitutional amendment which provided the Commonwealth government with the only power which approximates a direct power in education.

The final and most significant non-democratic, democratizing act of the High Court, in constitutional terms, was its decision in the *Koowarta Case* (1982). The decision in this case had the effect of importing civil rights for the Australian people into the legal and political domain without a formal change to the constitution. The High Court decided in *Koowarta* that the national parliament had the power under the external affairs provision in the constitution (s.51 (xxix)) to pass legislation which would implement the substance of *bona fide* international agreements. Australia had ratified a number of international agreements originating in the United Nations Organization, the United Nations Educational Scientific and Cultural Organization, the International Labour Organization and other significant world and regional organizations, in both general matters, and those affecting education and schooling. This 1982 ruling of the High Court enabled the national government to intervene in state law in the interests of the people to ensure that rights not provided for democratically were legally theirs. This was a rather tortuous path to a conclusion not so straightforward as that in Article 57 of the Law of the Russian Federation on Education (1992), which provides for the recognition for the people of internationally agreed provisions not contrary to this Law. Nevertheless, given the history of Australian constitutional provisions, the result in this country is noteworthy, particularly so when it is acknowledged that the body responsible was the non-democratic High Court of Australia.

The Political Framework of Australian Education

The political framework for schooling in Australia parallels the constitutional developments described above. Prior to 1901, schooling was the responsibility of the individual colonies. With the advent of federation, it remained the concern of the newly emerged states and also attracted the interest of the national government. Whilst the latter played little part in determining school policy before 1945, the last fifty years has seen an ever increasing involvement. Whilst the politics of schooling in Australia merit considerable attention in a detail which cannot be begun within the limits of this chapter, it is proposed to address four significant aspects of those politics. These are the bureaucratization of education, the politicization of education, educational choice — especially the State–Church debate — and federal–state relations in education.

The Bureaucratization of Education

The bureaucratization of education was first evident in a major way in the decades before Federation. The period from 1870 to 1900 was one in which the colonies moved towards the provision of schooling which has been traditionally described in Australia as 'free, compulsory and secular'. (A close analysis of the legal provisions suggest that there are flaws in this description but it remains the 'myth' of Australian schooling in the public domain.)

More important than identifying the main traits of primary schooling, this period also saw the cementing of the governance of Australian schooling in a bureaucratic mould. The beginning of schooling had been attempted in some cases in the context of local government administration. In Western Australia, for example, the 1871 Education Act asserted in its preamble, 'Whereas it is expedient that the people should have a more direct control in the management of the Public Elementary Educational system. . .'. Fletcher (1979) notes, 'The extent to which local communities were once involved in the management of the education of their children may be a matter of some surprise'. Early education in some colonies was community-based with district boards being established comprising elected members and with powers to operate school systems. However, they were always subject to the rules of the central board and had no independent financial resources.

Within twenty years, the principle of governance by the people had varied considerably. As colonies gained parliamentary independence, the tradition of ministerial responsibility — that is, a responsibility exercised by a Minister accountable to the electorate through the Parliament — superseded the notion of local representation. In addition, the loss of confidence in local boards on the one hand and the expansionist interests of central authority on the other hand spelt the end of governance of education so directly by the people. Although the boards lingered on until 1922, the politics of education was firmly embedded in a central authority. This authority comprised a Minister of the Crown responsible to Parliament and a Department of Education under the control of a statutorily appointed Director, which exercised wide-ranging control over the provision of primary and later secondary education.

The Politicization of Education

The highly centralized bureaucratic control of public education remained in place in Australia until the 1980s when a major change took place, which has been characterized as the politicization of education. In essence, Ministers of Education became active in their portfolios. They began making very direct decisions affecting the provision of education, no longer being prepared to rely on and percolate the advice of professional bureaucrats. In the process which followed, the management system of education was varied in at least two major respects.

In the first place, there was a major restructuring of the various state systems of education, with ministerial advisers rather than public servants providing advice. Senior officers were evicted or transferred from positions, corporate management styles replaced governmental bureaucratic forms, and security and trust gave way to doubt and *angst*. These changes were political, but not in the sense of partisan politics. Both sides of the political fence engaged in such activities. In two states, New South Wales and Victoria, changes of government saw no discrimination in the politicizing of education.

The second aspect of the change in the political climate was the movement towards devolving the school system from its centralized orientation to more domestic control. Variations in the form of the devolution were evident in the different states. Common to most was the attempt to put more educational power in the hands of educators at the local level. In particular, school-based governance, policy-making and decision-making were advocated.

The politicization of school education, so briefly canvassed, has attracted a considerable literature. Issues have been raised as to its worthwhileness from a political, far less pedagogical view. Questions have been addressed as to its success in management terms, given that the apparent democratization of the system was rarely supported with adequate financial sources or powers. Evidence has been proffered to suggest that the democratic principles underpinning the process were not necessarily sought or wanted by major participants in the system, including teachers and principals.

In general democratic terms, little changed for those for whom primary and secondary schooling was provided — the children and the parents. In some instances both were offered change and choice but with little enlightenment as to the scope and implications of their decisions. Although parents were enabled to participate in school-based decision-making groups, their voice was that of the lay person amongst the professionals. Power remained with the latter, many of whom, in turn, deemed that the power remained where it always had — at the 'Centre'.

The politicization of education has left an impression — perhaps not indelible — on the administration of Australian education. While remnants of it are in evidence at the time of writing, it would seem that what has occurred is a revision of the bureaucratic domination rather than its replacement. In terms of the democratization of Australian schooling, there has been some, but relatively little, change.

Choice in Education

The third feature in the political scenario has been the issue of choice in education. As summarized by Austin and Selleck (1975), the period from the founding of the colonies after European settlement to the time of Federation was characterized by the issue of Church versus State.

> For the first three-quarters of the century the problems of religious instruction and State aid had dominated educational politics, but in the last twenty-five years the debate, though not ended, had quietened considerably. State after state resolved to exclude religious instruction from the public schools (or to permit it only on a very restricted basis) and to withdraw government assistance from church schools. Thus, for better or worse, the problem was removed from the centre of the educational stage and educators were left free to concentrate on what was happening in the classrooms of the national elementary schools. (Austin and Selleck, 1975)

The state-aid issue came to a political head again in the 1950s when national and state politics were rent asunder by the question. Whereas conservative parties were finally able to accommodate the notion of state aid (state support for non-government religious education), their political counterparts were very divided, especially given the very Catholic basis of the Australian Labor Party. Beginning in 1964, national governments of all political persuasions committed themselves to providing financial support for religious schools, following decisions already made in some states by other governments.

If democratization is defined as the greater participation by citizens in choosing the form of education they want for their children, the 1950s and 1960s were such decades in the history of Australian schooling. But they were also very divisive years as parents and teachers arraigned themselves against each other publicly to argue the issue as to whether governments should do more than support the free, compulsory, secular ideal. No single election can be claimed to have been fought on this issue. But it was significant in the ballot box in several elections as conservative governments came to power on the basis of the preferential system of voting. This system allowed those who favoured state aid to vote for a splinter Labor Party — the Democratic Labor Party — which cast its preferences for the conservative parties.

The issue of choice in this religious sense came to a head with the mounting of a challenge in the High Court of Australia in what became known as the *DOGS Case* (1981). It is not proposed to discuss the case in detail here (Birch, 1984), but merely to note aspects of it which affect the issue of democracy, namely the plaintiffs to the case and its outcome. The plaintiffs to this case comprised three distinctive groups — and strange bedfellows they were. The first group comprised the principal plaintiff, a member of a Christian Church to the right of the ecclesiastical centre, whose commitment to the task was such that he undertook a law degree to ensure he knew his ground. Other members of this group were concerned that state aid would injure the integrity of the Church. A second religious grouping of somewhat less theoretical orientation was simply suspicious, to say the least, of the benefit which was flowing to the Roman Catholic Church as a result of state-aid policy. A third group comprised unionists and others with no affiliation with religious groups and no connection with their cause. These were opposed to the proposition of state aid on the grounds that it divided society by supporting the rich and depriving the poor.

The High Court decided that the grants made by the Commonwealth government in support of aid to students in Church schools were constitutionally justifiable. As conclusive as the decision was, it only applied to the laws of the national government. The states were under no similar restraint, although the decision may have had some persuasive effect in Tasmania, a state which had in its constitution a provision similar to Section 116 in the Commonwealth constitution. The Court's decision paved the way for government support of religious schooling, which enabled parents to choose the education they preferred for their children. But although seemingly dead, the issue of state aid in Australian education is not yet buried.

Federal–State Relations in Education

The final political dimension deserving of mention is that of federal–state relations in education and their influence in the democratization of education. The Australian Education Council, a non-statutorily appointed conference of Australian Ministers of Education, was founded in 1936 and Commonwealth–state relations in education began to evolve from 1949. However Australian schooling was not directly impinged upon by national policy in terms of the democratization of schooling until 1972, when issues of equity, equality and equal opportunity became more prominent.

The national involvement in the provision of schooling has grown and expanded considerably since that time. Australian education has entered an era when the issues are national curricula, appropriate national teacher education, competencies of school graduates being determined by national committees, national assessment criteria and a national determination of the schooling agenda. Such forces are being supported and resisted on many fronts. In support are governmental institutions and 'peak' employer organizations, and employee unions and federations. Resisting are state governments; educationalists; the private schooling sector, which provides places for more than one-third of the secondary school population; and parents' groups.

In one very real and important sense, this is democracy at work. People are arguing about school policy and its implementation. In another sense, the democracy of choice as far as the parent and child is concerned is a façade. The democratization of school education is not, however, merely limited to inter- or intra-governmental arguments about policies for school education. One significant movement in Australian schooling is the pursuit of education by means other than mainstream government or private-sector schooling. Only now coming of age in Australia are provisions such as that in Article 52(3) of the Law of the Russian Federation on Education which provides for home schooling. The democratization of education interpreted as genuine public choice may be deemed to have become available only when a range of schooling opportunity, including home schooling, is genuinely made available to parents and students.

The Legal Framework of Australian Schooling

The legal framework of Australian schooling has inevitably been touched upon in the foregoing sections addressing the constitutional and political frameworks for such schooling. But still more needs to be said. Obviously it is the legal process which further integrates the constitutional provisions with the community. Likewise, the process takes political policy and implements it by way of law making.

Law-making procedures follow upon constitutional provisions and political determinations. Thus the form of school administration is passed into law. Further, particular aspects of schooling policy are given a legal mandate. These will include the role to be played by and the discipline to be imposed upon teachers, the extent of parental involvement in education, the rights and duties accorded to, and required of, students — to mention some of the participants in the school system.

Leaving aside the law, which establishes the school administrative framework, there is a range of law which covers other facets of education. For example, the requirement that parents must cause their children to attend school is a legal one both in terms of that prescription and its enforceability. Excuses for non-attendance are also legally provided for and penalties are prescribed for parents who fail to cause their children to attend school or children who fail to attend of their own volition.

The law also addresses the meaning of school attendance by prescribing the length of the attendance required both in terms of the years of attendance and numbers of hours per day of attendance is required. By law, exemption from attendance is permitted in certain circumstances. Further, Australian school law provides for a range of circumstances in which parents may employ their children. The concern of the law is that employment does not interfere with education. But the present restrictions vary across the states, with the minimum criterion being that children may not be employed in school hours. Outside these hours, such employment should not interfere with the capacity of the child to enjoy the full benefit of the schooling provided.

In more recent times, laws have been made which attempt to allow and involve parent involvement in the school decision-making process. Committees of parents, teachers and principals have been appointed to prepare school-based programmes. But whilst such involvement suggests progress in the democratization of education in allowing a significant parental input into the school process, the result has been minimal in terms of the critical ingredients in the schooling process such as in determining the curriculum, appointing teachers and principals, and controlling the school budget.

As has been mentioned above, Australian constitutional law is not noted for its provision of rights or its protection for abuses of the apparent rights of children. This has been addressed to some extent in the legal requirements related to the discipline of children. Corporal punishment is now generally not available to teachers or principals in government schools by decision of the school administration. The same may be said of the private sector in general, although it is important to note that provisions within the criminal law of the states may well allow for corporal punishment. Policy with regard to the disciplining of children has been incorporated into law, which provides for a range of options to be exercised, ranging from withdrawal from a class to exclusion from a school. The extent to which such a provision assists in providing democracy in education is debatable. Laws need to be framed which preserve the rights of those who attend school according to law and of those who are alleged to be offenders in the school context.

An important issue in terms of democracy in education is the extent to which children at school are entitled to the protection of the provisions of natural justice — the right to know what the charges are when they have been laid, and the right to be heard with respect to them in an unbiased manner. Whilst much current Australian legislation has incorporated these concepts into the legislation with regard to discipline, it is still doubtful whether children in Australian schools may claim rights to natural justice. Those in the private sector have little recourse to such an appeal: those in the government sector may have more grounds for hope following the decision in *McMahon v. Buggy* (1972). Overall, however, the outlook is bleak, and children in Australia may well lose their claim to rights when they pass beyond the school door.

Teachers in government schools in Australia are virtually employees of the Crown, with their conditions of service, salaries, appeals and the like being provided for in law. Although there have been legislative moves in the past to have teachers formally registered, this is not now the case, either in the public or the private sectors of schooling. Whilst the law in Australia tends not to prescribe what teachers are to teach in school, a range of subsidiary law makes provision for the curriculum to be taught and the subjects prescribed for examination. There are critical points of testing for children in school, such as at the end of primary education, the conclusion of compulsory education and the completion of high school, with entry into tertiary institutions as a key examination point. The examination system and, therefore, the requirements on teachers for 'hard' assessment in Australia is not as demanding as in many other countries, where tough criteria for annual examinations, and rules for children who fail or repeat grade are the norm.

To some extent teachers are responsible for their professional action. For example, government school teachers are liable to be disciplined for breaches of professional conduct. Such accountability is always limited in terms of the processes to be followed and the penalties to be imposed for breaches of conduct. But the procedures available provide some avenues for members of the public, aggrieved by the actions of teachers, to make teachers accountable for their actions. However, there has been no success in legal terms in Australia for parents or students to call teachers to account for their professional waywardness. Teachers' rights are limited. Whilst teachers may hold more influential positions than parents, it is often the case that they are as powerless in terms of determining educational policy. By law, teachers are essentially employees, whether in the government or the private sector. In either sector, the teachers' professional expertise is not utilized greatly, in terms of educational policy-making. One particular matter of concern for teachers is the extent to which their behaviour in their private lives may effect their employment. Both the Russian Federation Law on Education and Australian law suggests that teachers are not immune from public action for what they may do in their private lives. The high standard expected of teachers, as with other government employees, makes them more obviously liable for their private actions, even to the extent of losing their employment for very non-professional reasons.

Negligence or malpractice is one area of the law in Australia where the rights of some — students, in particular — have been protected against the wrongs caused by others — usually, but not only, teachers. In *Ramsay v. Larsen* (1964), the High Court of Australia broke new ground in determining that state education authorities, or other employees of teachers, were liable for the negligent acts of their employees, the teachers. In a succession of cases, this position has been reaffirmed and expanded. In the most recent case of this kind (*Introvigne*, 1982) decided in the Court, it was asserted that:

> There are strong reasons for saying that it is appropriate that a school authority comes under a duty to ensure that reasonable care is taken of pupils attending the school . . . The immaturity and inexperience of the pupils and their propensity for mischief suggest that there should be a special responsibility on a school authority to care for their safety, one that goes beyond a mere vicarious liability for the acts and omissions of its servants.

The run of cases in Australia since 1964 on the issue of the care owed by schools to students has provided the opportunity for parents and pupils to obtain legal redress against teachers who have been negligent in their employment. The number of cases has not been large over the past twenty-five years. This is attributable to a number of factors, including the cost of such litigation, and the difficulty involved in pursuing an area of alleged negligence given that one has to prove a case on the balance of probabilities and bear such cost as is apportioned, should the case be lost. Despite governmental inaction on the issue, the decisions of the Parliament with regard to future financing of education leads one to conclude that the directions taken by the courts in some instances have improved the provision of schooling. The High Court's decisions have reflected a major pedagogical and practical concern that persons wronged by the system should be recompensed for the wrongs they suffer.

Conclusion

The evidence from the foregoing suggests that, while Australian constitutional provisions may be restrictive — and that is still a very debatable matter — they cannot be said to be restrictive of the provision of education according to whatever counts as democratic. Whilst a more desirable constitution might be proposed, Australia is not in the position of the Russian Federation, namely drawing up a national law or constitution which recognizes federal and state competencies in the context of a new world order. The constitution of Australia is some 90 years of age and is representative of an era and tradition. The era was one when compulsory schooling was only emerging: the tradition one which did not lend itself to allowing for a body of rights to which citizens might appeal to obtain their justifiable ends. Nevertheless, changes made to the constitution, particularly those 'changes' brought about by the interpretation of the High Court, have provided the prospect of Australian citizens obtaining educational rights by way of the international conventions and agreements to which this country has become a party. Whatever the merits of 'changing' the constitution in this way, the benefit to citizens is that they have managed to appropriate some rights in education. As limited as the constitution has been, its limiting power has been somewhat diminished by decisions of the High Court.

As between the legislative and judicial arms of government — apart from the constitutional cases mentioned previously — it would have to be said for Australia, in contradistinction to countries such as the USA, that the democratization of education has relied more on the political rather than the judicial process. In this country the term 'democratization' was very much in vogue in the 1940s. At that time, with the Labor ('socialist') government in power, the educational area most in need of democratization was that of university education. The context in which the term was used was one in which university education was seen to be the domain of the rich — so much so that in 1943 the Labor government introduced both a scholarship programme to enable poorer but eligible students to attend university, and a quota system to ensure that only the best students obtained places.

As far as school education in Australia was concerned, democratization might be applied to the very early process by which free, compulsory and secular schooling was introduced into this country. In more recent times democratization has taken a legislative form in the extent to which minority groups and multicultural education have been promoted and protected. This has been achieved by legislative means partly through active decision-making, partly as a reaction to the decisions of others. For example, industrial courts have ruled that migrant workers are entitled to free tuition in the English language to enable them to be both competent workers and to enjoy a safe working environment.

Despite the argument that the political rather than the legal domain has provided the most likely avenue for the democratization of education in Australia, the courts have played a not insignificant role, as has been demonstrated above. The irony of this, which has also been mentioned, is that the courts are essentially non-responsible, in the political sense. The fact that decisions have been reached which have advanced the democratic nature of schooling can only be applauded. But it is also fortuitous that this is the case. A different set of judges operating in a different context may have arrived at different conclusions. One only needs to be reminded that the Supreme Court ruled in *Plessy v. Ferguson* (*US Supreme Court*, 1896) that segregation by way of the provision of separate facilities for black Americans was constitutional, and then in 1954 (*US Supreme Court*, 1954) that such an arrangement was unconstitutional. The Court comprised different members in the two cases: the political and social context was considerably different. The membership of courts and the context of the cases before them are factors likely to contribute to the decisions likely to be made in other instances.

The issue is whether democratization should be left to such a fragile, non-democratic, non-responsible (in terms of answering to the people) institution. The answer is No! The people's avenue to democracy and responsible government in the Australian system is the legislature, even if they and it suffer from some constitutional limitations. In terms of the democratization of education, therefore, the focus has to be on the legislature and its capacity to effect democracy in education by making laws appropriate to that end.

The problem is, however, that Australian legislatures have not demonstrated any great competence at democratizing education. Bureaucratizing, yes. Democratizing, no. Such a claim can be simply tested, for example, by examining the legal provisions for schooling by establishing a ranking of the participants in it and the rights enjoyed by them. This may be done by determining the occurrences of the words 'shall' (a mandatory term in Australian law) and 'may' (a permissive term) and the extent to which Ministers, bureaucrats, principals, teachers, parents and students are the subject or predicate of these uses. The managers of Australian education have mainly permissive duties, the consumers the obligations.

Does school law necessarily have to be of this sort? Clearly not. Were principles such as the interests of the child or the participation of parents — democratic concerns in other words — central to the making of school law, much of the present legislation would require extensive review. Where, of course, the maintenance of the management system is the paramount aim, the present law is quite supportive. Democratic practices in education should reasonably have the underpinning of democratic legislative provisions. Whilst some have emerged in Australia's statutory provisions in education, too much has been left to occasional judicial intervention and too little initiative taken to change the status quo at the political level.

References

AUSTIN, A.G. and SELLECK, R.J.W. (1975) *The Australian Government School*, Carlton, Pitman Pacific Books, p. 62.

AUSTRALIAN HIGH COURT (1896) *Plessy v. Ferguson* 163 US 537.

AUSTRALIAN HIGH COURT (1900) *Commonwealth of Australian Constitution Act*, (63 and 64 Victoria, Ch. 12), Canberra, Government Printer.

AUSTRALIAN HIGH COURT (1920) *Amalgamated Society of Engineers v. Adelaide Steamship Company* 28 CLR 129.

AUSTRALIAN HIGH COURT (1920) *Engineers Case*, see *Amalgamated Society of Engineers v. Adelaide Steamship Company*.

AUSTRALIAN HIGH COURT (1926) *Roads Case*, see *Victoria v. Commonwealth*.

AUSTRALIAN HIGH COURT (1926) *Victoria v. Commonwealth* 38 CLR 399.

AUSTRALIAN HIGH COURT (1945) *Attorney-General for Victoria (ex rel. Dale and others) v. Commonwealth* 71 CLR 237.

AUSTRALIAN HIGH COURT (1945) *Pharmaceutical Benefits Case*, see *Attorney-General for Victoria (ex rel. Dale and others) v. Commonwealth*.

AUSTRALIAN HIGH COURT (1954) *Brown v. Board of Education* 347 US 483.

AUSTRALIAN HIGH COURT (1957) *Victoria v. Commonwealth* 99 CLR 575 at 605.

AUSTRALIAN HIGH COURT (1964) *Ramsay v. Larsen* 111 CLR 16.

AUSTRALIAN HIGH COURT (1972) *McMahon v. Buggy* Unreported case from the New South Wales Supreme Court No. 2095.

AUSTRALIAN HIGH COURT (1981) *Attorney-General for Victoria (ex rel. Black) v. The Commonwealth* 33 ALR 361.

AUSTRALIAN HIGH COURT (1981) *DOGS Case*, see *Attorney-General for Victoria (ex rel. Black) v. Commonwealth*.

AUSTRALIAN HIGH COURT (1982) *Commonwealth v. Introvigne* 56 ALJR 749.

AUSTRALIAN HIGH COURT (1982) *Introvigne*, see *Commonwealth v. Introvigne*.

AUSTRALIAN HIGH COURT (1982) *Koowarta v. Bjelke Petersen* 39 ALR 417.

BIRCH, I.K.F. (1984) 'State-aid at the bar: The DOGS case', in PALMER, I. (Ed) *Melbourne Studies in Education*, Melbourne, Melbourne University Press, pp. 31–54.

BIRCH, I.K. (1990) 'Australia', in BIRCH, I.K. and RICHTER, I. (Eds) *Comparative School Law*, Oxford, Pergamon, p. 143.

FLETCHER, L. (1979) 'Community Involvement in Education: The First Hundred Years', in NEAL, W.D. (Ed) *Education in Western Australia*, Perth, UWA Press, p. 63.

LAW OF THE RUSSIAN FEDERATION ON EDUCATION (1992), English translation.

SINGHAL, R.P. (1990) 'India', in BIRCH, I.K. and RICHTER, I. (Eds) *Comparative School Law*, Oxford, Pergamon, pp. 255–74.

UNITED STATES SUPREME COURT (1896) *Plessy v. Ferguson* 163 US 537.

UNITED STATES SUPREME COURT (1954) *Brown v. Board of Education* 347 US 483.

Chapter 6

Democratic Values in Russian Education 1955–93: An Analytical Review of the Cultural and Historical Background to Reform

Alexander I. Adamsky

Introduction

How do democratic values become integrated into education? If the backgrounds of educational systems, cultural-ethnic backgrounds and democratic values meet at school, as parts of the whole, the result is a school of a civilized society. If they don't meet, there won't be a civilized society. This is the case because:

- democracy is possible only when education is built on democratic values — freedom of choice, self-determination, sovereignty of the personality;
- in education, these values, in contrast to totalitarian ones, are impossible to impose — they emerge themselves, at schools, from real educational practice.

Democratic educational values cannot be born and cannot survive in 'obedient' state schools. At least, not in Russia. If these premises are true, it is reasonable to assert that in a democratic civil society, the school can't belong totally to the State.

Two explanations to the reader are necessary here. In this chapter I have chosen to focus on the period 1955–93. I chose this period for a simple reason — this is the time of my generation; I was born in 1955. My parents, during all my life, worked in schools. I became a teacher at 18. This, in part, explains my approach to this chapter — an attempt at personal reflection.

My main hypothesis, that a school with democratic values can't belong totally to the State, has proved to be correct in the case of the network of schools which are involved in the first non-government in-service teacher-training institution, the Eureka Free University. In this chapter I examine the difficult fate of these schools.

An Analysis of Innovative Tendencies in Russian Education (1955–92)

The Thaw

The 'thaw' is a word used by Ilya Ehrenburg to mark the end of the short period termed the 'people's tyranny'. Three years had passed since Stalin's death when in 1956 the communists gathered at their XXth Party Congress and Nikita Kruschev bravely pronounced the 'half-truth' that shattered the myth of totalitarian invincibility. A new cultural wave appeared — the generation of the 1960s — poets, writers, actors, journalists. These were outstanding people and they became well-known all over the world after, and because of, 'the thaw'. Despite the influence of this generation nobody seems to know of any outstanding educators of the 1960s. The public glory — authority and recognition — didn't come to a single one. Does this mean that they didn't exist?

In the 1960s everything began to change, 'a heavy ice began to stir', as Ehrenburg wrote, but school and educational science seemed, publicly at least, to remain dead, petrified. But when the whole river is drifting with ice, one place can't remain unmovable. In 1953–9 the fundamental trends in modern education — collective creativity in technology, the methodology of thought activity and teachers' innovations — were born.

The Communards' Movement

In 1956 the Frunze Commune was founded. Two educators, Igor Ivanov and Faina Shapiro, created the commune in the Leningrad House of Pioneers in the Frunzensky District, giving it the name 'Commune' in memory of Makarenko. It was a children's club, where children had discussions and evening parties and went hiking. The commune promoted the view that one lived one's life for the sake of others, that one must always value sincerity — if not, then what was life for? This was the main law of the Communards.

The Communard movement, a special educational method aimed at enhancing the collective creativity of children, quickly spread across the country. It was a very effective social technology based on collective planning of the life of the children's collective, and creative fulfilment. It also involved detailed investigation of who participated in the collective creative work and how they participated. Collective planning, collective creativity, collective analysis — these constituted the Communards' upbringing. For the first time in a Soviet children's collective, the value of human relationships was acknowledged. 'Tell me about me.' Communards would ask their friends during evening reflection. 'Who am I for you, how do you feel about me?' The Communards broke away from the gloomy space of children's upbringing based on categories of 'need' and 'must'.

The main event in the Communards' life was the Communards' assembly, the main ritual of which was the so-called 'eaglet circle'. At the beginning of the 1970s, the centre of the Communards' movement had become the Pioneer campus 'Eaglet', and the number one person in the Communards' movement had become the chief of one of the groups — Oleg Gazman. When Communards made a circle, put their arms around the shoulders of their friends and sang the Communard songs, there was no stronger fraternity in the world.

There were many rules, laws, and rituals created by Communards and transmitted from one group of children to the next. Children created the norms, an unprecedented and unheard of situation in post-Stalin Russia, in which everything, even the last social screw, was worked out by a 'brilliant leader'. Traditionally in children's collectives it was the custom to follow the laws, demands and rules made by adults. If you did everything well, you were good, you had friends. If you broke the rules you were faced with investigation, trial and boycott. The Communards' groups were designed by children and lived according to the original children's constitution. Children themselves were the authors of their life inside the Communard unit. These norms were transmitted to the next group of children as a tradition and discussed at the general Communards' assembly. The ways of doing things together could then be shared and mastered. The Communards' movement changed from being an experiment to becoming established practice. 'Live for the sake of others' happiness' became the main communard of thousands of children. From the Communards' movement the pedagogy of 'human relationships' grew up, the pedagogy of collective creative life exemplified in the schools of V. Korakovsky, A. Tubelsky, M. Schetinin and A. Pazuhnin.

Methodology of System Thought

At the beginning of the 1950s student-philosophers and psychologists at Moscow University began to reread Marx secretly. Famous philosophers such as Llyenkov, Zinovijev, Shedrovitsky, and Mamardashvili suspected that there was something wrong with the way Marxism was being realized in practice. On the basis of Marxist theory — the only scientific material available to them — they attempted to build a system of reflection and prognosis of reality.

From this movement, three trends emerged. The first trend was the system–thought–activity approach (STA) — system analysis plus thinking as an activity. Methodologists (they assumed such a name) established thought activity as a theoretical concept, which gave them a powerful method of penetration into the essence of the things and, at the same time, a method for constructing other concepts. The form of such construction and penetration became the 'game' (second trend), but the game was a serious activity, an organizational activity game. The initiator of this trend is considered to be George Shedrovitsky. Peter Shedrovitsky, Gromiko, Popov and Anisimov became his followers, leaders of the 'second wave'. The third trend was a focus on meta-subjects, on the basis of which it was possible to form the activity of learning — not a set of subjects, but the meta-content of thinking techniques, accumulated and grown by the culture. The methodological axiom was to master such techniques and methods of thinking as options for penetrating and understanding culture. Such work was done by Gromiko.

Methods and ways of organizing activity games became popular in education. So in 1986 a series of organization-activity games in Krasnoyarsk led to the opening of the psychology-pedagogical faculty at Krasnoyarsk University. Some time later, when some educationalists from the Eureka movement adopted the methodology, there appeared centres for organization-activity games. (V. Lozing in Kemerovo; in some way T. Kovaljova in Tomsk; the methodological lycée of D. Dmitrijev in Moscow.) The main concept, brought by the methodologists in the modern Russian educational context, was the value of the collective thinking activity.

Teachers-innovators

> Weak people in rebellion lead to devastation, but the rebellion of strong people leads to illumination. (S. Solovejchik, 1986)

The main problem Shatalov and Lusenkova solved was how to teach everybody according to the school curriculum — neither refusing to admit students, nor sending them to specialized classrooms, but teaching everybody. The basis of their method was so-called 'supporting signals' and schemes, which Solovejchik (1986) wrote about. Shatalov began work on his method at the end of 1950s. According to Solovejchik:

> The main thing in the Shatalov method is a 'system of signals' or 'system of notes'. The lesson plan is a result of a teacher's hard work. On the page are brief key-words, separate words with exclamations, maths notations, figures which the teacher needs to remember, charts the teacher will need to explain. The material is carefully organized using different lines and colour. Everything is thoroughly prepared in advance and is the basis for a twenty-minute lesson which might include a story, algorithm or reflection. It's not an elaborate lesson plan (plan on the left, paraphrase on the right), it's a modern, workable businesslike system of notes. The maximum amount of information is included within a minimum of space; it is a summary code understandable only to the initiated — a perfect business summary. (Solovejchik, 1986)

Lusenkova sought a method of teaching all the students in the classroom. She taught children how to think aloud, to accompany every action with a word

— again the idea of a note-scheme, a scheme for recording the child's thought was developed. Lusenkova worked out special schemes for every action and children followed the patterns, explaining to themselves and others what they were doing.

Teacher-innovators, V. Shatalov and S. Lusenkova, for the first time brought into education the idea that you can teach *everybody*. The concepts of collective thinking activity; human relationships and community life; and education for everybody were the main ideas which appeared during the last thirty-five years of Russian education. But, let's add two more ideas which are the result of scientists' and teachers' efforts during the last fifteen years — theoretical thinking and dialogue. Both of these are associated with the concept of developmental teaching.

Developmental Teaching

In 1959 in Moscow, secondary school N91 (Arbat Street) and the Scientific Research Institute of General and Pedagogical Psychology (Academy of Pedagogical Sciences) began an experiment. The aim of the experiment was to prove that it's possible to develop a theoretical type of thinking in primary-age children. The leader of the experiment was Daniil Elkonin, a student of the outstanding Soviet psychologist Vygotsky. The head of the laboratory which devised the Russian language curricula was Vasilij Davydov. Davydov was very close to the Moscow group of methodologists which influenced the following events. Many members of this circle decided that the most effective method of bringing about social change was to create a 'new education'. The school was chosen as 'fertile soil' for social change. Evald Llyenkov began to work with the problem of teaching deaf mutes, and Shedrovitsky with the methodology of shifting educational paradigms. The experiment, launched by Elkonin, continued successfully till the end of the 1970s.

Three educational approaches were developed in the Vygotsky cultural-historical conception: the Davydov–Elkonin system, the Zankov system and the Galperin system. What these three systems had in common was an understanding of a child's personal development in terms of his or her movement towards the Vygotsky's zone of 'approximal development' as a result of group/common activity. Inherent in the system was the principle of moving from abstract notions to concrete thinking, and Elkonin's periodization of age.

Key concepts in developmental teaching are:

- Vygotsky's notion of the developmental nature of teaching — teaching should lead development.
- Developmental functions of teaching are realized through building the content of knowledge, which is theoretical even with primary-school children.

In 1983 all the experiments on developmental teaching were stopped. The Davydov laboratory and its branches were closed and Davydov was excluded from the Party and removed from his position as Director of the Institute of General and Pedagogical Psychology (Academy of Pedagogical Sciences). The final crushing defeat for the Moscow psychological school occurred in 1983 at the all-union Congress of Psychologists. In addition, the hot-tempered Davydov quarrelled with his academic colleagues, some of whom were very influential and supported by the Central Committee of the Communist Party of the Soviet Union (CPSU). Theoretical arguments turned into personal rows, with the winners making short work of the losers. Not only were the scientific laboratories closed but experimental work was stopped in schools. Teachers in one school in Kharkov continued this work, but they had to keep traditional textbooks on the tables (in case the inspector came to check on their teaching). But in 1986, under the influence of the *Teachers Gazette*, a renaissance in developmental teaching began. Now, developmental teaching in all its variations is the most promising new system of teaching, the only one in which modern conceptions of personality development have been adequately reflected in the curriculum — at least in the primary school.

Splash and Fade of the Public Educational Movement in Russia (1986–9)

In December 1988 the Central Committee of the CPSU closed down the *Teacher's Gazette* and ended the brief renaissance of the public educational movement in Russia. It had begun in 1986, when the *Teachers' Gazette* editor-in-chief, Vladimir Matvejev, made two decisions which nearly changed the fate of the Soviet school. The decisions led to the closure of the newspaper and ruined Matvejev himself. Schools after that rushed from the party captivity, but didn't succeed. Matvejev some months later was sent to hospital with cancer and didn't leave.

The events were as follows: in summer of 1986 Matvejev invited a man, Simon Solovejchik to the newspaper. He told Matvejev about the work of Suhomlinsky, Shatalov and Lusenkova (a leading educational publicist). By the winter, Matvejev agreed to use the newspaper to promote 'clubs of creative pedagogy'. Matvejev called these clubs 'Eureka'.

Clubs of creative pedagogy became a very powerful force, a movement. Solovejchik succeeded in getting a number of progressive pedagogical thinkers to cooperate in the creation of a series of manifestos. These were pedagogical declarations which enabled teachers and parents to absorb the new, non-Soviet, pedagogical ideology. They were published in the *Teachers' Gazette* and received a great deal of support and interest. Neither the Ministry of Education nor the Academy of Pedagogical Sciences could compete with the newspaper when it came to its influence in schools, and on teachers' minds and souls. But that was only half of the trouble. The Communist Party realized that it was beginning to lose its power over schools, and schools in the USSR belonged to the Party. Anybody who encroached upon this power encroached upon the Party.

This raised the question: Who runs the school? Formally, the school was managed by a headteacher (principal). It appeared that it was he or she who published instructions, led meetings of the staff, defined the number of working hours for the teachers. In fact, none of that meant anything. Real school life went on according to an agenda set elsewhere. There was a Communist Party Secretary in every school. He or she was a liaison person between the school and the district Communist Party organization, sometimes even making the decisions. In any case, nothing substantial could happen at school without the sanction of the Secretary of the Party organization.

Rewards for students and teachers, appointment of tutors, places in the queue for a flat or a car, excursions and topics for teenagers' essays — all that could happen only with the permission of the Party secretary. And if something happened outside the Party ambit there was an immediate investigation. If anything happened in any school without Party permission — and this was seldom — the Central Committee of CPSU became aware of it immediately.

The system of Party control worked efficiently and quickly. In Donetsk (Ukraine) teacher Shatalov began to teach according to his own original methods. In Georgia, Amonashvill dared to change authoritarian pedagogy to humanistic pedagogy. In Moscow, teacher Lusenkova began to work according to her own curriculum. Immediately — children could have hardly left the lesson — everything was known in a grey building in the Old Square, and in the School Department of CPSU they were discussing the fate of these 'recanters'. Nobody discussed educational values. The fact of unsanctioned innovations was sufficient crime in itself. And if an article about any of these courageous people appeared in the newspapers, both the author's name and the innovator's would turn up on the list of rebels. To declare a teacher an innovator could cause only concern to the School Department of CPSU. Pedagogical academics were appointed with the support of the Party, and the innovators were attempting to cast doubt on Party-endorsed educational 'truth'. To doubt Party-appointed academics meant to doubt that Party decisions were correct. And the Party never made mistakes.

Simon Solovejchik had been looking for creative teachers since the 1970s and, being an educationalist himself, wrote about such teachers and opened the eyes of countless other teachers to what real school meant, but to the Central Committee this meant only one thing — he was against Party direction. It seemed that all these people were saved by the *glasnost* declared by Gorbachev, and the arrival in the CPSU of new people who were more tolerant. But the tolerance didn't last long.

Eureka Clubs Movement

On 30 January 1986 there appeared in the *Teachers' Gazette* the first announcement for teachers to gather for a discussion of school problems. The report of this very hot discussion involving fifty people from all over Moscow was interesting for the readers, and the editor-in-chief suggested having regular meetings at the Eureka Teachers' Club, and publishing articles about them. It is well-known that newspapers are not only collective propagandists, but also collective organizers. The fate of the Eureka clubs proves the truth of this idea of Lenin.

In summer 1986, in Pushino, not far from Moscow, the first all-union Eureka seminar, 'School of the Future' was organized. After that there was the Eureka seminar 'Days of Creative Lessons' (February 1986) which was barred at first by the pedagogical administrators but later, after Matvejev's efforts, was allowed to proceed. For the first time, teachers showed their lessons to their colleagues from all over the country, discussing them freely, with interest. Following the success of the first seminars there were hundreds of seminars during which teachers showed lessons to each other, shared their projects for school transformation and argued with administrators.

The most outstanding innovation of Eureka clubs was the 'Authors' school' competition. We couldn't imagine then that there were educational systems other than the traditional school. We knew we needed to build a better school system, with any alternative being thought of as a single system — but we were wrong. We suspected, that in the Soviet Union there were already schools in which children studied in a different way and most importantly, they learnt different things. The newspaper ran a competition for those schools who considered themselves schools with alternative education. These were the 'Authors' schools' and that was in January 1988. After the announcement of the competition, the principal of one of the Moscow schools phoned the newspaper and said 'There will be not a single fool who will declare his school an Authors' school'. The newspaper got 300 applications! There were three stages to the competition. First of all several groups of experts worked through the applications. They chose thirty. After that, in April 1988, in Kransnoyarsk, there was a meeting of the thirty applicants. They decided among themselves who deserved to take part in the next stage.

At last, in August 1988, Eureka organized a pedagogical 'island', of six schools: the Tubelsky school; the Dialogue of Cultures School (Kurganov–Bibler); the Dmitry Lebedev School; the Sergey Marjasin School; the E. Fremina School; and the Nikolay Guzil School. The main idea at this stage of the competition was that of school modelling. Besides the representatives of each Authors' school there were about 300 teachers and principals from other schools involved with this pedagogical Eureka 'island'. They acted as the students of the six Authors' schools. The idea of the seminar was that these 'students' would be able to feel the atmosphere of the Authors' schools, to understand how these schools were organized, what kind of philosophy they had, and what their curriculum was based on.

Tubelsky was the only principal of a real school then. The rest were struggling for such a possibility. All the authors were declared winners. All the projects were published and recommendations made for putting their ideas into practice. All of the authors, except Dmitry Lebedev and Serjey Kurganov, became principals.

We thought then that Authors' schools would be schools where teachers and principals would work out philosophical backgrounds, psychological conceptions and the whole curriculum themselves. But later we realized that it is impossible to do this with only the help of teachers. Today I would name A. Tubelsky and M. Schetinin as Authors' schools. Dialogue of Cultures School attracts a lot of teacher academics, even now, for its development. And Authors' schools face the same problem as developmental teaching and the Dialogue of Cultures school: teacher training and retraining — in other words 'self-transmission'.

Is the phenomenon of the Authors' school a typical Soviet or Russian thing where teachers, without the help of academics, try to work out the concept of a new curriculum? Now the idea of Authors' schools has nearly died, as have the majority of innovative ideas of that period of time. However, the attempt to establish the public, pedagogical movement wasn't in vain. It turned out that the Eureka movement was a necessary part of the whole system of education development. The Authors' schools movement supported the most innovative teachers. They were able to reveal themselves, not only at school but also outside its boundaries. In the clubs they were able to obtain both the acknowledgment and the criticism that they couldn't get from school colleagues. Without the public pedagogical movement those values which were born in the new school would not have been retained; they would have faded. In May 1989 Eureka clubs, Communard's units and family clubs united to form the Creative Union of Teachers. On the eve of the disintegration of the USSR the teachers tried to unite but failed. The USSR Creative Union of Teachers existed for no more than two years and vanished without having achieved anything substantial.

I can see three main reasons why the USSR's Creative Union of Teachers broke up. The first related to the political events which were the background for the birth of the union. With the disintegration of the USSR, came the stratification of educationalists according to their political persuasion. The Communist Party, whose ideology was the ideology of the school, vanished. The second reason for the failure was that the *Teacher's Gazette* ceased its activity as a union organizer and coordinator. This led to the fading of the Eureka movement and weakened the interaction of teachers with the union. The third reason was that the Creative Union of Teachers was created according to the model of a public organization in a totalitarian society. In such an organization, in reality there are always struggles for power, destruction of enemies and, only in the last instance, the implementation of declared values into school practice. This is the tragedy of all public organizations which were created even under the totalitarian regime. Structure is a means of struggle for power. It is badly adapted for normal positive activity.

Now we are at the point of deciding upon an appropriate model for a teachers' union which will allow us to unite educationalists around democratic values, and to implement without fuss these values in schools.

Mechanisms for Development of Education in Modern Russia (1993)

After the catastrophe of the public pedagogical movement, the brief renaissance in education finished at the beginning of 1993. On the surface it was symbolized by the retirement of the first democratic Minister of Education in Russia, Dr Edward Dneprov. Dneprov's reforms failed to create a workable mechanism of school change. The reformers themselves irritated officials, deputies and the population, and were banished from the Ministry.

The Russian system of education is now in a state of disillusionment because of insufficient funding. Mechanisms which feed this embitterment are the Russian Law on Education; the Ministry of Education; the statement on the system of teachers' evaluation; and state standards of education. Russia remains a country where the diplomas of higher education are not acknowledged by the world community. In Russia you need a certificate of secondary education to enter university. So-called home schooling is unachievable in Russia, even though such a possibility is declared in the Law of Education. So-called 'non-skilled' schools, are referred to in the law, but it is impossible for such schools to exist where there are no curricula and no textbooks. Schools can't register as educational establishments unless they have written curricula.

The development of any state-authorized way of educational development in Russia now is impossible. The official system of education is finished but there is still a reactionary thicket of officials. The only possible way that education can develop in Russia today is through innovative communities and non-authoritarian educational unions which can support informal association in the organization of alternative schools, colleges and universities.

The Prognosis of Educational Development in Russia (1993– . . .)

The educational situation in Russia in 1993 is grim. This can be seen in the management of educational institutions and the content of education.

Management

There is a strengthening of the centralized system of management in education. This can be seen in the reinforcement of the mechanisms for checking the observance of the Educational Law, the new wave of teachers' accreditation, the introduction of state standards in education, and the reinforcement of state influence as a whole. The weak scientific and methodological base in the Russian regions, and the monopoly the central publishing houses have on textbooks won't allow 'rebellious regions' to throw off the strong grip of the Ministry. Cultivation and acceptance of the united federal programme for development of education in Russia also reinforces centralization.

Content of Education

'The good old days' are coming back. Society is convinced that the educational reforms have not been effective and the slogans under which school change occurred have been discredited. The English catchcry is repeated in Russia — 'back to basics'. People say, 'As soon as innovations started, everything became very bad, so what do we need innovations for?' Moreover, it is argued that to enter university we need skills, not independent thinking.

The old barriers to innovation will all be universally adopted: stable programmes; uniform textbooks; minimum of experimentation and maximum of so-called differentiation; and streaming by 'ability'. (This does not include gifted children who should be taught separately, but those children with whom the teacher can't cope.) Regression in education will also be reinforced because of the strong competition between political parties. Each of them tries to offer educational policies that are simple and attractive, and which can be accepted by the majority of the population. And the majority of the population does not like to pay for schooling, does not like a lot of money to be spent on research, and does not want to choose between schools — let everybody study in the same way. The population doesn't like to take responsibility for children. 'We've given you the children — it's your task to teach them.' I expect that half of the alternative schools soon will be closed, some for financial reasons, some because they won't be able to get registration, and some which won't pass a special test. This will also reinforce a reactionary mood in education. 'Come on, wise men, have you tried? You didn't succeed! There you are!' The preservation of an untalented system of teacher training will ensure the reproduction of traditional teaching methods.

Despite the depressing educational situation in 1993 in Russia, some form of renaissance of the public pedagogical movement may yet begin. It will probably happen through the creation of alternative trade unions, financially supported by the West. It may also happen because of an emerging scientific-pedagogical union with western scientific-educational communities. The main directions of this renaissance are likely to be defined by a search for funds for the financial support of:

- real alternative and innovative schools;
- alternative teacher-training centres;

- an independent publishing house to publish textbooks; and
- an independent Russian trade union of teachers.

Conclusion: A Dialogue of Educational Values

Let's compare two systems of pedagogical values. On the one hand (right) is a successful, powerful, qualified traditional school teacher. On the other hand (left) is a Russian innovative teacher, who has come from the alternative traditions of the Communards' movement, developmental teaching, the Eureka movement, and the pedagogy of cooperation.

Commandments of the Right Hand

You always need to know how the child should behave. The system of demands is the main thing in your work. Manage your staff in a skilful way — this is your weapon. Ensure there are collective influences on the child: through this collective your demands will be met. You should always know the right answer to any questions you ask.

You are the guardian of knowledge, the guardian of the right answer. Don't allow the student to hesitate about whether you are right. To study is the main thing in the life of the child; it is the child's duty. A good student is a good child, a bad student is a bad child. Everybody should be attentive during the lesson and listen to you and only you. Those who are not attentive should be punished. Wrong answers must be punished; lateness must be punished; shouting, running, breaking the rules must be punished.

Investigate any disobedience thoroughly. Find the guilty one, and if you can't, punish everybody. Parents are your allies. Make them control their children and give you information about their behaviour at home. Let children know that you and the parents are one united force. To study well means to follow your instructions well. Collect as many difficult tasks as possible. Work hard to perform them yourself perfectly, then you can demand perfect performance from others. You are an example — your task-solving, your literacy, your skills are an example. If you lose your leadership, you are not a teacher any more.

Commandments of the Left Hand

There are no right or wrong answers. It makes no sense to ask a child a question to which you do not know the answer. Don't check the child but look for the answer together. Before solving a problem, discuss it with students: 'What do we need it for?' If the problem is not worth investigating, refuse the task. Trust the child more than yourself, more than the administration, more than the rules. Recoil from distrust: if the child has broken rules, there was probably a reason. The right of the child to make a mistake is to be respected. Trust and sincerity are always risky. Freedom for the child is always risky. To admit the child's sovereignty is more risky than to control every step. Parents are not enemies of their child; don't make them inform on and betray the child.

Be prepared to admit your own lack of knowledge and your own weakness. Refuse definitions — simple information is no substitute for depth of knowledge. Don't ask to learn rules by heart — knowledge doesn't lie in rules, but in the ability to discover and to use it. Don't compare children — everybody is good in different ways. Compare the child of today with the child of yesterday. Don't follow a set plan that belongs only to you; it hasn't come through mutual content with children.[1] The way we discover is more important than what we discover. Knowledge comes when we have understood and when it is interesting to understand. You don't have the right to judge what is right or wrong in your students' answers and deeds. They are not mistaken, they are seeking their way.

And now I ask a simple question: 'Where do values live? Where do different values live?' Do they live in that state school which in Russia strictly observes state policy in the sphere of education and strengthens the State? The State machine needs tiny screws. And it was always so. Aristotle wrote: 'State aspires to everybody being equal and the same but this is an attribute of ordinary people.' So the natural composition of the State will inevitably lead us to the conclusion that the State consisting of ordinary people will have the best regime.

The authoritarian State and its school don't need 'left hand' values; the State tries to make the school a factory of uniform citizens. In Russia, everything has changed — politics, economy, art; only schools remain the same as they were, the true guardians of the totalitarian regime, authoritarian customs, 'right hand' commandments.

There are two distinct types of education in Russia today: the etacratic school of totalitarian values, and the alternative school of civil-society values.[2] In a civil society, every person has the right to an education that is independent of state demands. It is impossible from my point of view to free a person politically and not at the same time free him or her from compulsory studies according to the state model. Yet Russian citizens can get only one type of education. Dialogue between the western style school with its democratic values, and the authoritarian state school in Russia is impossible; it would be like attempting dialogue between a Kibbutz and a reform school. Here and there people live and work together, but in the first case, as far as I know, they are free and choose to work together, while in the second they are forced to do it.

The 'Dream of the Mind' is coming to an end in our country and the age of civilized democracy is beginning. It is a paradox — the state school will be the last place to be democratized. But before this triumphant moment has come we need to initiate real dialogue with democratic schools of the West. Western educational systems are being adopted now in Russia: the Waldorf School, the Montessori system, family schools, free schools, Frene schools. In Tomsk the 'Eureka-Development' school of Leo Tolstoy has been restored to life — a real life, not an artificial one.

Not everything is controlled from the school department of the Central Committee of the CPSU any more. There isn't a single *Teachers' Gazette*, for centralized management is finished. But the age of centralized influence is finished too. It is silly to imagine that only one Union of Teachers is possible for the whole Russia. It is silly and naive to think that it's possible to fascinate all teachers with only one method or educational system, however outstanding.

This doesn't mean that we can't plan for the development of education in Russia. On the contrary, we must plan, otherwise the blind will lead the blind. But the organized movement of schools and teachers in just one direction, however wonderful, is impossible now. Besides, it is now clear that values grow from the dynamic school life. Schools and moral values are interrelated. Without schools any values become the subject of theoreticians' speculation. We may only guess what new values will appear in the next thirty-seven years — it depends upon the type of schools yet to be born.

Notes

1 Content in Russian means keeping together, something mutual for everybody.
2 Etacratic school means state school.

Reference

SOLOVEJCHIK, S. (1986) *Eternal Joy: Stories about School Life*, Moscow.

Chapter 7

Government Policy and Democratic Reform in the Russian Educational System

Yelena A. Lenskaya

A democratic society grows from the roots of a democratic school system. If a society wants to make itself free, it gives more freedom to schools. The prerequisites of a free society, such as respect for human rights, free choice of career and lifestyle, personal decision-making, civic education and respect for democratic laws are developed mostly through the educational system. If schools are to be able to develop the concepts and skills their students need to become members of a democratic society, schools should themselves be governed by democratic laws and organized according to democratic patterns.

Until recently, because school life in Russia replicated the life of a totalitarian society, it mirrored the same patterns and dogmas which were predominant in the society. The totalitarian regime was constantly trying to make our schools a weapon for its criminal activity, committing crimes against personality, against childhood, against science and culture. The unitarian State's 'ownership of the school' resulted in its structure being a closed, almost prison-like institution. The interests of an individual and the interests of a community were not its concern. Its function was to address only the needs of the State. Accordingly, a teacher was deprived of the right to creative work and became nothing more than a civil servant, a state employee.

A system of triple alienation was built: schools were alienated from society and their communities, students from schools and teachers from students. As a result of schools becoming state bureaucratic offices, they began to function in a mode of standard thinking, standard behaviour and unitarian administration. They neglected the diversity of culture and traditions of a multiethnic society composed of more than 120 different ethnicities speaking different languages and sharing different religions: the school was standard for every region of Russia. Standard curriculum, standard textbooks, even standard lessons were all meant to develop a standard personality, a 'cog' in a huge state machine. By cutting the historical and social roots of nations and ethnicities, the intellectual potential of the society was diminished. An authoritarian style of teaching was predominant: top–down control promoted authoritarianism in management which was automatically projected onto the classroom.

Schools were dominated by Marxist ideology; every school child was supposed to become a 'Pioneer' and later a 'Komsomol' member. If children did not follow this pattern there were serious implications for their future careers. Every academic discipline, especially humanities, was taught in the context of Marxism and dominated by Soviet propaganda. Even foreign language textbooks referred more to the Soviet Constitution and Komsomol leadership than to the country of the language being taught. The voice of the school party leader counted more than the voice of the school principal, and the teaching staff was administered mostly through party channels. Those who did not conform could be easily fired, regardless of their professional skills. Schools were militarized: military training was obligatory for girls and for boys. Schools served as agents for military recruitment committees.

Children with physical handicaps or behavioural disorders were segregated and isolated in special institutions which did not permit them to integrate into comprehensive schools or into society. Vocational schools, no matter what slogans were proclaimed, were just another type of segregation. They did not provide quality academic training. Moreover, the vocational training they provided was very narrowly specialized and served to satisfy the immediate needs of industries with a low-qualified labour force.

Schools provided almost no choice within the curriculum; individual needs or learning styles being almost totally disregarded. Teachers were never trained to address every child in the classroom, only a non-existent average student. The school system was a closed one. Teachers had practically no access to foreign educational experience and had no opportunity to exchange ideas and practices with their colleagues abroad.

From the portrayal of the school presented thus far, it is clear that a new society in Russia could not be built on the foundations of the old school system. Therefore, because education is not only a leading factor in personality development, but also a key factor in a society's development, educational reform in Russia is a precondition for the success efforts of radical reform in all spheres of social life.

In Russia, we are now in the process of building a bridge from a side-road of world civilization to its main highway. Education is the main foundation for such a bridge. It is the system of education that will provide much needed changes in the social attitudes and the elimination of old stereotypes. It is this system that will provide a road for democracy, for a new political culture and for market literacy among the population. This idea was very clearly stated in the first decree of the President of Russia, Boris Yeltsin.

The dominant features of the new school policy are as follows:

- Schools are to become society-oriented rather than system-oriented.
- Realism is to be substituted for social myth-making.

- School policy is no longer to be an interpretation of Party and government decisions, but a vehicle for the democratic policy of society.
- The cornerstone of this policy is the evaluation of concrete results, the identification of needs, and the development of strategies to better serve these needs.

Ten basic principles determine key priorities for the reform of education in Russia. These principles are multitargeted. They determine the ideals and goals of the reform, but they also provide guidelines for their implementation into practice. Moreover, these principles simultaneously address society, the State and the system of education; they are interdependent and interconnected.

Democratization of Education

This is the first priority to secure development of the democratic society. It implies:

- doing away with the state monopoly on education and the transition to public–state ownership of educational institutions, i.e., to a paradigm within which the State, the individual and society are equal partners;
- decentralization of management as opposed to the 'leadership' and dictatorship of the State in everything to do with school education. This means the redistribution of functions between federal, regional and local authorities with maximum delegation of management functions to lower levels;
- municipalization of education, i.e., participation of local authorities and local communities in managing education through both municipal legislative bodies and school-based management, accumulating additional resources for the efficient development of educational system, stimulating interest in educational problems in the local community and its active involvement in campaigns for quality and equity in education;
- self-determination of educational institutions with regard to strategies, goals, content, organization and technologies of their functioning, and their legislative, financial and economic operations;
- teachers' rights to creativity; to an individual style of instruction; to professional freedom in the choice of methods, textbooks, teaching aids, and ways of assessing pupils; and participation in school management;
- students' right to select a school and school profile; their right to choose education in private institutions and, if need be, for education at home, accelerated education or education according to individualized curricula; and their right to participate in school management. (*National Report of Russian Federation on Educational Development,* 1993).

The implementation of these goals requires a complex approach. Democracy is the most important criterion of school efficiency, since a non-democratic school cannot be truly efficient. There is no such thing as too much democracy. Every society that wants to become democratic starts by democratizing schools.

Yet, there is the danger of democracy being seen as total disintegration of the system, with lack of feedback and support between the levels of educational management. Regional and local legislation is not yet fully developed. There are some responsibilities for which delegation to lower levels is not seen as reasonable nor in the interests of better quality education. For example, many territories have assumed full responsibility for licensing schools, but have lacked qualified staff for this task; consequently a number of new private or semi-private institutions have been licensed which do not comply with the minimum curriculum requirements. The rights of children for good quality education are violated because of this. However, there is some resistance to delegating licensing activity even to interregional level, where it could be exercised with greater efficiency.

There is an even bigger danger involved in the fact that local authorities are now campaigning for responsibility for vocational and teacher-training institutions to be decentralized to the regional level. If this were done, it might cause the closing down of some training institutions, though these might be essential and irreplaceable on a national level, because the region has more pressing economic priorities. The implications are that educational institutions will lose valuable, well-trained staff who will go into other fields. Moreover, because a majority of regional and local administrative staff is not properly trained for the new functions they are now performing, local managers often tend to regard educational policy as just a method to solve immediate economic problems rather than strategic problems associated with the development of all citizens in a democratic society.

Still, there is probably only one way to democratize schools: to practise democracy, which means learning to be responsible for freedom, to make long-term strategic decisions and, most importantly, to accept the fact that democracy is possible only when it is shared by all participants in the educational process.

Pluralism, Diversity of Education and Multiple Sources of Educational Finance

This is a cardinal change from the former unitarian and standardized system into a diverse and polyfunctional one with multiple goals and diversified curricula, different ways of organizing educational processes, varied technologies and instructional designs, and various forms of ownership of education and educational institutions.

These forms of ownership reflect not just the proprietary ownership of educational services (state and non-state, including private educational institutions, home schooling, etc.), but also the multiplicity of subsystems within society which have been disregarded for too many years. Major lifestyle differences according to social status, ethnicity, region, urban–rural setting were neglected in the past.

Variability and diversity within education are necessary if choice is to be exercised. Alternatives within the system of education such as state-owned, nonstate-owned and home schooling provide for competition in the educational system. Competition ensures progress and development. There was no competition within the Soviet educational system whatsoever. Recently the system of alternative education has begun to develop rapidly. The number of alternative educational institutions which can be termed 'non-state owned' rather than 'private' is increasing every year. The number of such institutions doubled in year 1992 and tripled in 1993.

However, there is always the danger of a too rapid development of non-state-owned educational institutions. Such institutions tend to be exclusive, rather than inclusive, which means that the selection of children within these institutions is always according to either the social status of their parents or their ethnicity, religion or other criteria. If this system develops into a really large system, this could lead to more stratification within society, which is definitely not an aim of the government. So, we have to be very reasonable in providing a framework within which these alternatives develop, yet providing as much support as possible for the government system of education. The state-owned system of education, therefore, should also have a number of innovative institutions capable of creating their own curricula, and working on alternative concepts of education. Being state-owned, they would still provide the possibility for all children to be admitted. The quality of education in nonstate-owned institutions has to be controlled and guided. The problem is that the licensing of such institutions is now mostly the responsibility of regional authorities. There is no provision in state law for closing down these institutions if they prove incompetent. The majority of regions lack qualified staff who can develop proper procedures for licensing. There is an urgent need to create interregional licensing bodies, or to establish a procedure for licensing under a government authority.

As far as home schooling is concerned, this certainly has to be limited to those families that can provide quality education at home in cases where parents do not work, or where a child is not easily adaptable to school conditions. A system of external examinations has to be developed properly, so that every child, even if educated at home part-time, can be evaluated on a regular basis. Unless the quality of home schooling is acceptable, parents cannot be granted the right to continue it.

The main task of the administrative bodies of education is to protect the right of a child to a quality education in whatever conditions provide optimum possibilities for its development.

Regionalization of Education

This provides the authority to the diverse regions of Russia to choose their educational strategy, and to add their own component to the federal curriculum in accordance with their needs.

Previously, within the republic of Russia, the curriculum, the textbooks and even the school buildings were standardized regardless of economic, geographical and historical backgrounds. This led to the unification of the educational system and, in fact, diminished the possibilities for people who lived under different conditions to obtain an adequate education that would respond to the needs of the area in which they resided. Although the necessity for regional programmes of educational development is indeed great, the capability of local authorities to develop such programmes is somewhat limited at this point because of their lack of experience in this kind of work. A major lack of proper training in the field of legislation has become apparent as the power to develop regional legislation is being delegated to regional authorities. This power is often misused because the people who perform this function are not literate in legal matters. That is why, in order to carry on the task of regionalization of education, we have to retrain the vast majority of regional authorities in legislation, educational finance, educational economics, educational management and educational leadership.

Another problem lies in the fact that the region is now responsible for the regional component of the educational curriculum, which now equals 25 per cent of the general curriculum. This regional component of curriculum is supposed to introduce subjects, subject blocks or components of syllabuses that cover regional geography, history, culture, language and other areas that are crucial for the particular location. Unfortunately, perhaps because the federal component of the curriculum is not yet stable enough, many regions tend to substitute basic subjects, such as maths, physics, chemistry, and the official language of the country by what might be regarded as part of national culture, and what is often irrelevant to the general education of a child. Occasionally, the curriculum includes study of tribal religions, different kinds of folklore, crafts, games and other things that are quite acceptable as options or choices, but can be hardly regarded as a compulsory part of the curriculum.

Regionalization of education should not lead to the disintegration of common educational ground. It is not by chance that many of the regions make agreements with central authorities, such as the Ministry of Education of Russia, to provide expertise for their plans and programmes of development so that there can be more consistency between the regions and within the country as a whole.

National Self-determination of Schools

This is an issue that is closely connected with the previously described one. It is a key principle in any policy of a multiethnic society. The school is inseparable from the native soil. Being rooted in national and historic traditions, enriched by world experience, schools become a powerful instrument of national revival, providing a necessary balance for interethnic relations. In a country as diverse as Russia, with 120 ethnicities permanently residing within the republic for centuries, it is impossible not to recognize these cultures and not to respect the rights of people to their own religions and traditions being represented in school. However, it is difficult for a country, the economy of which is in a state of transition, to provide the necessary financial support for developing a sufficient number of textbooks in different languages for every ethnic group.

There is also debate about how much native language there should be within a school curriculum. Our psychologists always claim that a child should be educated in elementary school in his native language, which is not necessarily the language of his ethnicity but the language that the child has learned to speak best by the age of 3. Unless this fact is properly recognized, later possibilities for the child's successful education are greatly diminished. Yet, if education in a native language continues until high school, this can diminish possibilities for further education, because while it is still possible to provide schooling in a native language in elementary and secondary schools, it is next to impossible to provide similar conditions in higher education. Moreover, it is probably not sensible to attempt to do so, because smaller languages have not properly developed sets of terms that would cover professional languages relevant to different spheres of life.

There is an acute need to balance native and official languages in schools, and there is an acute need to balance other rights and obligations children have regarding language. Some of the territories that have suffered formerly from the imposition of the Russian language as the only language of schooling are now hastily substituting the ethnic language for the Russian language regardless of the interests and needs of their own people. People who claim to be Yakutians in their passports often have Russian as their first language so that if their children are sent to schools that start schooling in Yakutian from the very beginning, they might encounter problems similar to those of children who speak Yakutian at home, and then must learn to cope with Russian as the language of instruction at school.

In the earlier years of *perestroika*, mandatory determination of the language in which the children have to be educated was not unheard of. There are fewer cases now. However, the separatist policy of several regions in fact imposes these choices upon parents. There is as big a need as ever for a balance of cultures within the school curriculum. With the world becoming more global, children cannot be restricted to just their local culture, or even to the culture of the country in which they reside. There has to be a balance between world culture, the culture of the continent, the culture of the country and the culture of the ethnicity.

Another problem is that people often tend to study the culture of the major nation, such as Russia, and do not know anything about the culture of their nearest neighbours. This is especially true where close neighbours speak languages of different language families and belong to different religions. However, there are some autonomous republics within Russia, such as Chuvashiya, which maintain a perfect balance of different cultures, and try to provide equal rights not just to representatives of their own ethnicity, but to all ethnicities living in the region. In some Chuvashian villages one can encounter Tartar, Bashkirian and Russian schools, or classes within schools for children of a certain ethnicity. This does not mean that children are segregated according to their nationality, rather that in elementary school they can be taught in their own language.

One of the possibilities offered by the West, which has not yet been thoroughly investigated in Russia, is bilingual education. This is potentially a major solution to many interethnic problems. Bilingual schools are just beginning to appear in big cities, where there are mostly schools that teach in Russian and foreign languages, but there are still no schools teaching languages of neighbouring nations in ethnic regions where understanding between neighbours is badly needed.

When we talk about national self-determination of schools, we often tend to talk mostly about the interests of minority groups within the republic of Russia, whereas there is as much need for the development of the Russian school as a school rooted in the traditions of the Russian people — not just cultural traditions, but also educational traditions that have been long neglected through the Soviet period. The schools that existed within the Soviet period of our history were not truly Russian, although there were accusations about the Russification of education. It is probably more correct to call it 'sovietization' of education, because the Russian people were as much deprived of their traditions as the rest of the country. The Institute of National Problems of Education within the Ministry of Education of Russia is now developing a concept of the Russian school, which can be applied and disseminated within the territories mostly populated by Russians.

Openness of Education

This implies raising ideological blinds, doing away with political and ideological dogmas. Education begins to address the holistic world, its global problems, and ranks the priority of human values higher than class and group interests. Our schools need to incorporate the best of European and world education. Such schools should be capable of preparing the world community to live comfortably together, to understand their neighbours and to be tolerant of their differences, to be able to resolve conflicts in a peaceful manner. When we are talking about openness in education, we should also bear in mind that, previously, Russian schools were closed not just to the outer world; they were closed to parents and community members. In fact, they functioned as regime institutions in which strangers were not welcome. If we are really thinking about promoting openness, it is the real partners of the educational process that have to be admitted to schools in the first place. Parents have the right to visit schools when they choose (although they probably have to follow certain procedures); they have the right to participate in school life, to be part of school councils and participate in decision-making, to be involved in the process of discussing school-based development. The concept of involving the community in school management and school development is not altogether alien within the Russian federation. However, involvement was previously understood as voluntary assistance from the community to the school in terms of finance, sponsorship, some school activity, and time and labour to provide for the maintenance of the school.

Another facet of openness is openness to different pedagogical technologies and concepts. For a long time the only accepted pedagogical concept of education was the one approved by the state authorities, which was standard for the whole of the country. The concepts of Maria Montessori, Rudolf Steiner, Charles Frene and other great educators of the world were known in Russia mostly through critical texts in textbooks on pedagogy. These concepts began to be recognized and mastered only within recent years. Yet, there is a great deal of interest in these concepts in Russia, and if we are really talking about choice for parents and choice for children in education, this choice should be provided within a range of different philosophies of education. Most of the schools that are now experimenting with Montessori or Steiner teaching are public schools, not private schools, which is different from the tendency in America, Australia and some other countries of the world. However, this is fully justified, because the majority of great educational scholars of the world did not develop their concepts for exceptional children. They were generally trying to address the needs of children who were socially deprived, who were special not in terms of their social status, but rather in their individual abilities and in the relationship with the teacher that they favoured. One possible danger in implementing the principle of openness is that the choice is often made without a real understanding of the impact of various theories, or without a real understanding of the necessary curriculum development work that has to be done in order to provide adequate interpretation of these theories in practice. Because of seventy years of isolation, schools which are not really experienced in making choices often select strategies that seem to be easy to implement and which, in their perception, involve less effort on the part of the school team. It is not by chance that many concepts which are not generally very popular in the West are disseminated within such schools, especially when support is being offered from their western advocates. In this case pedagogical concepts are often just translated and not adapted. They are often borrowed without real understanding of whether the goals of these philosophies really respond to the needs of the children and the parents. The major necessity here is to restructure teacher training so that future teachers are trained to make a choice that corresponds with their individual qualities, the needs of their neighbourhood and the environment in which they will practise their skills. These schools already exist in a number of territories of Russia: Krasnoyarsk's school 'Universe' should probably be mentioned in this context as one of the most successful examples. It provides a real choice of pedagogical strategies within one school. It also provides possibilities for the university students to assist school teachers, i.e., to try their hand in teaching while they are still in the university. These training institutions are also valuable for retraining purposes, because every pedagogical concept can be best understood after having been introduced to the practice of teaching.

Humanization of Schools

This implies first, and foremost, doing away with the main drawbacks of the old school — its standard image. The main idea behind it is that the school should become child-centred and respectful of the child's personality. It should have trust in the child's abilities and an understanding of his or her personal goals, demands and interests. When school is child-centred there are no authoritarian methods of teaching; there is team work and real partnership between teachers, students and parents. A child-centred school promotes co-operative learning, individual choice and flexibility within a school curriculum. One of the biggest needs, if we are to humanize education, is to create appropriate conditions for the development of children's abilities and gifts, for living a normal life at different stages of their development, for their self-determination and confidence.

A child-centred school should also provide possibilities for children with special needs to be mainstreamed and integrated into the normal life of children and, further on, into the normal life of the society. It is not by chance that the departments which were training people for special education in Russia were called 'defectology' departments. Mentally and physically handicapped children were segregated and assigned to special institutions which provided, in many cases, proper care for their physical health, but no psychological rehabilitation and no skills that would be valuable for their future life in society. Boarding houses, which in the Russian language are called *internats* (another symbolic word that originates from the verb 'to intern', 'to isolate') were the kind of institutions that many of these children had to attend for their whole school life. A society cannot regard itself as humane unless every citizen of this society, especially those who are less fortunate, has the full right to education and development of his or her personality. This goal cannot be achieved through segregation. That is why one of the biggest tasks for the future is to provide mainstreaming, a legal basis for schools to accept children with special needs, and proper care for these children. Given the scarcity of educational funds now, these goals certainly cannot be achieved overnight. There is a need to investigate intermediate stages, such as resource centres, which can assist teachers, students and parents towards the successful integration of children with special needs into normal school life, which would monitor and observe. The child's development would be monitored and observed and assistance would be provided to any child if the family or child is not satisfied with the progress being made at school.

Another important goal in this context is to train teachers within teacher training institutions to address the whole class, which means every child in the classroom is taught in a way which is informed by individual strategies of learning and is responsive to individual educational needs. At present, teachers of the Russian Federation lack these skills because the goal of addressing the whole class, which includes children with special needs, has never been a part of general curriculum guidelines in pedagogical institutions. There is still a debate between those who support the concept of special educational institutions and those who promote mainstreaming. The former claim that special institutions can provide proper care for children with special needs and can hire appropriate staff. However, if we do not train every teacher to address children with special needs, we will always face the problem of a lack of appropriate personnel, and we will continue to segregate children.

Humanization of Education

This principle does not just represent an opposition to technocratism, and scorn for the individual and the human values of our former educational system. This principle is in accordance with general global changes in the modern man's mentality. Such mentality abandons the traditions that were accepted in the previous world system of education of the past 200 years, and which had been inspired by a rational and technocratic world outlook. The world had been considered an inhuman object that could be further subdivided into mechanical parts in the process of cognition. These parts could be a person, a society or a culture. Humanization is meant to reorient education towards the development of a complex and yet holistic picture of the world; it is the world of culture, of the individual person, of humanization of knowledge and of the progress of humanitarian and systemic thinking. It implies a higher status for humanities in the school curriculum, while the content of learning is radically revised.

Humanization of education is seen as filling the spiritual vacuum caused by the collapse of old ideological dogmas, as an instrument to form a new social ideology, capable of changing mental stereotypes of our society. Another important aspect of humanization is to overcome consumer attitudes towards nature and to improve ecological literacy. Technocrats, party ideologists and bureaucrats do not take responsibility for history, nature, society and mankind.

Humanization of education implies that subjects such as physics, chemistry and maths should not be taught as the basics of an infallible science. They should be properly recognized as a certain type of human cognition which should be mastered, and a special language which should be learned. It is no coincidence that when we launched a nationwide competition for writing textbooks in the humanities, many applications suggested the development of textbooks in humanitarian physics, humanitarian chemistry and the like. The purpose of school is not to train a specialist in an infallible science; it is to teach creativity, cognitive skills, critical thinking. Curricula in natural sciences and maths should provide for that. Wrongly understood, humanization of education sometimes means decreasing the number of natural science and maths teaching periods within the school curriculum, which is explained by the adherents of this strategy as respecting children's individual choices. What many of these adherents often claim is that not every child is interested in maths or physics or chemistry, and this is why these subjects should not be regarded as compulsory, at least in high school. But these subjects are irreplaceable in terms of promoting critical thinking and cognitive skills, if, of course, they are taught appropriately.

Another important thing is that these subjects are practice-oriented and provide knowledge that can be later applied in an unexpected environment or unexpected conditions. The major drawback of the Russian school was the fact that although it provided great knowledge of facts — probably greater than in most countries in the world, and skills for establishing connections between the facts, it provided much less expertise in applying this knowledge and these skills in real life. The evaluation done under the sponsorship of IEA showed a big difference between the maths results of children in OECD countries and children in the countries of eastern Europe, precisely in these terms. Whereas the children in eastern Europe knew more facts, they could apply these facts in their real life to far less an extent.

Humanization of education is especially difficult in a country which has been trained in standardized ideology for years and years. Even with the best intentions, curriculum developers tend to provide ready-made answers to many eternal questions that have no answer whatsoever. The new textbooks in history or social sciences often have the same drawbacks as those which existed in past years. They suggest that there is one single ideology, and lack respect for individual choice both in mode of life and way of thinking. Though western curricula are not easily adaptable to the Russian environment, there are cases in which these curricula are welcome in the Russian educational market as alternatives to the one-way thinking of many Russian scholars.

Differentiation and Flexibility of Education

These imply the creation of a spectrum of possibilities to realize individual educational goals, and to satisfy interests, abilities and inclinations of students in accordance with the psycho-physiological characteristics of different age groups. Differentiation is meant to provide a market of necessary educational services and products. The market will react to the educational demands of the different social and professional groups of the population in a flexible and mobile way. Yet the development of a differentiated system should be based on the cornerstone of state educational standards, and so provide diversity, accessibility and quality of educational services. The former unitarian school that provided no choices for an individual is replaced by a diverse, multi-patterned school system that services the interests of different personalities.

The major goal of differentiation is to provide a variety of choices within a single school, and to provide for individual strategies of learning for every child in a classroom. Not long ago schools started introducing choices and options within the curriculum. But so many of these options and choices are not those that children and their parents want. Moreover, what many schools began to understand as differentiation is in fact tracking, which means that children at a very early stage of their education are streamed into a certain kind of curriculum, providing more humanities or more maths and science or more physical training and arts. Because this streaming is done at an early stage, children cannot make a sensible choice, and the more they progress within a certain curriculum, the more difficult it is to change, if they realize they have made a wrong choice. Many schools are reporting now that they have introduced differentiation, whereas in fact there are very few that are not confusing differentiation with tracking. Differentiation is a difficult concept to implement. What is most needed is for teachers to be trained to implement different strategies of teaching according to different personality types in a classroom. They should learn to address particular difficulties and needs that any child might encounter on his or her educational route. Career orientation at later stages of education is an important part of differentiation of the educational system. The more flexible this career orientation and the wider the range of professions it addresses, the better for the future life of a child. Because the economic system of the country is unstable, and because the economy in the future will demand multiple skills that provide for quick reorientation in the professional field, it is often desirable that vocational education be merged with general secondary education, and that specialization is provided at the latest stage possible.

Developmental and Active Character of Education

This is in opposition to the mechanical memorization of facts and the traditional lecture method of teaching that was meant to provide transmission of selected portions of knowledge. Knowledge that in no way corresponds to the stages of a child's development, that does not provide learning skills, is infertile knowledge. A person whose brain is full of memorized but unneeded facts is not capable of self-development or creative activities and is unprepared for changes in his or her professional career.

A child's activity is a key factor in his or her development. Thus the content of education, as well as forms and methods of learning, should be mastered in an active way. Teachers should stimulate what a great Russian scholar, Ushinsky, called 'an inborn human striving for activity'. It is important to bear in mind when talking about the developmental character of education that the goals of education are set on both social and individual levels. Whereas the society mostly demands competencies to be developed within the school curriculum, the individual need is for the utmost development of potential. There is a constant tension between these two goals in any country. The extremes of competency-based education tend to neglect individual needs, whereas extreme individualistic tendencies tend to disregard the future socialization of a child. The need to balance these two tendencies is indeed acute, and the appropriate balance differs according to the developmental age of a child. The Vygotsky school of Russian psychology recognizes the fact that every stage of personality development is characterized by a predominant activity. If this predominant activity is not recognized within an educational process, if it is not the foundation for the kind of activity the child performs through his or her education, individual potential cannot be properly developed. There are unique schools within the Russian Federation that have implemented the theory of age development in school practice, achieving significant results. This is probably the future for schools as a whole — not just for the republic of Russia, but for the whole world, to adjust the process of education to the natural development of a child, and to promote the multiple intelligences that every child possesses.

Continuity of Education

This provides the interconnection between the different stages of education and multiple individual possibilities: it can be either gradual walking up educational steps or taking time for mastering. It should be possible not just to continue a certain type of education, but to change a pattern; that is, a person should be able to switch from one sphere of activity into another.

The principle of continuity of education changes the goal and the nature of the educational process. You cannot get education for a lifetime in this new era. The knowledge that you acquire at school today wears out sooner than a schoolbag. Education must become a lifelong process. Thus stimulating the critical thinking of a child or a teenager, helping him or her to acquire learning skills, and to understand the necessity of continuous learning becomes a major task of a school.

To implement the principles of continuity of education it is important to provide a natural transition from one educational pattern to another, from general secondary education to vocational education if need be, or to higher education, and within every stage of schooling. If we are talking about equity in education, we have to ensure that no matter in what school a child has been educated previously, he or she can move into a different pattern or into a different kind of school with as little difficulty as possible. This implies a need for preparatory stages or courses for every type of school, especially middle or high school, which would assist a person to redesign his or her educational trajectory in a way that corresponds with individual choice. Continuity of education should also provide for every adult person to come back, to resume education at any stage of life or professional development. There should be a variety of possibilities for doing this in full-time institutions through distance education, evening courses and the like.

The concept of adult education is not very widespread in Russia now. Previously it meant mostly providing people with the possibility of receiving a certificate of general secondary education, or undertaking narrowly specialized training courses. There was almost no provision for mastering particular skills or attaining particular kinds of knowledge in cases where people were not going to implement this knowledge and these skills in their immediate careers. There was very little provision for the kind of flexible training for adults that would help them gain basic competencies which they might need in a wide variety of jobs. Unless these possibilities are provided, the system of adult education will continue to be a waste industry, consuming a lot of money and effort, and providing very few outcomes for a particular personality.

Conclusion

The interconnection and integration of the above-described basic principles constitute the ideology and moral values of the new educational reform in Russia. The core of it can be described by two key words: democracy and humanism. But the way from democratization to democracy and from humanization to humanism is steep and thorny. Any society, unless it is seriously ill, is continuously dissatisfied with its schools. Schooling cannot remain unaltered in this constantly changing world.

However, schools inevitably oppose change due to the conservatism of their staffs. There are two reasons for conservatism. The first is the institutional stability of schools, which can be regarded as a positive factor: schools resist uncontrolled social experiments that can be harmful to children. The second is resistance to change because of egotistic clan interests within schools: any serious innovation requires a lot of effort and it is always easier to question the reform than to take the trouble to consider the benefits and try to implement it. This is true worldwide, as an analysis of the tendencies and the outcomes of major world educational reforms, be they in Russia or Australia, will clearly demonstrate.

Reference

Russian Education Federation (1993) *National Report of the Russian Federation on Educational Development*, Moscow.

Chapter 8

The Structure of Democracy in Educational Settings: The Relationship between the School and the System

Jeffrey F. Dunstan

An analysis of the structure of democracy in educational settings, and in particular of the democratic relationship between a system and its schools, requires an analysis of complex political and educational developments which have occurred and are reflected through structural arrangements, decision-making processes, participation policies and practices, and devolution effects. The objective of this chapter is to describe and analyse significant developments which have enhanced democratic structures and processes in the conduct of government schools in the State of Victoria, Australia. The developments have been selected because they illustrate best the marked changes in the breadth of participation in decision-making at central, regional and school levels, as well as the range of decision-making now devolved to school level.

The democratic relationship between schools and the education system in Victoria has not been static. It has been a dynamic relationship marked by consistent and deliberate changes in processes and structures, aimed at increased participation at all levels.

The Centralized System

Historically, the state education system has been highly centralized. The primary, secondary, technical and special services divisions of the Education Department controlled their schools across the State through a set curriculum; an inspectorial system; centralized staffing arrangements; uniform buildings and equipment schedules; and provision of supplies from a central store. Local school and teacher discretion was restricted, with schools being reviewed and teachers being assessed on the basis of system requirements. There was little room for local participation, other than on the primary-school committee and high-school advisory council, where decisions were limited to safe local issues like accommodation for the teacher and minor maintenance work, or the technical school council where budget and finance decisions were more substantive. Schools were conducted within an authoritarian structure in which senior central office personnel implemented their policies through a hierarchical system of inspectors.

Centralization had been firmly established in Victoria as early as 1878 when Royal Commissioner Pearson (Education Department of Victoria, 1973, p. 313) reaffirmed the liberal belief that 'Equality before the law is the leading principle of democracy.' He remarked that the planners had 'sketched an admirable outline for future administration', but he decided that, 'despite the faithful service of the many . . . an unhappy centralisation principle had been adopted at the expense of local cooperation.' Part of the fault, he asserted, lay with the Act which failed to specify definite powers allocated to Boards of Advice. 'As Departmental officials drew more power to themselves and thereby so overloaded the central machine that breakdown now seemed imminent, local support dwindled and failed.'

Hunter (1983, p. 54) argues that 'Centralisation places a high premium on conformity by the majority with control in the hands of the few. Bureaucracy has little time for participation.'

Thus all elements of school administration were standardized so that the relationship between the school and the system was clear, ordered, unequivocal and consistent. The fairness and equity required in a democratic society were the overriding objectives.

Jean Blackburn notes that:

> An aspect of our public provision [of education] of which we may be justly proud is that a wide tax base with a commitment to equality of opportunity has brought about a rough equality of provision in richer and poorer districts, in sparsely populated areas and in areas of population concentration. The wide tax base and the commitment to equal provision are fairly substantial in the democratic commitment which is Australian public education. (Blackburn, 1990, p. 4)

Harman quotes Partridge on this same issue of equality when he says that:

> Perhaps the least that can be said for Australian public education is that one does not find the disparities between schools of different regions and districts that one finds in the United States or even in the United Kingdom; the quality of schools, the wages, competence and morale of teachers, do not vary according to the resources of a district or the willingness of the state, county or district authorities to spend money on public schools. (Harman, 1990, p. 66)

Harman (1990, p. 66) also notes that the Australian school system was a 'school system with a high regard for ordinary people and their needs, wherever they might live, that emphasized equality of services across a vast colony or state, that stressed common academic standards, and that provided bureaucratic rules to protect teachers from the whims of local communities.'

Democratization: Changes in Processes

In an analysis of processes, democratization of the system may be viewed as involving two complementary elements. The first element was the movement to devolution and decentralization; the second was the introduction of participative decision-making. Devolution of decision-making to schools began in the late 1960s when schools were encouraged to develop their own school policies reflecting local circumstances, interests and strengths; schools were given small school grants as a basis for local financial decision-making; and school-based curriculum was introduced. Decentralization of administrative decision-making to regions began in the early 1970s, when aspects of resource allocation and school support were delegated to regions.

The second element, participation in decision-making, was a natural corollary, leading in the early 1970s to a range of opportunities for participation through a multiplicity of committee and board structures at system and school level.

As Hunter points out:

> In Victoria, there was increasing opposition to the bureaucratic and centralized approaches to administration of education. A central feature of such opposition is a desire for greater participation, the constant participation of the ordinary man in the conduct of those parts of the structure of society with which he is directly concerned, and which he has therefore the best chance of understanding. (Hunter, 1983, p. 51)

Governments of both political persuasions moved to enhance devolution and increased participation in decision-making. A White Paper on education in Victorian government schools published in 1980, when Hon Alan Hunt was Minister of Education, included in its broad objectives the need to 'encourage increased community participation in consideration of educational issues, educational decision-making, and the life of schools' and to 'develop a more co-operative, caring and democratic community concerned with the welfare and optimum growth of all its members'. These were translated into specific objectives which included a determination to 'decentralize the administration of education wherever appropriate to allow local communities as far as is possible to share the responsibility and accountability for local educational policy and for decision-making in local schools'.

Following the change of government in 1982, Education Department Ministerial Paper No. 1 (1983, p. 1.1) was released. Entitled 'Decision Making in Victorian Education', it stated unequivocally that 'The Government will implement a system in which people affected can participate in the decision-making process.' Specifically in relation to curriculum, the Ministerial Paper advised that:

> It is the Government's intention to encourage and extend decision making related to school-level choice, content and methods in order to further involve parents, teachers, other community members, and, where appropriate, students. Effective involvement and participation occur when all groups establish agreement on what they want to accomplish, have access to stimulating ideas and support from wider community and systemic sources, and together have the opportunity, over time, to achieve their common objectives. (Education Department, 1983)

Robert Fordham, Minister of Education after the change of government, stated the new government's philosophy very precisely (Frazer, Dunstan and Creed):

> There must be a genuine devolution of responsibility by Government, and the active participation in our education system by parents, teachers and the wider community. Educational decision making at all levels should be public and participative. (Fordham, in Frazer, Dunstan and Creed, 1985, p. 58)

Democratization: Changes in Structures

By the 1990s, action relating to each of these process elements, participation in decision-making, and decentralization and devolution of decision-making, had progressed significantly, being well supported by structures which went hand-in-hand with processes. At school level, school committees and advisory councils had given way to school councils with a range of working committees, and school staff had become involved in local administrative committees.

In a memorandum concerning school councils in April 1977, the Director-General commented that 'The new circumstances can bring new satisfactions to members of the school community. Individuals now exercise a wide range of choices. Prescriptions for the future cannot be made effectively at a central point to serve every school situation' and, further, that 'The changes made to the nature and functions of school councils bring areas of significant decision making closer to the school.' The cautionary note was added that 'School councils will need to keep in mind the fact that we have to provide an overall system of education capable of serving our children wherever they happen to reside in the state.'

School-council structures, roles and responsibilities were strengthened further by the release of the Ministerial Papers in 1983. Ministerial Paper No. 3 specifically addressed the new arrangements for school councils, emphasizing that:

> School councils will have the major responsibility for deciding the educational policies of their school. The provisions of membership will give formal expression to the Government's belief that the most effective educational program depends on a process of consultation and negotiation among those vitally affected, so that the policies adopted will reflect their values and goals, thus increasing the prospect of wholehearted support. (Education Department, 1983, p. 4.5)

At regional level, system administration was also blended with active involvement of school and community personnel, and democratic structures were established to support the process. Participative committees, involving administrators, principals, teachers and parents were established in all regions in 1974 to undertake decision-making in relation to capital works and building maintenance, in-service education planning and provision, and the 'Disadvantaged Schools' Program' with additional areas of responsibility progressively being decentralized. Resource allocation was decentralized to regions, and a new set of relationships was able to emerge between schools and the decentralized system. It was a relationship based on the democratic principle that decision-making should involve those most affected by the decision. Many schools took the opportunity to nominate parents and teachers to regional committees in an expansion of democratic opportunity.

The regional-committee structure evolved by the mid-1980s into the establishment of regional boards of education, participative groups at regional level providing a mechanism for collective decision-making by school councils within the region. These boards, according to Education Department Ministerial Paper No. 5 (1984, p. 5.5) were 'an important component of the Government's program to develop an administration which is both responsive to the needs of schools and shaped by collaborative decision making between the school, the region and the centre'.

Thus the boards introduced a new and increasingly democratic relationship. They comprised elected parent, teacher and student representatives of school councils, representatives of statewide principal, teacher, parent and school-council organizations, the regional director, and representatives of the regional community. A school could be represented on the regional board by its principal, an elected teacher, an elected parent from the school council, or an elected student. The boards became the mechanism by which regional collective planning and decision-making occurred in relation to all areas of decentralized administration. These areas, by 1984, included selection of regional staff; long-term strategic planning; state-funded regional programmes and activities such as building and maintenance works and the 'School

Improvement Plan'; Commonwealth-funded projects such as the 'Participation and Equity Program', the 'Country Education Project', the 'Professional Development Program' and the 'Supplementary Grants Program'; and the allocation of school and student-support personnel.

Regional boards were expected to report regularly to the school communities in their region as well as to the central office of the Education Department. Education Department Ministerial Paper No. 5 affirms that:

> The requirement to develop a responsive bureaucracy is a system-wide requirement and not simply a requirement of any specific part of the system. The major characteristic of a responsive bureaucracy is that it focuses on the needs of clients, rather than on the needs of the system. It requires, therefore, both a desire and a capacity to respond quickly and flexibly to the needs of schools. It also requires a policy development process which allows those who are to implement policies and those who will be affected by policies to participate in their development. (Education Department, 1984, p. 5.5)

These affirmations relating to the development of responsiveness are at the heart of democracy, and the establishment of such participative bodies is the very essence of democratic structuring. On this basis it is of interest to note that regional boards were removed from the structure in 1989 because by then they were seeking to take unto themselves greater powers than the Minister and central office were prepared to devolve to them. In addition they were advocating to the central office and to the Minister the needs of schools in their regions far more effectively than they were advocating to schools the policies of the government and the central office. Specific-purpose committees were reconvened to ensure continued participation in decision-making.

At central level, participative structures were also clearly in place, evidenced most clearly by the establishment of the State Board of Education and a wide range of operating committees which included representatives of parent, teacher, school council and principal organizations as well as administrators. A State Board of Education was established, according to Ministerial Paper No. 3 (1983, p. 3.3) 'to provide for parent and community participation in decisions about the future of primary and post-primary education in Victoria. The Government believes that such collaborative decision making will lead to a progressive improvement in all facets of schooling.'

The State Board incorporated representation of all major interest groups in education, both government and non-government. Jean Blackburn, later a Chairman of the State Board of Education, commented on its role and operation as follows:

> The Victorian public system also, more vigorously than any other such system in Australia, has balanced bureaucratic power with

> participatory arrangements at system and school level. These extend the ownership of educationally important decisions with a correspondingly higher prospect of their successful realisation. The State Board of Education is unique as a representative, continuing review of the system, as a non-bureaucratically based dispenser of information about it, as a stimulator of wide engagement with educational issues and as the meeting place of government and non-government schooling. (Blackburn, 1990, p. 4)

It should be noted that following the change of government in 1992 the State Board of Education was discontinued.

The importance of achieving the delicate balance necessary between central, regional and school decision-making was stressed by Chapman and Dunstan (1990, p. 2): 'The tension emerges in decisions about how much control central authorities should retain and how much autonomy should be granted to regions and schools.' The present trend is to err on the side of giving significant additional powers to schools themselves.

Initially, the only democratic structures in place in education were at the peak of the political process. What occurred, particularly under Liberal education Ministers Lindsay Thompson and Alan Hunt and the Labor Government of the 1980s, was the extension of democratic processes throughout the whole education structure. It is this development which, according to Hunter (1983, p. 65), led one principal, emphasizing the increasing democratic nature of his school's organization, to stress that, 'In a democracy I have learnt that I can only rule with consent.'

Significant benefits have resulted from the new democratic relationships brought about between schools and the system. Hunter notes that:

> Democratic approaches have allowed the introduction of such qualities as innovation, participation, co-operation, autonomy, individualisation and initiative in both staff and pupils as characterising the ethos of a successful comprehensive school, for it is these qualities which can support the democratic principles of tolerance and equity between human beings. (Hunter, 1983, p. 52)

The present government's policy of encouraging schools to become 'Schools of the Future' is based strongly on schools being self-managing, developing their own specific charter, engaging in their own strategic planning, receiving lump-sum budgets as a basis for resource decisions at local level, determining their own curriculum arrangements, and generally becoming more independent. The expectation is that the democratic participation of school communities in decisions about the school's operation will lead to improved student outcomes and increased effectiveness.

Implications of Democratization at Central Level

At central level, implications of decentralization, devolution and participative decision-making have been progressively addressed. The need for a clear presentation of policies and guidelines within which schools could exercise their local discretion became a high priority. A wide range of support materials was published, including Ministerial papers, documents establishing curriculum frameworks rather than prescriptive courses and syllabuses, and manuals providing advice concerning the administration of finance, facilities, school councils, curriculum and school operations. The number of referrals from schools to central office on operational issues declined markedly as schools assumed increased responsibilities. This allowed a focus on policy determination and strategic planning at central level so that a basis could be provided, initially with regional support, for school self-management and self-reliance, and a reduced dependence on central administration.

The inevitable outcome of greater devolution, increased decision-making at school level, the elimination of inspectors and school reviews and an increase in powers of school councils was a reduced emphasis within schools on accountability to 'the Ministry', and an increased emphasis on accountability to the local community through the school council. This divided accountability created significant difficulties for some principals who found it hard to share responsibility with teachers and parents, and for some senior central administrators who no longer had unquestioned authority over action at school level.

A later and related outcome was a significant reduction in the size of central and regional administrations. With decision-making increasing markedly at school level, there was less justification for large teams of support personnel in regional and central administration. The result has been a reduction in non-schooling staff to a quarter of the level it had reached ten years ago. Major reductions have been made in the number of curriculum consultants and student-support consultants, in staffing of finance and facilities branches, in staff previously involved in school review and teacher assessment, and in curriculum research and development.

The cost of greater involvement has been considerable. Meetings at regional and central level involving large numbers of representatives involve a great cost in time and travelling and accommodation expenses, as well as in preparation of papers. Criticism has been levelled at the Ministry for involving representatives of principal, teacher, parent and school-council organizations in such decision-making as selection of senior staff, resource allocations, curriculum-frameworks developments, facilities-priority determination, and school-improvement policies and practices. It has been argued that such involvement slows the decision-making process and includes in the formulation of key decisions people who do not necessarily appreciate the full context in which decisions need to be taken.

Despite these criticisms, the participation of large numbers of personnel across all areas of administration has led to fuller understanding of the issues involved, a broader range of potential solutions, and a greater commitment to, and ownership of, the final decisions. Nevertheless, a number of key issues emerge.

Emerging Issues

Dual Responsibility and Accountability

Dual responsibility and accountability need to be addressed as changed relationships and governance are introduced. Tensions are apt to arise when principals are required to report to two masters, the former 'master' in a vertical, bureaucratic line relationship to the employing authority, and the emerging 'master' in a horizontal, participative line relationship to the school council and school community at the local level. Already there is evidence of conflict where, for example, a school council has tested its muscle by intruding into professional areas of learning and teaching, or where a principal has maintained an authoritarian role and resisted referring to the school council issues which were properly within its domain. Induction and development activities should be planned for both principals and members of school councils if effective understanding of changing roles and relationships is to be achieved.

Local Development of Objectives

There is potential for tension between the provision of system objectives and the encouragement to local schools to develop their own objectives. It is critical that objectives developed locally are within the guidelines and parameters established by the system if the goals of equity and access in a statewide system are to be maintained. However, the constraints on a school's freedom must not prove too limiting or the value of devolution of responsibility to schools is lost. It is necessary for self-managing schools within a state system of education to realize that they are not independent schools, but that they do have freedom to act within boundaries established through the political process. A government school in Victoria cannot, for example, determine as one of its objectives that it will not enrol students from within its own neighbourhood catchment.

The Motives for Devolution and Decentralization

A further issue is addressed by Chapman and Dunstan (1990, p. 2):

> Problems also emerge from suspicions about 'motive'. Is the intention in relocating decision making to the local level supposed to increase

> democratic approaches, or to contain expenditures and to allocate resources more effectively and with less opposition?

It can also be asked whether the initial momentum to decentralize and devolve responsibilities was related to the unmanageable size to which the system had grown, and a resultant need to limit the number of complaints and inquiries being received at central office. It is fair to assert that whatever the initial motive, benefits are accruing from increased democracy, from improved resource allocation and from more localized handling of complaints. It is constructive to address problems emerging from initial suspicions about motive, but if the analysis of those problems reveals a broadening of benefits, including greater use of democratic processes, then the suspicions referred to can increasingly be allayed.

Participation as a Legitimating Tool

It is possible for participation to be used as an exercise in social control or engineering, a legitimating tool, introduced to provide back-up support for the introduction of minority views or unpopular policies. Where this is the case, it can only be seen as patronizing and dishonest. Hunter (1983, p. 59), in a specific school case study, refers to such an instance, pointing out that 'Even though there were many meetings, many of the staff did not feel that they could influence events'; that 'It's like banging your head against a brick wall. They never take any notice'; that 'It does you more harm than good to speak your mind'; and that 'It was quite common for opinions which flourished in the semi-privacy of small groups in the staff room not to be forthcoming in open meetings. Apathy, timidity and caution were some of the reasons presented, the latter reason some claimed through experience.' Schools and systems must guard against token participation or participation used simply to legitimate a leader's whims.

Progress to More Democratic Processes and Structures

The attention drawn by Grant Harman (1990, p. 65) to the criticisms expressed by Professor Freeman Butts during his visit to Australia during the 1950s is pertinent, when Butts was 'repelled by the high degree of centralisation in the governance of education'. He criticized the high degree of administrative centralization from several points of view: one was that of democracy. He noted:

> The basic questions are these:
> Are decisions made by a relatively few people in a centralized system more likely to be democratic or undemocratic?

> Is centralisation necessarily democratic or undemocratic?
> Will an exclusively centralized system of decision making ultimately serve the cause of democracy in a society at large?
> Do Australians miss something of the vitality, initiative, creativeness and variety that would come if the doors and windows of discussion were kept more open all the way up and down the educational edifice? The two-way flow of education ideas might lead to more broadly based decisions and therefore more democratic ones. (Butts, 1955, p. 17)

The subsequent action by governments in Victoria has done much to address the concerns raised by Butts, by focusing on regional and school participative decision-making, and by establishing increasingly democratic structures in our education settings. Refinement, consolidation and extension remain a high priority.

Case Study

The following case study illustrates the changing structure of democracy in educational settings in Victoria. It involves Golden Sands Primary School, a hypothetical government school in metropolitan Melbourne. Golden Sands Primary School was established in 1930. It has operated throughout its sixty-four year history as a government school, continuing to provide primary education for all students in its neighbourhood. It has always maintained very high standards, giving the school a proud tradition and a well-known high reputation.

In 1928 the local community used the democratic process to draw attention to their need for a primary school. They garnered support from all local parents, they held meetings to which politicians and senior education officials were invited, they wrote letters and submissions in support of their case for a school, and they continued to lobby for their school on the basis that there were sufficient district children of school age to entitle them to a neighbourhood school. Furthermore, the school to be provided, in a democratic system based on equity for all, should be of similar quality to those provided elsewhere in the State, and with an equitable share of staff, finance and curriculum support. Thus, in the case of Golden Sands Primary School, a government primary school was established, staffed and resourced on the basis of a request of local parents using the democratic process. But that, in 1930, was where democracy in education started and finished. The whims of local communities were kept securely in check.

For its first forty or fifty years of operation, relationships between Golden Sands Primary School and the system were based on a top–down model, whereby government policies were imposed on schools, and their implementation was ensured by inspectors. The democratic trigger for this top–down relationship was the mandate for its education policy won by the government through a majority vote of the people at elections. This characterizes a model of democracy based on representation at political level only. Jean Blackburn (1990, p. 4) states, however, that 'Public schooling has other democratic dimensions. It is organized as a system, responsible through a minister to parliament. This makes it public in a unique sense . . . it is responsive to agreed public commitments to a unique degree.'

Golden Sands Primary School, like other government primary schools, had a school committee comprising elected local parents. The committee had a support role, but no decision-making related to the school programme, staffing, finance or operational matters. The principal and staff worked within strict guidelines issued by the Education Department, the system, in all functional areas and they were not free to vary these arrangements. Such variation, it was believed, could jeopardize the equity of provision of education.

By 1966, Golden Sands Primary School was a pilot primary school, invited by Primary Schools' Division of the Education Department to develop a school policy which reflected its own goals and objectives, taking into account local considerations. By 1970, it had been allocated, with all other primary schools, a school grant which provided a limited amount of recurrent funding to be spent at the school's discretion.

In 1975 when school councils were introduced to replace school committees, Golden Sands Primary School Council was established, incorporating teacher representation as well as parents and the principal. The school council was given considerable additional decision-making responsibility, including overall planning and policy, financial matters, buildings and school–community relations. In 1975 also, when regionalization of educational administration across the State was completed by Education Minister Lindsay Thompson, Golden Sands Primary School suddenly found there were opportunities for participation and for shared decision-making in areas that affected their school. They had the opportunity to be represented on the regional board and regional committees by their principal, an elected teacher, and an elected parent from the school council.

The momentum for local decision-making gathered significantly through the 1980s, and the relationship between Golden Sands Primary School and the system changed dramatically as a result. Golden Sands Primary School Council became responsible for the school's education policy, the selection of the principal and deputy principals, its budget planning and financial policy, its curriculum policy, and buildings and grounds. All school councils now comprised parents, teachers and principal, and in post-primary schools, students. The level of the School Grant increased enormously, with Golden Sands Primary School now receiving from central office well over $100,000 per annum, which the school council is responsible for administering. The school council pays the electricity, gas and telephone accounts, it meets all costs of administration, library provision and minor maintenance works. Furthermore, as one of the pilot 'Schools of the Future', Golden Sands has been able to develop its own charter, describing how the school 'combines local and system requirements to deliver quality education to the local community' (Department of School Education, Victoria, 1994, p. 2).

Democratic decision-making at the school level has arrived, based on general policies and guidelines established at system level to ensure maintenance of overall equity. The rationale for the structure of democracy now in place is that those affected by decisions should participate in the making of those decisions.

What has been noted about the potential for an enhanced democratic relationship between Golden Sands Primary School and its regional and central administration also applies to secondary colleges in Victoria. These former high schools, although they had advisory councils rather than school committees until 1975, followed similar patterns to primary schools in their increasing democratic opportunities. In relation to the former technical schools, however, successive chief inspectors (later, directors) of technical education testified to the close, harmonious and productive relationship which operated between the central administration and support bodies like the Technical Schools Association and school councils. The director, Mr Ted Jackson, in his 1968–9 report to the Minister, asserted that 'our technical schools have never operated as closed shops but have traditionally maintained close contact with what were quite wrongly referred to in some quarters as 'outside bodies' (Johnston, 1992, pp. 84–5). Clark (1929) affirmed that 'The tendency of any department is to become bureaucratic and ignore outside assistance. Unfortunately also, the more pronounced central administration becomes, the less pronounced local interest becomes. Experience has clearly shown this to be subversive to the best interests of technical education. No department is infallible.'

Bill Johnston (1992, pp. 62–5), writing of the history of the School Councils Association, notes that 'It really is quite remarkable, looking back to those early post-war years, to see the number and variety of proposals, now accepted as normal, which originated from the Association.' Examples cited include 'the local selection of principals, university recognition of, and credits for, technical school qualifications, the establishment of regional technical colleges and regional councils, and payment of equipment grants direct to schools.'

Yet there remains much to be achieved. Golden Sands Primary School is now declared a 'School of the Future' by the Department of School Education (1993) whereby:

- parents will be able directly to participate in decisions that affect their child's education;
- teachers will be recognized as true professionals able directly to determine their own careers and future and with the freedom to exercise their professional skills and judgment in the classroom;
- principals will become true leaders in their school with the ability to build and lead their teaching teams;

- communities, through the school charter, will be able to determine the future destiny of the school, its character and ethos;
- within guidelines, schools will be able to develop their own curriculum programmes to meet the individual needs of students; and
- schools will be accountable to the community for the progress of the school and the achievements of its students.

Whilst the detail of these more democratic approaches to schooling is still being determined, there is being maintained a strong momentum to grant to Golden Sands Primary School increased responsibility for decision-making associated with its own school community, within parameters and guidelines established to ensure ongoing equity and access in relation to other government schools in Victoria.

Through these processes and structures, everyday practice in attaining democratic behaviour is provided. Schools and systems are constantly being encouraged to create a democratic atmosphere in their operations, so that the products of democracy may be more visible: justice, equality, tolerance, respect and mutual benefit. There is encouragement for the acceptance of minority opinion, for the mature acknowledgment of differences, for innovation and divergence, for the coexistence of both conformity and consistency on the one hand and freedom on the other, for the presence of contradictions. Democracy is to be understood through practice, and where better than in our schools and school systems?

References

Blackburn, J. (1990) *Public Schooling: The Democratic Commitment*, Melbourne, State Board of Education.

Butts, R.F. (1955) *Assumptions Underlying Australian Education*, Melbourne, Australian Council for Educational Research.

Chapman, J.D. and Dunstan, J.F. (1990) *Democracy and Bureaucracy: Tensions in Public Schooling*, London, Falmer Press.

Clark, D. (1929) *Some Notes on the Development of Technical Education in Victoria*, Melbourne, Working Men's College Printery, p. 45.

Department of School Education, Victoria (1993) *Schools of the Future, Preliminary Paper*, Victoria, Minister of Education.

Department of School Education, Victoria (1994) *School Charters: Information Package for Consultation and Promotion*, Victoria, Department of School Education.

Education Department of Victoria (1973) *Vision and Realisation: A Centenary History of State Education in Victoria*, Blake, L.J. (Ed), Melbourne, Government Printer.

Education Department of Victoria (1983–4) *Ministerial Papers No. 1–5*, Victoria, Minister of Education.

Frazer, M., Dunstan, J.F. and Creed, P. (1985) *Perspectives on Organisational Change: Lessons from Education*, Melbourne, Longman Cheshire.

Harman, G. (1990) 'Democracy, Bureaucracy and the Politics of Education', in Chapman, J.D. and Dunstan, J.F. (Eds) *Democracy and Bureaucracy: Tensions in Public Schooling*, London, Falmer Press.

HUNTER, C. (1983) 'The Politics of Participation: With Specific Reference to Teacher–Pupil Relationships', *Reflective Readings in Educational Administration, EED431/731 Introduction to Educational Administration*, Victoria, Deakin University.

JOHNSTON, W.H. (1992) *Technical to Post Primary: A History of the School Councils Association (1914–90)*, Melbourne, Association of Councils of Post Primary Institutions in Victoria.

Chapter 9

Democracy in the School Setting: Power and Control, Costs and Benefits

Brian Spicer

Over the past two decades there has been a powerful and at times almost euphoric movement towards greater democracy in all aspects of society and in all forms of organization. In some countries, such as the old Soviet Union, Yugoslavia and East Germany, the democratic movement has caused massive political upheaval and the redrawing of national boundaries. It has also caused, or been associated with, dramatic changes in thought as to the way organizations should be run and the way various social or community services, including education, should be delivered. However, while the media worldwide have been dominated by the political changes in these countries, the national press in countries like Australia and the United Kingdom have recognized the equally important shifts in thought, policy and action taking place in their own established democracies. Whereas the former 'Eastern Bloc' countries have been seen to be the focus of political change from communism to democracy, the western world has been seen as the focus for organizational change in which workplace democracy has been replacing an array of bureaucratic, authoritarian management structures in both government and private industry and commerce. Put very simply, the proposition has been put forward and adopted that increased employee participation in decision-making — in other words increased workplace democracy — will enhance organization effectiveness and efficiency and lead to greater productivity of higher quality at a more competitive cost.

This proposition has been increasingly applied to all forms of government and business in Australia and is now being rigorously adopted in the educational sector. However, while many of the proponents of such a strategy base their support on the apparent democratic basis of such an approach, critical appraisal suggests that frequently the motives have little if anything to do with democracy, often much more to do with 'new power', and certainly much to do with the more fundamental tenets of economic rationalism. Furthermore, whatever the results of such an appraisal, there is, as yet, only limited evidence to support the view that such strategies will produce the results which are expected. In education there is little substantive evidence to support the view that greater workplace democracy has enhanced the quality of the school product; even in the industrial sector some of the exemplary organizations of the 1980s (Peters and Waterman, 1982), with their flatter non-hierarchical structures and devolved power, failed the test of the recession of the late 1980s and early 1990s. Despite the appeal and strength of the democracy argument, the costs and benefits of the democratic school are still far from clear.

This chapter focuses on the school and school system in an established democratic setting, and tries to explore the reality of the democratic movement and of democratic processes in school education in Australia and to take some assessment of the costs and benefits which may accrue to the school and school system in such a setting. Inevitably, because the writer has had greater experience in one state of Australia — Victoria — the data for the chapter and for the arguments contained therein are essentially Victorian. However, the evidence suggests that while each state of Australia has its own idiosyncratic features, the essentials of their development paths in education over the past ten to fifteen years have reflected a marked conformity of view and underlying philosophy.

In any government-controlled public-education system it is inevitable that the organization and administration of schools will mirror to a great extent the structures typically in place in the broader society and economy. Similarly, the values which will be articulated in schools will strongly reflect the values of that society and the policies of government, and it will be exceedingly difficult for the mainstream of education to adopt and pursue goals or adopt structures and processes which may challenge it in any fundamental way. But education is about change and therefore such challenges may be unavoidable and may even be desirable.

This chapter then, while seeking to provide greater understanding of the costs and benefits of the democratic school, also highlights and confronts some of the dilemmas and paradoxes which inevitably arise when issues of democracy, participation, individual rights and freedoms are considered in the context of a publicly funded and government-controlled education system.

Responsibility, Democracy, Participation and Power

From an administrative perspective, schools and teachers in the government system can be viewed not just as public institutions and public employees, but as 'agents' or 'servants' of society. Therefore, it can be argued that it is society, acting through its democratically elected government and legally appointed administrative structures, that in the end should determine the key elements of the education system — including the goals of education, the administrative structures and the responsibility and accountability provisions. It follows too that in a democratic society the school and its teachers are responsible and accountable to both the local community and, through the government, to the society at large.

Until the 1980s the government's control over, and accountability for, the operation of the school system and for the work of schools and teachers was not questioned. Even within a democratic country like Australia the need for centralized, even bureaucratic, organizational control was not seriously challenged. The so-called 'democratization' of schooling in Australia in the 1980s was not so much to do with changing from this fundamental position as it was concerned with moving the locus of control for several key areas of decision-making from the centre to the school site, an inherent part of which involved a realignment of power which gave far greater power to members of teacher unions and parent associations than bureaucratic officials.

The push for a shift in the locus of control occurred about the same time as the movement in the business sector for devolved management and control structures. The government recognized the potential benefits, especially with a rapidly increasing and well-qualified teaching personnel, of allowing and even encouraging a greater level of participation in decision-making. These benefits included improved staff morale and reduced industrial unrest. Business, especially in the USA, had already moved to encourage greater levels of worker participation by devolving responsibility to small cost or profit centres in a search for higher productivity and higher quality of output.

In the broader manufacturing and commercial context, the previously hierarchical management structures gave way to flatter, more participative structures with great emphasis on the role of the team. 'We only survive and prosper by working with others — we never do it alone' (Kovach, 1989, p. xii). This was the direct response to the Japanese threat to US industry and to US leadership of the world economy. Australian industry and government enterprise have taken the same path towards the devolution of decision-making and the education sector has followed.

However, while there has been this process of devolution, the fact that the overall responsibility for education in the community has been given to government by society through the democratic process, means that the government *must* maintain ultimate control and responsibility for the education system and for the work of the schools. The reasons for devolution have been far more related to issues of productivity, efficiency, 'value for money' and power than they have been to democracy.

Control is exercised at the school level through a number of key mechanisms, all of which embody democratic principles but somewhat paradoxically maintain central power, and each of which has evolved to levels of great significance in the 1990s:

- the organizational mechanism — legislative and other strategies to determine the broad character of school governance;
- the resource mechanism, including staffing, school funding through the Student Resource Index and quality provision strategies;

- the curriculum mechanism, including strategies at both the federal and state levels of government;
- the accountability mechanism; and
- the marketing or competition mechanism.

Within the parameters set by these mechanisms the school does have significant and increasing primary control over curriculum; student grouping; class organization; resource allocation, including staffing, maintenance and site development; marketing; and the school and community interface. However, it is the mechanisms themselves that create the paradox of central control and central power within an ever-widening panorama of devolution.

The Mechanisms Examined

The Organizational Mechanism

Over the past fifteen years in Victoria and in other states of Australia, the organizational mechanism has moved consistently along the pathway towards greater decentralization and devolution of the school system. In the early stages the approach by government was to encourage community participation through developing and enhancing the role of school councils and increasing the role of teachers in school governance by encouraging the use of administrative structures which called for greater teacher participation in decision-making. However, while there was clear devolution of some aspects of administrative decision-making and control, the power of the Labor government of the time was secured by the key role it gave to teacher union representatives on school administration committees and by the reduced status it implied for school principals. For example, Clause 12.8 of the Primary Agreement 1990–3 reads as follows:

> The Principal/Head Teacher/Officer-in-Charge shall have ultimate administrative and operational responsibility for the work location and this responsibility shall be exercised in consultation with the Union branch. (Federated Teachers' Union of Victoria, 1992)

Decentralization of the administrative arm of the Department of School Education (DSE) to regional and subregional centres, as well as the growth of centrally determined and funded support services meant that the bureaucratic power of the centre was diffused but not reduced. The so-called democratization of the decision-making processes in education was really little more than a shift from central bureaucratic control to control by local unionists. It would have been extremely difficult for any school to develop policies, structures and approaches which were in conflict with the government's philosophy.

The philosophical linkage between government and the teacher unions meant that the early steps towards devolution were certainly a shift in the locus of control but were equally certainly not a shift towards full participative democracy. The power remained strongly entrenched in the centralist forces.

In the 1990s, with a change to a conservative Liberal government, the process of devolution continued and the pace of change accelerated. The numbers of people employed at both the central and regional levels have been dramatically reduced and the transfer of key decision-making power to the school site has continued. However, while these latest developments have been accompanied by the rhetoric of democratization, the reality is that the new focus of controls is not determined by the exercising of equal rights by all stakeholders, but is firmly centred on the parent community through the enlarged powers of the school councils. Whereas the previous Labor administration saw devolution to the school site as a shift in the locus of control to government-friendly unions and teachers, the present Liberal administration sees the local parent communities as being more aligned with, and accepting of, its philosophy of economic rationalism, quality performance and accountability.

That power is still strongly in the hands of the government through the Department of School Education (DSE) and is evidenced by the use of key strategies such as a school charter, which must be developed by each school and is the basis for a signed contract between the Minister and each school council. Each charter clearly asserts that 'The school council is accountable for the overall governance of the school' (Victorian Ministry of Education, 1993). Responsibility has shifted but ultimate power has not. The government has moved to reinforce this centralist control by adding to the power of the community in selecting the school principal and other senior staff while at the same time reducing the power of the unions and the teachers. Under new selection guidelines, no teacher from the school which is seeking a new principal appointment is able to be a member of the selection panel. Teachers from other schools may be on the panel but only in their capacity as parents of children attending the school and as members of the school council. Effectively, the process of principal selection has disenfranchized not only the union representatives but also the teaching staff in general. The fact that two school principals may be on selection panels, one representing the DSE and one as a 'critical friend' of the school concerned, must reinforce the tendency for councils to appoint new principals who accept the importance of the school charter and who are committed to making the school achieve in accordance with the charter and the criteria for quality performance, effectiveness and efficiency. That is, there is a reasonably high probability that councils will appoint principals who accept and conform. It appears that the latest developments on the devolution pathway have increased the role and responsibilities of school councils, but, allowing for the reality of only limited parental representation and participation in the work of school councils, this is not necessarily an exercise in greater democracy. From the perspective of the many teachers who are no longer represented in such deliberations, the opposite is true.

One further way in which the organizational mechanism has been structured to encourage the support and adherence of school principals to ministerial and departmental goals and to the school charters is through the use of performance incentives or salary bonuses for principals who meet the Department's performance criteria. This, combined with new powers for principals in the selection and hiring of new staff and the removal of unsatisfactory teachers, has added significantly to the power of the conformist forces in Victorian education. The organizational perspective has been the devolution of much of the formal responsibility, but it has not seen a major diminution of power at the centre.

The Resource Mechanism

While over the past decade the organizational dimension has perhaps offered the most to schools by way of a real transfer of power and responsibility, the resources dimension has remained very much the absolute responsibility of the centre. School financing has been centrally determined with a range of specific grants to schools to cover various aspects of the normal day-to-day operations. The grants have been tied so that there has been little freedom for schools to shift funds from the designated purpose to another deemed to be of higher priority. The only funds which have been 'free' in the sense that the school is able to determine the uses to which they will be put have been those raised directly from parents, usually as fees, and the community. In the latter case, the use of funds is usually determined by all members of the school community acting together through the school council and other committees. Funds for staffing, including funds for replacement teachers, were never at the disposal of the school. Even where the school community was involved in staffing selection or promotions, or the allocation of higher-duties allowance, the funding or resourcing decision was a central decision, not one for the school. In this way the school was isolated from the financial impact of its staffing decisions. The control of resources, from the initial budget allocations by the government through to the specific grants to schools, very much reflected the central bureaucratic assessment of needs and effectively ensured central control over school practice through control of the purse. In the more heavily devolved school organization of the post-1992 era — that is, since the election of the Liberal government — the resource dimension is also undergoing dramatic change and realignment.

The 'Schools of the Future', as the newly devolved schools in Victoria are known, will receive from the beginning of 1995 a single line budget, determined by a Student Resource Index (SRI), which will cover all operating and general maintenance costs. Only major renovation and capital costs will be excluded and remain under direct central control.

The SRI will comprise a number of elements, but the key provision is for a payment to the school for each student enrolled, with the payment for students attending secondary school significantly higher than the payment for students attending primary school. The rationale for this differential is the more diverse curricula of the secondary school, and the acceptance of a more favourable teacher-to-student ratio for secondary schools than for primary schools. While the SRI will include some provision for students with handicaps or learning disabilities, for special curricula programmes and for geographical isolation and/or specific community disadvantage, the key principle is that each primary student will receive through the school grant the *same* direct educational funding or resourcing as every other primary student, and similarly for secondary-school students. How schools then distribute the total sum of their resources among their various activities and priorities is for their school councils to decide in consultation with their school principals. This represents a dramatic change in the nature and dimension of the school's resource allocation and distribution functions, and a major increase in the direct responsibility of the school council. The resource mechanism clearly shows a shift in the locus of control from the central bureaucracy towards the school site.

However, it would be an error to believe that this shift is based on a concern to build a more democratic school or education system. The primary motivation for changing and shifting the control of the resource provision is to ensure greater local responsibility and accountability for educational decisions and the concomitant resource decisions, but within the context of agreed school charters which reflect state, national and community expectations. In an economic period in which the community is seeking evidence of financial prudence on the part of governments and government authorities, and when there is considerable pressure on stable if not reducing resources, it is a sound political as well as social strategy to let communities make some of the harder decisions in relation to educational priorities. Power over some very difficult school-resource allocation decisions may well be a pyrrhic victory for those champions of democracy in education decision-making.

Of course, while the rationale behind the devolution of resource decisions to schools may be anything but the activating of the democratic principle, there is no doubt that such devolution does transfer considerable power to the school councils and to the school principal. The ability of the school principal through the council to determine the numbers and mix of teaching staff is considerably strengthened by the new procedures. While in the short and long-term this may open up teaching opportunities for younger graduates who have struggled to find employment in a period of stable enrolments and decreasing resources, it will add to the insecurity of teachers who fear that their rights of tenure are being permanently eroded for fiscal rather than educational reasons.

The considerable fiscal freedom which school councils and principals now have will almost certainly be reflected in the way the curriculum is supported through various resourcing decisions. Councils which seek to influence the change to new priorities such as technology education or physical education, will be able either to hasten or retard development by their resource-allocation decisions. Over the medium-term, say the five-year period of a principal's contract, it may well be that a school's resourced or supported curriculum could change quite dramatically away from the balance as indicated in the published or stated curriculum. Areas perceived to be of lesser priority may well be the losers in this type of financial or resource environment. While government and school policy will continue to support the need for a 'broad and comprehensive' curriculum, the desire by schools to be seen to be 'top performers' in the areas that are perceived to be government and community priorities may effectively narrow curriculum choice. At the level of the ordinary classroom practitioner, teacher influence over resourcing decisions is probably not enhanced and may even be reduced when compared to the previous phase of devolution.

The Curriculum Mechanism

The curriculum mechanism has been subject to considerable change and variation over a period of almost thirty years. The immediate post-war decades of the 1950s and 1960s were primarily years of total central control over curriculum at all school levels. The formal curriculum-management structures were extremely hierarchical, and the classroom teacher had only limited autonomy in the selection of teaching strategies and very little control at all over the substantive and conceptual content of courses and lessons. The area of decision-making available to classroom teachers was generally related to the way(s) in which the experience of the child could be integrated into the study unit. In larger schools, even this could be a subject-department decision rather than the decision of the individual teacher. The central influence over textbooks and the greatly maligned inspectorial system further reinforced conformity to the set curricula. Then, in the late 1960s and 1970s, control over much of the curriculum passed quite overtly from the central bureaucracy and its various curriculum agencies to the schools and essentially to the teachers. The only exceptions were in regard to the curriculum specified for the pre-university certificate examinations.

The underpinning professional rationale and management philosophy was that teachers, as well-trained professionals, are those best able to determine the actuality of the curriculum in the context of official policy and course guidelines, the nature of the school itself, the local environment as well as the background, needs and aspirations of the students and the community, and with due regard to their own personal expertise, skills and interests. Thus teachers were freed from the need to conform rigidly to externally determined programmes and instead were encouraged to 'customize' their curricula to their students and classrooms. The removal of the inspectorial system and reduced emphasis on the formal evaluation of classroom teachers, except in the context of promotion, gave added impetus to this move to professional autonomy. Teachers were, for the first time, holders of real curriculum power. But, they achieved that power, not as a result of deliberate democratization of the curriculum process, but as the result of the acceptance of a new management strategy. Unfortunately, the curriculum mechanism of the late 1960s, 1970s and early 1980s, was essentially one of *laissez-faire,* in which the acceptance of the doctrine of professional autonomy gave teachers almost free rein with little or no concern for the totality of the product.

Paradoxically, in the 1990s, we can recognize a return to more central curriculum control albeit while maintaining the rhetoric of decentralization and devolution. This change is a response to several powerful forces. One such force has been the widespread community belief that the schools have failed Australian youth by not equipping them with the skills and competencies which are necessary for a high quality and successful workforce (Mayer, 1992). This view has been strongly supported by the rhetoric, policies and actions of all Australian governments in the 1990s whether Liberal or Labor (Borthwick, 1992). The work of the Australian Education Council (AEC) in seeking to reduce interstate differences in key curriculum areas, and in promoting the concern for essential skills and competencies has been an added impetus for more central control of curriculum. While not possessing the rigid conformity of the British National Curriculum, and not seeking to eliminate local and regional differences in curriculum, the AEC statements and profiles are part of an attempt to 'develop a more common view of the purpose of schooling and of the shape of the curriculum' (Hannan and Wilson, 1992, p. 2). A related force has been government and community acceptance of the need for higher standards of accountability for the use of resources and the quality of output. Finally, there has been a recognition by many in the teaching profession that the era of freedom was not without its difficulties and failures and that many schools and many teachers were not ready for such important new responsibilities.

Indeed, the realization that serious problems were accompanying the transfer of curriculum power from the centre to the schools led, in the 1980s, to the introduction in some states of curriculum statements or frameworks produced by the State Education Departments and covering a range of curriculum areas, e.g., language; the study of society; mathematics; science and technology; the arts; physical and personal development; etc. These documents sought to bring a greater degree of centralized control to curriculum and to ensure an acceptable level of congruence both in the scope of the curriculum offered across the states and within the various subjects themselves. They were also designed to ensure that schools paid greater attention to specific areas of study such as languages other than English (LOTE), technology and music, which may otherwise have been given a lower priority. The schools then had the management responsibility to ensure that the policies and educational goals presented in these documents and other departmental and ministerial papers were reflected in the policy documents and curriculum programmes developed by teachers, administrators and parents working collaboratively.

In Victoria, this process and relationship has been further developed in the new school charters, which clearly outline the curriculum areas and structures which form the basis of each school's educational programme and their accountability to both the community and the government. In addition, a new curriculum body, the Board of Studies, has been established. 'Operating under its own public charter the Board will provide leadership and expert assistance to schools for the development of a curriculum that will meet the continuing needs of all students' (Victorian Ministry of Education, 1993). Schools can either adopt Board of Studies accredited courses or they may submit their own courses to the Board for accreditation. The Board will have a key role in the evaluation of courses and the assessment of student performance. 'It is intended that Board of Studies courses will occupy 80 per cent of curriculum time allowing flexibility for schools to emphasise curriculum areas appropriate to their school community needs' (Victorian Ministry of Education, 1993).

When taken together it seems that the effect of all these changes has been, on the one hand, to devolve power and control to the schools, the teachers and the community and to build a foundation for the self-governing state school, and yet, on the other hand, to return to the centre the power to determine the focus, structure and even the content of the curriculum. Responsibility has been devolved. Power and control have been maintained. Clearly, on the curriculum dimension, there are strong centralist forces which are now finely balanced alongside the forces for decentralization and devolution. It is difficult to support the contention that the changes in curriculum power over the past two years have represented a shift towards greater democratization of schools and schooling.

The Accountability Mechanism

One of the major issues which has dogged the path of the decentralization and devolution movement in Victorian schools, and for schools in other states, has been that of accountability. How can the government, as the key provider of formal education and as the custodian of the public purse, effectively shift, devolve or delegate, decision-making powers and responsibility to the school site and the school community without setting up appropriate and workable accountability mechanisms? The perceived failure of our schools to meet national, community and individual needs and aspirations has added strength to the call for the implementation of such mechanisms. The 'Schools of the Future' have been created amid such pressure and concern.

An examination of the literature — policy and working documents — which has accompanied the establishment of the 'Schools of the Future' bears out the view that the government regards accountability as a necessary and vital part of any further journeys along the devolution pathway. The documentation reveals quite precisely the government view that while 'Schools of the Future' are self-managing, they continue to be part of a statewide system of education and therefore the controlling body, the DSE, has a responsibility to ensure that a quality education is being delivered by schools. To this end the Victorian Ministry of Education (1993) states that schools will be involved in monitoring:

- student-learning outcomes;
- student-participation outcomes;
- school-learning environment;
- financial and asset management; and
- community satisfaction.

Performance indicators will be developed to provide benchmark and comparative data in each of these areas. Other procedures to be adopted as part of the accountability strategy will include school reviews, which will have both an internal and external component. The internal component will be concerned with annual monitoring of programme effectiveness, classroom practice and progress towards goals established in the school charter. The external review will take place every three years, will be managed by the Schools Review Office and will involve Directorate personnel together with the school community. The external review process will culminate in the development of new school charters.

Performance appraisal for principals as well as for all teaching staff will become standard practice, while the Board of Studies will be involved in standardized testing programmes in key learning areas at various year levels (P–12) as part of the overall monitoring strategy. Continuous monitoring in the areas of finance and personnel will be facilitated by the general use of sophisticated technology and software. This specifically designed technology platform will provide for centre–school links to support information transfer and accountability processes.

Much of the detail of the accountability mechanism has yet to be finalized but there is no doubt that, at the level of principle and policy, the shift to school-site accountability has been even more apparent in recent rhetoric than the shift to self-management itself. In many ways, this new orientation to accountability mirrors the shift in business corporations from a management concern for the profitability of the whole. Whereas previously it was the DSE and the government that had to carry the burden of poor performance and non-attainment of goals, the new approach places the locus of blame firmly with the schools. While school councils may have to accept some of the blame for poor performance, it is certain that most will fall on the shoulders of principals and teachers.

It is interesting to reflect on the fact that the concerns which many now have about the accountability provisions for 'Schools of the Future' are similar to the anxieties expressed when the previous Labor administration proposed very similar strategies in 1986 (Victorian Ministry of Education, 1986). Parent organizations at that time expressed considerable concern at the increased burden and responsibility that the government was trying to put on to school councils. As a result of the pressure from school councils, teachers and unions, the 1986 proposals were withdrawn. It is unlikely that the same fate will be suffered by the current proposals.

The Marketing or Competition Mechanism

The final mechanism which operates to control schools in an era of devolution is that of marketing or competition. The public nature of the accountability processes outlined above, combined with the freedom which parents have to choose schools for their children and the fact that a school's size not only determines its level of resourcing but also its ultimate viability and survival, means that for the first time government schools are in real and serious competition with each other. It is difficult to predict the overall impact of this competition but it is possible to put forward some suggestions as to what might happen.

First of all, the effect of competition will almost certainly be to reduce the extent of real difference between schools. In the initial marketing phase, a school wanting to be successfully competitive will have to be better at doing those things that the public believes schools should be doing. The right to be different and the ability to sell that difference as a positive attribute in the market-place will only follow a clear demonstration that a school is among the best in the conventional sense. Not only will this have the effect of reducing school difference, it will probably mean that many government schools will take on, or try to take on, the characteristics of those non-government schools which have traditional high status in the eyes of the community. It is reasonable to believe that this will lead to an initial conservatism in the way the newly emerging self-governing government schools will approach all decisions, from principal selection to teacher selection, curriculum development and resourcing. It will almost certainly lead to a greater emphasis on the achievement of the traditional academic goals which are reflected in many performance indicators used in educational settings.

Secondly, the effect of competition will be to leave some schools stronger and some schools weaker on both the enrolment and resource dimensions. This in turn will provide its own motivation and pressure for further rationalization of resources and encourage closure of the weakest schools and, through amalgamations, the establishment of multicampus schools which can build on traditional strengths and use the resulting economies of scale to provide greater curriculum breadth and depth. In an era of great concern for fiscal responsibility, the competition and marketing mechanism will almost certainly work to lower average costs per student and therefore contribute strongly to a maintenance of the government's tight budgetary policy. But, whereas in the traditional scheme of things governments made savings by cutting expenditures, under the new order the school communities themselves will provide much of the pressure for economic rationalization. Unfortunately, as the research suggests, while the size of schools will increase and there will be savings to the public purse, there is no evidence to support the view that beyond a certain middle size of enrolment, say 400–500 students, there will be a significant increase in the diversity and depth of curriculum offerings (Fowler, 1992).

Thirdly, there will be a diversion of funds, at least in the short-term, away from the learning needs of the students towards the financing of better public relations or advertising materials. Schools will be tempted to produce bigger and glossier school handbooks and prospectus documents in order to create a more positive image in the wider community.

Overall, the marketing or competition mechanism will almost certainly have the effect of increasing school size, reducing school differences, reinforcing a concentration on key curriculum areas and on student attainment in academic subjects, and cutting average costs per student — all of which are congruent with general government strategy. It is indeed a powerful form of control and an important form of central power.

Internal Autonomy Versus External Control: Paradox and Tension

What appears to have happened in the case of Victorian education is that after more than a decade of increasing devolution and decentralization, albeit with minor and major setbacks and with various levels of opposition, the stage has been set and the gates opened on the pathway to the self-managing government school. At first glance this would suggest a major shift towards the democratization of schooling, but a second more penetrating examination suggests that this is not the case. School communities and school principals have gained increased powers in many areas of school governance, especially in relation to staffing and resourcing, but these new powers have not been freely given. A variety of mechanisms have been established and operationalized to ensure that with the new powers have gone increased responsibility and accountability. This accountability mechanism means that the government has maintained its central power and control over the direction, structure and operations of the schools while still meeting its policy goal of enhancing and expanding the role of the local communities in education. This paradoxical relationship between internal autonomy and external control is already creating tension among the stakeholders in school education. It also supports the contention that many of the recent changes in school governance have been created out of concerns for control and power rather than for democracy.

However, irrespective of the motivating forces which have spurred the change to self-management, it is possible to identify a variety of potential costs and benefits which need to be considered when any school system moves along the devolution pathway. Many of these have been mentioned previously in this chapter but they are the single focus of the final section.

Benefits

- Some key decisions are made at the school site by those most concerned with the particular issues and their outcome. There is no doubt that school-site management has the potential to allow school communities to make important priority decisions taking greater cognizance of local needs and special local or regional factors. If the plethora of other controls allows this to happen then we might expect those decisions to have widespread acceptance and to generate widespread commitment.
- Participation and collaboration in decision-making is encouraged and enhanced. This is the fundamental rationale for a more democratic workplace. It does allow for all stakeholders, at least potentially, to be a part of the decision-making. In practice, this means that usually a representative form of democracy develops and it may well be that, depending on the nature of the representation, some groups will still feel isolated from the decision-making process. At times in Victoria, the power given to union representatives has worked to alienate other non-union staff members and, while giving the impression of greater participation and collaboration, has actually reinforced special group power. Theoretically, the move to self-management and greater workplace democracy should encourage more and better team play within the organization and a higher level of commitment and goal achievement.
- The shift to self-managing schools will lead to greater recognition of the professional skills and professionalism of teachers. Again, this may or may not happen. Senior staff may be able to use their professional skills to influence the decisions of school councils but the current developments in Victoria seem to have actually worked to limit the extent of such influence for the majority of teachers. One can also argue that the new concern for accountability, while justifiable on grounds of principle, also represents an overt expression of a central government or bureaucracy policy to reduce the autonomy of teachers.
- The role of the principal is enlarged and enhanced. This is certainly true in the 'Schools of the Future' in Victoria in the 1990s, but it was not so true of the earlier phases of devolution in the same state. To the extent that the principal has high-quality leadership and management skills, then this enhanced role may be of benefit to schools. However,

it does demand a great deal from principals, many of whom have not been given the necessary and appropriate management and leadership-development support. For those who aspire to the role of principal, the changes, including the performance bonuses, will make the position even more appealing as a career goal and, provided that appropriate selection procedures are employed, it might be expected that posts will be taken up by the very best people available within the DSE.

- Poor performance is more likely to be recognized and remediated. One of the greatest perceived difficulties associated with the management of schools and the whole public-education system during the past twenty years or more has been the apparent inability of schools or the system to identify problem teachers and then to do anything to rectify the problems. In a system where schools are self-managing and accountable and where principals and councils have greater power in the way the schools are managed and staffed, then the desire and commitment to achieve a higher level of performance will act to support staff appraisal and staff development. Schools will simply not be able to afford to have continuing poor performance by any staff member. The ability of a school to market itself effectively would be reduced if public perceptions of poor teaching surrounded its operations. One must hope, of course, that the desire to have a school perform at the highest possible level will not mean a reduction in loyalty to teaching staff and lead to teachers losing their positions without serious effort being made to improve their teaching. Using appraisal in such a punitive fashion would seriously reduce morale and also work against the development of the commitment which government policy seeks to encourage.
- Resources are more likely to be allocated to meet and support priority needs, and resource rationalization is possible. Earlier discussion in this chapter has supported this contention. However, there is a down side, in that areas of lesser priority will find it harder to increase their share of resources and may even find it difficult to maintain an equitable allocation. It is possible also that some student groups, such as those with learning difficulties or physical handicaps, may not receive the positive discrimination in terms of resource allocation that their individual circumstances demand and deserve.
- Important goals are likely to be pursued with vigour. The school charters, the nature of the agreements between the Ministry of Education and the school councils and the accountability processes virtually guarantee that the mission and goals of each school will be pursued with determination. Marketing, competition and the associated public scrutiny of school performance will add to the pressure for schools to attain their goals. The danger is that some goals, especially values-oriented goals, for which success in attainment is less easily measured, might be downgraded in the short-term, although the longer-term

effects of any decline in the standards of values would certainly impact negatively against the school in the marketing arena.

- The government and the bureaucracy are distanced from the decisions made at the school site. In tough economic times this is a real advantage for any government which does not wish to be perceived by the voting public as lacking concern for, and commitment to, public education.

Costs

The discussion of potential benefits arising from the change to school-site management has in itself raised the spectre of serious potential costs or disadvantages. Some of these are explored in more detail in the discussion which follows:

- Time, effort and money. First of all, the increased participation and collaboration which the self-managing school may encourage and develop through the use of teams and other strategies does require time, effort, commitment and skill on the part of principals, staff and parents. True self-management is not an easy or restful task.
- Loss of morale and increased stress. As a result of the increased workload and the pressure from other new provisions and controls, staff morale may actually decline. Uncertainty as to how the self-managing school with greater financial power and flexibility will seek to balance budgets and priorities will increase the insecurity of many teachers. The hidden costs of stress resulting from such changes may be very high.
- Loss of curriculum diversity. Curriculum diversity may suffer as schools seek to strengthen their market position. Conformity, rather than bravery and initiative, may be the short-term result as schools seek to gain competitive advantage.
- Diversion of resources from learning. The process of participation, if it develops as many policy makers suggest, will take up resources which may have been available to support learning in other ways. The skills associated with building effective teams, programme budgeting, etc. have to be learnt.
- Student versus school. The individual student may suffer because of the concern for overall school performance.
- Good teaching requires initiative and creativity. The 'critical environment' is not easily created and may also be jeopardized by the tendency to conform.
- Potential financial inequities. Formula financing on a per capita basis may still disadvantage some schools while preserving the notion of equity.

Conclusion

True democracy in public schooling is probably impossible. While there have been dramatic shifts in decision-making power and responsibility between centre and schools in recent years, it is questionable whether such shifts have been motivated by a concern for democracy or by a desire to make schools more productive, more effective and more accountable to both the government and the public. Over the past twelve years, firstly under a Labor administration and now a Liberal government, the rhetoric has been remarkably similar with clear policies for the devolution of power to the school site. However, there is plenty of evidence to suggest that for neither government there has been a desire or an attempt to establish autonomous public schools. Schools now have greater powers than they possessed twelve years ago and these powers cover many areas previously the exclusive domain of the central bureaucracy. But these powers are not, and have not been democratically shared among all the stakeholders, and the schools are now far more accountable for the quality of their performance than ever before. Paradoxically, the transfer of some decision-making powers to the school site may well have ensured greater central power and control overall.

References

BORTHWICK, A. (1992) 'A short tour of the findings of the Mayer Committee', *Curriculum Perspectives*, 12, 4.

FEDERATED TEACHERS' UNION OF VICTORIA (1992) *Primary Agreement*, Melbourne, FTUV.

FOWLER, W.J. JR (1992) *What Do We Know About School Size? What Should We Know?*, A paper presented to the American Educational Research Association, Annual Meeting, San Francisco.

HANNAN, B. and WILSON, B. (1992) 'The development of a national curriculum framework', *Curriculum Perspectives*, 12, 2.

KOVACH, B.E. (1989) *The Organisational Gameboard: Winning the Game at Work in Changing Times*, Englewood Cliffs, New Jersey, Prentice-Hall.

MAYER, E. (1992) *Employment-Related Key Competencies: A Proposal for Consultation*, Melbourne, AGPS.

PETERS, T.J. and WATERMAN, R.H. (1982) *In Search of Excellence: Lessons from America's Best-run Companies*, New York, Harper and Row.

VICTORIAN MINISTRY OF EDUCATION (1986) *Taking Schools into the 1990s: A Proposal from the Ministry Structures Project Team*, Melbourne.

VICTORIAN MINISTRY OF EDUCATION (1993) *Schools of the Future: Working Documents*, Melbourne.

Chapter 10

The Development of the Management and Self-government of Russian Schools and Pupils

Oleg Gazman

School Management: Yesterday and Today

The term 'school management' was introduced in education theory in Russia only in the 1970s. Until then the term used was 'school administration'. School life was centrally regulated and administered throughout Soviet history. Every problem of organization and management was decided in accordance with standard regulations, rules and acts that came from the central organs of government. We had standard regulations for planning school work and for controlling principals and teachers. The topics and dates for meetings and conferences of school staff, teachers' councils, parents' meetings, school parties, were all prescribed. Even the date of the school graduation ball was the same for all schools. Thus, obeying orders was the primary function of the school principal, who was allowed no initiative. Schools were managed by the undivided authority of a principal. No collective leadership in school teams was allowed. Teachers' councils and parents' committees existed in a formal sense, but they followed the orders of the principal. The undivided authority principle was understood very primitively: order verification, sanctions and incentives. Administration functioned according to a military pattern. Principals gave orders to their assistants; assistants gave orders to teachers and class organizers; and teachers gave orders to pupils and their parents. Principals were responsible for verifying that what went on in the school was in accordance with central regulations. Verification was carried out by principals and their assistants, by:

- checking documents (plans, class registers, diaries, exercise-books and tests of pupils);
- checking the content and form of lessons and visiting extra-curricular activities;
- observing pupils' behaviour at school; and
- obtaining information from meetings of parents, etc.

There has never existed (nor does there exist now) an effective way of collecting and processing such information. Thus principals were often very subjective in their judgments. Where they were unable to obtain objective information, they often listened to the judgments of rival groups of teachers; then snooping and reporting on each other became quite frequent. As a result the psychological climate in schools was often not very healthy.

In the early 1960s new administrative bodies were set up, such as 'administrative councils headed by the principal', which were groups with responsibility for certain operations of the school. However, the administrative councils, consisting of the principal, the assistants and representatives of Communist Party and trade-union committees, were purely consultative organs in all respects. Their most important function was to compile a general school plan, embracing all issues of school work, according to prescribed regulations. School administrators have always had a fetish about planning because they perceived it to be the main principle of a socialist government. The exact fulfilment of a plan was the true criterion of the good work of a principal, a teacher, a school. Any deviation from the plan was illegal and punishable. One of the big tasks of the school reform movement of the 1980s was to eliminate this top-down planning of all aspects of school life. As a consequence of this reform such an approach to school management is not recommended any more.

The democratic reform also rejected prescribed forms of school assessment. Under the old system, if the school was to be assessed as successful, not less than 90 per cent of the pupils had to receive pass marks in all subjects. This led to a situation where principals and local education authorities were competing not to produce the highest quality of pupils, but to be able to report the highest possible marks of pupils. The typical pass rate on school reports was around 96–98 per cent, even though many pupils did not know the three Rs. There was a special term for this phenomenon in school practice: 'per cent mania'.

Making a written report was an important function of the school administration. This report was always full of self-praise, and only positive trends were registered. It was, therefore, an inadequate means of management analysis. Because 'successful' plans and reports guaranteed an easy life for school staff, there was always a big gap between real school life and its reflection on paper. The school reform has meant that all types of reports except statistical ones are now abolished.

Professional activities of teachers and even their moral qualities were regulated by special instructions issued by the Ministry of Education. Similar rules for pupils were issued as well. Of course, some of the more reasonable of these rules are still valid today. Since 1943 a standard set of 'Rules for Pupils' for all schools of the country had been in operation. They were adopted not just by the Minister (known at the time as the Commissar) of Education but by the highest executive body of the republic — the Council of People's

Commissars of the RSFSR. Thus their compulsory nature for all educational institutions was stressed. In 1972 new 'Standard Rules for Pupils' were issued. They were not as strict, but many of the provisions of 'the rules' of 1943 still regulated the life of pupils, having become institutionalized. Among the 1972 rules were the following:

- Right after the bell rings you should be in the classroom and take your place. You are not allowed to enter or leave the classroom during the lesson without the teacher's permission.
- You must sit straight during the lesson, not leaning on the desk or sprawling. You must listen to the teacher's explanations and the answers of your comrades attentively. No talking on outside matters is allowed.
- When you are answering the teacher's questions you must stand straight and you may be seated only with the teacher's permission. If you want to answer or put a question to the teacher, you are to raise your hand.

Pupils who did not behave according to the rules during a lesson, during break or even in the street — if they spoke rudely to a teacher or comrades, or broke some school property or committed any of the 'crimes' children so often commit — could be punished in various ways.

Today, the Russian Ministry of Education has rejected the policy of imposing rules of behaviour and punishments on the pupils. Officials suggest that appropriate regulations should be agreed upon in a democratic way by administrators and teachers, together with the pupils and their parents. The Ministry is on record as stating that there must not be excessive punishment. Pupils are to be punished only in exceptional cases and punishments should never be degrading; they must be fair from the point of view of the pupil, not only the teacher. We must find ways to do away with such practices as the public 'trials' by peers of misbehaving pupils; blaming and insulting parents in the presence of their children; giving pupils lower marks in school subjects not because of inadequate knowledge, but for improper behaviour.

School-based Management

Site-based management is a feature that must become characteristic of any institution. It is of the utmost importance for an educational institution because it serves two functions: first, it provides for self-regulation, and second, it helps participants to develop certain personal qualities such as civil and public responsibility and leadership.

The theory and practice of pupil self-management have been widely popular in the Soviet educational system for some time, although the goals were not very democratic. But at the same time the necessity for, and the problematic character of the school-based management idea for teachers and school staff was never seriously considered. Why was this so? Probably because the idea of self-management for the pupils was regarded only as a useful strategy in the upbringing of young people. Thus, it presented no danger to the totalitarian State. But self-management of teachers would be destructive of education as a part of the totalitarian system chain.

Russian educational reform has now proclaimed school-based management as the most rewarding strategy for educational management. This concept implies participation in school management by community members, parents and pupils. Teachers are to take a leading role in this management, both quantitatively and qualitatively, because their impact upon school strategy is the greatest. The basic organization and operation of school-based management is very simple. It can be realized in many different ways; it can develop in accordance with the development of the democratic culture of the adults and children involved.

According to the reform initiators, the highest organ of management is the school conference, in which teachers, pupils, parents and interested community members participate. Delegates to this conference are elected at the meetings of pupils, teachers and parents. The main task of the conference is to adopt proposed school rules. These rules determine the school's individual ethos, proclaim its independence and confirm proposed structures of self-management. The conference is to be held at least once a year, to approve proposals for better schooling and decide what should be amended and changed, and to decide what problems need to be worked on.

The school council is the highest executive body of the school. It is elected by the school conference and the principal executes its will. The council provides for the social protection of the pupils, controls, the observance of the school rules by everybody, and confirms the school-based curriculum in which both parents and pupils are interested (this curriculum is devised by the teachers' council). It decides upon the profile of education, controls the school budget and financial policy, raises additional funds, hears the reports of the principal, etc.

Teachers' self-management is enabled by the teachers' council, groups of subject specialists, commissions, etc. Teacher trade unions can also be represented in this structure. In 'The Regulations on the Teachers' Council' of 1952, this council was described as a consultative body for the principal, i.e., the principal could choose whether or not to follow its advice. According to these regulations the chairman of this council was not elected; the council was always chaired by the principal. The council heard and discussed the plans and reports of teachers, principal's assistants, class organizers, Pioneer leaders, etc., but it could never interfere with the financial activity of the school. Under 'The Regulations' of 1970, the teachers' council had the right, not just to advise the principal, but to make decisions about the following matters:

whether to allow a pupil to sit final exams, whether to promote a pupil to the next grade, whether to expel a pupil or punish a pupil in a particular way. In practice, the teachers' councils often took it upon themselves to reprimand misbehaving pupils.

The Provisional Act on State General Secondary Schools of 1991 makes the teachers' council more democratic by transforming it into a structure of school-based management. The chairman of the teachers' council is now elected by teachers, and any teacher, or even community member, can become a council chair. The main functions, as stated in the new regulations for the teachers' council, are as follows: to choose curricula, programmes, textbooks, methods and forms of the teaching–learning process, depending on the local conditions; to organize in-service training of teachers; to select innovative activities for school teams; to assess teachers, taking into account the opinions of parents; and to make proposals as to categories of teachers' qualifications. The school itself can decide whether the functions of the teachers' council should be broadened.

Parents' committees were initiated by the Act of 1947. From that time until now they have acted as social organs, assisting the school in organizing all kinds of activities except educational activities (attendance, extra-curricular activities, work with parents, behaviour control, school meals, excursions etc.). According to the new legislation, parents are considered to be the main customers of educational services (together with the State) and participants in managing educational institutions. They are represented in the top organ of the school-based management conference, the school council.

But the real impact of parents upon the work of an educational institution depends not so much on the rights that are given to them, but on their cultural level, the level of their public consciousness, and their interest in studies of not just their own children, but others as well. Unfortunately, such active participation by parents is rather infrequent in modern schools.

Pupils' Self-management

After the October Revolution (1917), the ideologists of Soviet schools, N. Krupskaya, A. Lunacharsky and S. Shatsky, enunciated self-management of pupils as one of the fundamental principles of education. From the point of view of the pedagogical theorists, the main purpose of pupils' self-management was to form socially active persons, able to participate in the building of socialism. Self-management was intended to cement a school body organizationally, to train all pupils in the skills of organizational work, and to be a means of social control.

In the history of Russian schooling, three main types of self-management are identifiable: imitative (play at society); pseudo-business (play at command); and democratic, aimed at moral self-training and self-organization.

Imitative Self-management

The first type of 'imitative' self-management involved the creation of a school community which imitated the state structure having the republics, parliaments, presidents, constitutions, courts, public prosecutors, police etc. In the first years of Soviet power, schools copied the structure of original democratic states, and children assimilated the political structure of the adult society through play. Such self-management methods have been described by Y. Korczak, B. Soroka-Rosinky, S. Rives, S. Shatsky and others.

Pseudo-business Self-management

Later on, with the development of the totalitarian State, the second type of self-management — bureaucratic, pseudo-business, appeared. In form, it reproduced the Soviet military State, and in spirit, the Communist Party organization. This type of self-management was present in Soviet schools until the middle of the 1980s. The creation of bureaucratic machinery in the children's environment for the realization of the social control of pupils' personalities became the end of such self-management.

General meetings of the public were declared supreme organs of self-management. However, general meetings existed only nominally and carried out puppet functions in the hands of the principal of the school and the teachers. (Voting had to be unanimous.) Real power belonged to the puppet committee of the Young Communist League, led by the Party organization of the school (communist-headmaster). The Committee of the Young Communist League governed both the pupils' committee and the soviet of Young Pioneer groups. Many soviets, headquarters and commissions were established to train activists-organizers, recruit active members and transform pupils into future social leaders, but they were not involved in any practical organizational activity. The public work of active members was limited to meetings and making demands on teachers and children.

Theorists devised a motto for such self-management: 'For each function — an organ', which meant that, as much as possible, each aspect of education (ideological and political, moral, labour, aesthetic etc.) should be controlled by a separate unit. For each aspect, there were separate self-managing structures. The services a school offered were measured by the number of its organs of self-management. And a lot of managers tried to increase this number. For instance, one school could work simultaneously on creating a headquarters of discipline and order; a headquarters of competition; a headquarters of Young Pioneer action; a headquarters of labour; a headquarters of duty; a soviet of political informers; museums of battle fame; a Lenin's room; different clubs; sport and art soviets and so on. One can see the formalistic character of such self-management. The abundance of organs of self-management could not be given adequate pedagogical support, and pupils, even senior pupils, were not able to manage these organs for long without assistance. Such self-management turned into a simple 'play at command'.

The administrators of schools never worried if their students didn't show independence; after all, society needed executors, not organizers. Because of this, a system of 'public assignments' was initiated. Each pupil had to have such an assignment. It was called 'public', but issued by the teacher. Here are some examples of assignments for pupils of a fifth grade (10-year-olds): group monitor, class janitor, group nurse, pupils responsible for wall newspaper, responsible for work with younger children, responsible for sports, responsible for amateur performances, responsible for political information, etc. In addition to these responsibilities, many 'chiefs' headed councils, committees and sectors at the school level. The activity of these children was minimal. They were oriented not to their comrades' needs but to the teacher's orders. But being a part of the governing elite stimulated a special type of personality development; this type of personality was especially needed for the State, and was typical of a bureaucrat.

Our main task today is to do away with arbitrary pupil assignments of formal work. The main fault of the above-mentioned approaches to pupils' self-management was the fact that self-management never really existed. The system was never considered a form of public organization designed to defend pupils from the arbitrary behaviour of adults and peers. Its secret task was to transfer the functions of the teachers from the area of organization of studies and school life to maintaining student discipline. Through so-called self-management, a mechanism was set up to ensure that pupils obeyed their teachers.

Real self-management begins when pupils understand their own interest in studies, clubs and public activity; when they learn and begin to defend their own interests. The structure of self-management and the process of its organization are of secondary importance in this endeavour, unlike under the old system where structure was considered primary in the system of self-management.

Democratic Self-management

The third type of self-management is recognized by its genuine commitment to democracy, with an orientation towards the protection of children's interests. Such self-management doesn't appear by order from above (from principal, teachers), but grows out of a necessity for children to organize themselves to achieve their own goals, and to realize their common purposes.

In order not to transform children into officials, not to label them or to teach them that the duties of a leader are a painful burden, schools which aim to establish democratic values use Makarenko's principle of an obligatory 'shift system of active members'. Children are chosen by the organs of self-management to carry out a concrete task for a relatively short time. Progressive teachers of the 1960s realized that it was pointless to engage children in organizing activities that should be performed by teachers. 'We name the goals, we build the programme, we organize and then analyse everything' — such was the logic of non-formal self-management.

Many schools are now rejecting the old stereotypes, where quality of school self-management activity was sacrificed to quantity. In school we now see a tendency to change permanent structures for temporary ones: if we have a problem of discipline, or we need to design a school interior, we elect a special committee. If we want to go hiking together or to organize a party, we organize on an *ad hoc* basis, then as soon as the problem is solved, the organizing body ceases to exist.

Another way of making pupils' self-management more democratic is to build up a sense of cooperation between children and adults. Instead of confrontation and the subordination of pupils' self-management organs to those of teachers, it is necessary that we create a joint self-management system of pupils and teachers — a union of representatives of different generations interested in each other.

Problems of and Prospects for School Life

The good intentions of the Russian government and public organizations to make school life more democratic face many difficulties. So far, those in the Ministry have engaged in a type of wishful thinking, and we are entering a stage when we must leave such thoughts behind and engage in reality. Of course, a victory has already been won with the translation of our wishes into legislation, but the genuine transformation of a mass educational system into a democratic and humane institution will require time and huge effort from government bodies.

What are the main obstacles in the way of democratic school renewal? The main one is the deteriorating economic situation and the growing poverty of the country. All the above-mentioned negative features of the educational system still exist. New schools are being built very slowly, which means there are too many pupils and insufficient resources in each school. At this point in time, we do not talk so much about the need of schools for more computers and audiovisual aids; rather we struggle to acquire the most primitive building materials, to train and place enough teachers, and to retrain the specialists (teachers, managers and principals) who are already in the schools.

If the material resources were available, it would be much easier to depoliticize the school, to change attitudes towards Pioneer and Komsomol organizations, to reject compulsory standard activities for schools and ingrained attitudes towards the education of children, schools and, especially, teacher–parent relationships. Such fundamental psychological shifts are not just a question of changing national and cultural stereotypes but of bringing about qualitative changes in social and economic life. It is difficult to raise these issues, however, when parents are too busy with their work, their living conditions are declining, and they are finding it harder to obtain food, clothes etc. Whatever changes occur in the society, we have to understand that schools still remain a place for caring of children, and they cannot avoid functions of providing care which includes the organization of extra-curricular activities for pupils.

The role and place of class organizers in school life are now being revised. We are considering freeing the organizers from teaching subject matter: we want them to become advocates of children's interests at school and in the community. Their main responsibility now is the psychological and physical health of the children, helping them to learn and to communicate. Their functions are therefore complementary to those of parents.

Principals also face grave problems. There are many enormous schools in Russia, where 2000–3000 pupils are being educated simultaneously. It was economical in the past to build such schools, considering the necessity of saving money for construction work, but such schools are anti-human, both for the school administration and for children. Principals spend 80 per cent of their time and energy solving the problems of materials and technical equipment of schools, just trying to maintain them at least in sufficient quantity and acceptable order. They have no time for organizational and educational activities. Thus there is a deficit of creative solutions for educational problems.

We have to do a lot of work in order to break down stereotypic authoritarian thinking and behaviour. Many people working in schools, including the principals, behave and administer according to the old rules; they demand the same old things from teachers and from children. Changing this is a big challenge for the system of in-service training. In spite of all the difficulties, we regard the situation with optimism. The announcement that education is a top priority of the government in the new Law on Education gives us hope that the future economic revival of the society will make schools richer. We can also hope for a change in school-management attitudes. Indeed, the change has already started.

Beginning in 1986, the *Uchitelskaya Gazeta* newspaper and other popular press organs launched a campaign aimed at directing public opinion towards the necessity for decisive school reform. The ideology of the campaign was concentrated in a programme called 'Cooperative learning'. The educational process is seen as a joint creative activity of pupils and teachers, a joint search for solutions to educational and existential problems. Looking for solutions, teachers and students act as partners, as friends. All partners invest whatever knowledge and creativity they can, given their nature and experience. The principle of cooperative learning applies not only to reforming school learning, but also to reforming school life and extra-curricular activities. 'Cooperative learning' has already helped to change the attitudes of many teachers and school managers. It has resulted in the creation of a number of pilot schools and experimental sites, where school staff have devised their own curricula and developed individual organizational visions for their schools.

The principles of school organization have changed dramatically through the renewal of the content of education according to the principles of civil and personality-oriented professional self-determination of pupils; the establishment of Steiner schools and joint-project work by teachers and students reflecting the 1920s experience; and the method of immersing pupils in the content of one school subject for a long period of time, etc. New curricula are to be developed; and new ways of group organization are already being practised, such as big groups for lectures and vertical groups for mutual education (the school of A. Tubelsky in Moscow, the school of M. Stchetinin in Krasnodar, the school of Froumin in Krasnoyarsk, and others).

Organizational freedom and the development of an orientation toward parents as customers, toward national customs, and toward a new way of life give rise to many different profiles and specializations in educational work. Some schools give priority to the culture of communication and behaviour; some to the revival of a national culture through studies of customs and folk arts, organizing hobby clubs of handicrafts (embroidery, woodwork, pottery, metal ceramics, etc.) and collecting folk songs and dances. The number of such examples is becoming greater every year. There are many schools in towns, villages or on the outskirts of big cities which double as cultural, ecological and hobby centres for their communities.

Finally, I would like to say that it is imperative to do away with the repressive school life that has existed for the past seventy years. I have emphasized the negative experiences of the past to show what we must reject. But we also now have the rich experience of organizing new types of schools and stimulating the independence and creative activity of school principals, teachers and pupils. This is one reason for an optimistic prognosis for Russian school development.

Chapter 11

Building Democracy in the School Setting: The Principal's Role

Clive Dimmock

It is normally assumed that schools in democratic societies reflect democratic characteristics in their organization and management and that students are exposed to curriculum experiences which develop in them a healthy respect for democratic ideals. Many generations of philosophers and sociologists have indeed espoused the prudence of schools and schooling mirroring society in microcosmic form. The reality, however, may be quite different from the ideal. This chapter explores, firstly, the extent to which practices in Australian schools reflect democratic ideals. It presents, secondly, a justification for building more democratic practices in schools. Finally, it suggests that principals in particular, through their leadership, management and organization of schools can exercise a substantial influence on the extent to which their schools are democratic.

Conceptualizing Democracy in Schools

Schools may be conceptualized as a number of educational arenas in which democratic practices and values exist to a greater or lesser degree. These arenas are:

- the classroom, in which teaching and learning take place;
- the department, section or team, in which groups of staff function;
- the whole school, all teachers and students; and
- the school council, in which representatives of school and community meet.

Major actors and participant groups in these arenas comprise students, teachers, principals and parents. Distinctions between professional and lay interests may be useful, as well as distinctions between the roles of students as workers, clients or consumers (Handy and Aitken, 1986).

It is not the intention or purpose of this chapter to explore the concept of democracy. Other chapters in this volume address that issue. Brief clarification, however, is helpful for purposes of the present analysis. Thus, democracy may be seen to include:

- prevalence of the will of the majority;
- tolerance and respect for the rights and values of all, including minorities;
- participation and/or representation in decision-making;
- delegation of responsibilities and powers with accompanying accountability;
- checks and balances to prevent abuse of power;
- sharing and dissemination of knowledge and information to empower people to make decisions;
- concern for equality and equity in decision-making; and
- ability and opportunity to make judgments and choices in one's own and others' interests.

Many of these are not exclusive to democracy, but by students of contemporary society and organizations they are frequently thought to reflect democratic values and principles.

Democracy and its Expression in Schools and Schooling

Students may come to acquire knowledge about the meaning, development and history of democracy in its various forms through curriculum subjects and syllabus content. A second way of demonstrating democratic ideals is through the administration of schools and, in particular, the organizational structures established. A third manifestation of democracy is in the activities, processes and procedures at the heart of the school and expressed through interpersonal relations in the four arenas — the classroom, where teacher–student and student–student interaction is most evident in teaching–learning, and the other three arenas, where decision-making assumes pre-eminence.

Democracy in Australian Schools and Schooling

Traditionally in western education systems at least two forces have coexisted with democratic principles — bureaucracy and expertise. Bureaucracy, or government by officers in departments, and expertise, decisions taken by those with more knowledge, ability, or experience, create tensions with many of the democratic values outlined earlier. Both tend to be characterized by top-down government with relatively few checks and balances and little accountability.

There is a dearth of research evidence on the extent to which democratic elements permeate Australian schools. This review and analysis is, necessarily, selective and partial, based on secondary data and personal experience. Situations also vary between the separate 'states' and 'territories' in Australia, each of which has responsibility for providing education. The following description applies the conceptual frameworks outlined earlier to, and structures its argument around, key issues at the levels of classroom, department, whole school and school council.

Classroom

Elements of democracy are reflected at classroom level in two ways — through curriculum subject content and the teaching–learning process. Students may be introduced to democratic ideas indirectly, through studying ancient and modern literature, or more directly, through social studies subjects such as politics, government and history. In neither case is there generally an avowed intention to influence the political values of individual students; in fact, it is generally agreed that the Australian curriculum is lacking in two respects — political education and ethics. The curriculum in Australian schools has never been formally acknowledged as buttressing the prevailing political ideology, although it would be surprising if it did not implicitly reflect many of its values. The curriculum is not generally seen as a vehicle for indoctrinating children in a political sense.

It is in the classroom arena where the processes and activities of teaching–learning have strong implications for the presence or otherwise of democracy. Australian classrooms still reflect a predominantly teacher-centred approach. Didactic teaching methods are commonplace, particularly in secondary schools. Moreover, clear division of labour in schools places expectations on teachers to teach and students to learn (Dimmock, 1993c). This inflexibility of role places teachers as experts imparting knowledge for students to consume. It is teachers' views and interpretations of knowledge which monopolize classroom learning (Boomer, 1991). Teachers act as mediators between knowledge and student understanding and interpretation of meaning. Traditionally, teachers have denied students the opportunity to construct their own meanings. In this sense they have denied students some of their democratic rights, especially respect for the rights and values of others, and the opportunity to form judgments and make choices in the interests of oneself and others. A similar concern focuses on the general absence in Australia of negotiated curricula between teachers and students.

This concern about due process at classroom level exemplifies well the tension in schools between democracy on one hand and expert and bureaucratic control on the other. Traditionalists argue that teachers possess expert knowledge, which should be transmitted in a structured and orderly way. Students are thereby introduced to a body of knowledge which is often seen as uncontestable and absolute, but which they acquire passively as inert knowledge. Teachers are assumed to know what is in the best interests of students.

The problem with this argument is that teachers cannot possibly know what is in the best interests of all students, especially if they are teaching 150 students each week. If teaching is the means of securing student learning, then it should be no surprise that so many students fail to learn in school. Students might conceivably learn more without formal teaching taking place. Furthermore, few would dispute that knowledge is complex, contestable and largely socially framed (Marton and Neuman, 1992).

Although considerably more needs to be said on these issues, it is clear that tensions exist at classroom level between democratic ideals and those of expertise and bureaucracy. In traditional classrooms the extent to which students have participated in deciding curriculum content has been minimal, especially at secondary level with prescribed syllabuses from state curriculum and examination bodies. Student exposure to democratic principles through the medium of curriculum subjects has also been largely unplanned and minimal. Teachers' expertise has dominated practice in the important teaching–learning domain. Teachers and students have rarely shared responsibility for teaching and learning and it is even less commonplace for students to be allowed the individual freedom or autonomy to form their own interpretations, judgments and understandings.

Whole School and Department Level

Democratic elements at both the whole school and department levels can be framed in structural and process dimensions. The department structure, particularly in secondary schools, is customarily a strong unit for exercising decision-making. Fullan and Hargreaves (1991) have described in pejorative terms the 'balkanization' of the secondary school, where departments constitute competing factions and prevent the formation of whole-school perspectives. Research by Wildy and Dimmock (1993) in Western Australia found relatively low levels of instructional leadership by principals and deputy principals. Instead, curriculum management was focused on heads of department, who were either delegated these responsibilities or, more usually, assumed them. Teachers, therefore, generally find more opportunities for involvement and participation in decision-making processes at the departmental level.

While structures incorporating the whole school normally function more effectively in small schools and primary schools, it is acknowledged that whole-school perspectives on educational issues are relatively neglected by school managers and leaders. Whole-school staff meetings are commonly cited as too restrictive an environment for many staff to make meaningful contributions. Consequently, most schools have adopted committee structures. Membership of these committees is usually by election or appointment. Cooption and voluntary attendance of other interested staff may be encouraged in some schools. These are not without their problems. Irrespective of the bases of their membership, criticisms are often made about their representativeness and the processes by which they reach decisions. In many cases there is disillusionment with the process when senior staff choose to ignore committee findings and impose decisions of their own. This use of committees is then seen by staff as a screen preventing genuine participative decision-making. Representatives of two of the most important participant groups — students and parents — are generally absent from such committee membership, even if the issues to be decided affect them.

Teachers and principals are often ambivalent about fine but important differences between consultative and democratic decision-making (Tannenbaum and Schmidt, 1958). Both are forms of participation, but with very different implications. Principals may consult teachers but reserve the right to make the final decision themselves. With democratic decision-making there is no such veto — the will of the majority of participants prevails. Many conflicts in schools arise because principals and teachers fail to clarify whether a particular decision process is consultative or democratic. Another common 'corruption' of democracy occurs where the decision-making process appears to be democratic, but decisions are taken which reflect the interests of a powerful minority of staff rather than the will of the majority.

For most of their history the control of Australian government school systems has been highly centralized. Decisions relating to school finance, staffing and to a lesser extent, curriculum (teachers have enjoyed representation on curriculum committees) have been the prerogative of bureaucrats in central state offices. Surprisingly little discretionary power has been delegated to school level. Principals have acted as line agents executing central-office policy. Parent and community involvement in educational decision-making affecting their children has been largely non-existent, apart from a fund-raising function enjoyed by parent and citizen groups. The exclusivity of power and control exercised by bureaucrats has deprived parents for more than 100 years of meaningful participation in school decision-making. As a consequence, many Australian parents are culturally inexperienced in educational decision-making.

Moves to decentralize Australian school systems began in 1973 with the Karmel Report. Since that time, states have begun to cut their own path towards loosening central control, but each has done so at its own pace. Western Australia, for example, began to decentralize as late as 1988. The process is proving difficult for many reasons. While it is probably true that the majority of principals and teachers favour the philosophy underpinning restructuring, there are many who view the states' imposition of the devolution and decentralization policy as an abrogation of their responsibilities. These groups, including the teachers' unions, maintain a traditional mindset in believing education is best run from the centre. They argue that this is the only way to ensure equity of staffing and resourcing between favoured and less favoured schools. Interestingly, advocates of decentralization propose the same arguments to justify their position. Decentralists argue that resources are most effectively and equitably allocated to meet diverse individual needs at the school level, where needs are best known. Centralists generally assume equity means equal resource allocation, whereas decentralists tend to believe equity means unequal resource allocation based on need.

Whether the policy intent of decentralization and devolution is to improve school effectiveness, or to allow schools and their communities genuine participation in school governance, or more cynically, to pass the responsibility for system shortcomings on to schools, important democratic implications follow from the policy. Centralized Australian school systems have minimized the democratic contribution of parents, communities and professionals in school governance. Insofar as central bureaucrats are still reluctant to devolve power to school level, despite policy rhetoric advocating devolution, they buttress bureaucratic at the expense of democratic control.

Poor implementation strategies by central bureaucrats have impeded the move to decentralization. Implementation has been hampered by bureaucrats' willingness to decentralize but not devolve. Many school personnel complain that while decentralization of administrative responsibilities has taken place there has been relatively little devolution of accompanying powers. The workloads of principals and teachers have increased substantially without extra powers and resources. A further difficulty encountered in policy implementation is that school communities have been deprived of the responsibility for decision-making for so long that they are now unfit to bear this responsibility.

School Council

Policies for restructuring Australia's state education systems commonly focus on a revised role for the centre — that of setting system-wide goals and benchmarks, and holding schools accountable by monitoring their performance. At school level the establishment of school councils promotes the involvement of parents, teachers, principal and local community in decision-making. Students may also have statutory rights to representation, particularly on secondary school councils. Principals and teachers owe dual accountability to the school council and the central office. Policies developed in school and school council are expected to fall within overall system-policy guidelines. School councils have been established in Australian states at different times and with different powers and functions. Victoria, for example, established school councils in the mid-1970s, whereas Western Australia introduced school councils in the late 1980s. In both Victoria and Western Australia, the powers and functions of school councils when first established proved to be limited. These powers, however, were substantially increased in Victoria during the 1980s, and it remains to be seen whether more powers will be conferred on school councils in Western Australia during the 1990s.

School-council membership is rarely representative of the diversity of the parent body and local community. It would be rare, for example, for six elected parents to represent the diverse views and interests of the whole parent body. Despite these shortcomings, decentralization and devolution may offer increased hope and scope for introducing more democratic elements into the running of schools. These include delegation of responsibilities and powers with accompanying accountability to grass-roots level, greater ability to make judgments and choices in the interests of the school, more knowledge and information available at school level on which to base decisions, more checks and balances to prevent abuse of power and a higher level of participation and representation in decision-making.

Expressed fears that parents lack the knowledge and skills to participate in democratic processes are admissions of the weaknesses created by bureaucratic controls in the past. If parents do lack the requisite knowledge and skills for decision-making, it is because they have historically been excluded from participation and they will only develop such skills when given the opportunity and appropriate training. Two other cautions, however, are worth noting. Decentralizing and devolving from the centre to school can mean simply transferring bureaucratic structures from the former to the latter. Relatively little attention has so far been given to decision-making structures and processes in school-based management (Dimmock, 1993a). How principals and senior staff share power and influence with teachers, students, parents and school councils is a key issue both now and in the future. It is clear that in the foreseeable future parents seem destined to play a more participative role in their children's education. In the longer-term, however, the spotlight may focus more on the contribution from students themselves, as consumers and clients of the education service.

A second concern is the extent to which democratic structures and processes are necessarily beneficial to schools and schooling. Some of the worst excesses of democracy are seen in schools such as Summerhill in the UK, where very little structure is provided, students are given excessive freedoms and arguably, quality of education suffers. In more conventional Australian school settings, as is presently argued, there is surprisingly little reflection of democratic principles and practices. Achieving a balance between elements of democracy, bureaucracy and expertise in Australian schools appears an important aim for the future. In clarifying this balance it is worth referring to the school effectiveness research, since whatever arrangements pertain, it is the quality of education experienced by all students which should remain central.

Justification for More Democracy in Australian Schools: School Effectiveness and Student Learning

Although school effectiveness research is acknowledged to have methodological shortcomings, there are some generally agreed findings which are accepted across cultures and systems. An accumulation of research findings since the late 1970s confirm that a student's social development and academic achievement may well vary, depending on the school attended (Reid, Hopkins and Holly, 1987). This confounds the conventional wisdom of the 1960s and early 1970s that the school had little or no influence on student achievement, when compared to the influence of the home and family background. Although the definition of what is an effective school is problematic and contested (Chapman, 1993), it is taken here to mean a school which obtains, for the majority of its students, achievements in learning which are above those expected, given the intake of students and resources to the school.

On the basis of American, British and Australian research it is possible to recognize key factors in school effectiveness (Mortimore, 1991). These key features include:

- leadership;
- management and instruction of pupils;
- management of teachers;
- pupil care;
- parent involvement;
- school environment; and
- school culture and climate.

For a school to achieve high levels of effectiveness it appears unnecessary for it to perform well in all of these areas. Research, however, has not weighted the importance of each factor, neither has it addressed in a convincing way the apparent importance of the interaction of the variables (Reynolds, 1993). Nonetheless, leading researchers generally agree about these key factors (Mortimore, 1991). It is worth investigating each to ascertain the connections with democratic values and procedures.

Leadership

A principal who is goal-driven but neither too authoritarian nor too democratic, and is able and willing to share ownership of the school with colleagues is important. There are occasions when the appropriate behaviour for principals is either more authoritarian or more democratic, but in general, research suggests a balance somewhere between the two is effective. Leadership qualities include the ability to delegate to others and to involve staff members in planning and managing the school. The ability to involve others and to gain their commitment and motivation to commonly agreed goals is a vital factor in effective leadership. Contemporary theories of leadership emphasize the leader empowering others rather than exercising power over others. As Fullan (1991) states, 'the principal's job is to ensure that essential things get done, not to do them all himself or herself' (p. 36).

Classroom Instruction and Management of Pupils

Classroom organization which encourages and rewards student involvement is linked to higher learning. Achievement is higher where students take responsibility for their own learning. Both of these factors support the case for developing democratic values in the classroom. However, student performance also improves when teachers assume responsibility with students for their learning, and when the management of student behaviour is neither too weak nor too harsh. These conditions provide structure within which democratic processes can operate.

Ensuring that lessons are structured and work-centred and that material to be learned is challenging but achievable is important. Empirical research on effective teaching (Fraser, Walberg, Welch and Hattie, 1987) advocates a number of teaching–learning strategies which support democratic notions. Among these are — individualized and personalized learning, cooperative learning, adaptive instruction and tutoring — all of which recognize the efficacy of teachers responding more to the learning needs and interests of students rather than adopting teacher-centred methods. Whole-class didactic teaching can also be effective in securing learning, providing it is enthusiastic and motivational, for limited periods, and displays good subject mastery (Porter and Brophy, 1988).

Management of Teachers

Where principals involve teachers in the corporate life of the school and encourage them to work collegially for the benefit of the school, higher performance of both teachers and students is achieved (Little, 1987, 1990). Research suggests that the ways in which principals interact with teachers set a model of behaviour for teachers to interact with students. This, in turn, influences the quality of student interaction with each other (Fullan and Hargreaves, 1991).

Pupil Care

Where students are treated with dignity and encouraged to participate in the organization of the school — even at primary level — they feel valued. Managing student behaviour positively, using rewards rather than sanctions, achieves the same effect on students. Above all, students need to feel that they are valued and that teachers genuinely care for them as individuals and are deeply concerned about their personal welfare (Mortimore, 1991).

Parent Involvement

Many researchers have found that the more active roles parents take at school, the greater the benefit of parental involvement for promoting academic and social change in schools (Comer, 1980, 1984, 1988; Leler, 1983). Parental involvement in schools may take many forms. On one level, parents attend parent–teacher conferences and open days. These provide opportunities for parents and teachers to render accounts to each other on schools and schooling, and for parents to receive reports on the progress of their own children. On another level, parents are represented on formal councils or advisory committees. School councils are forums for parents to participate in school policy-making. On a third level, parents may perform more active roles, serving in the classroom or assisting on field trips, in which case they are likely to have more direct influence on student learning, and possibly on the curriculum. These are qualitatively different contributions. Parental involvement in school councils may contribute relatively little to enhancing student learning, at least directly. On the other hand, school councils and parent participation in them introduce a greater likelihood that democratic structures and processes will characterize school governance. Involving parents as partners in school affairs is likely to improve community confidence in, and support for, the school. It is also likely to generate more resources for the school.

School Environment

A safe, orderly, attractive and stimulating environment, where students' work is openly exhibited and explicitly valued tends to have a profound effect on student attitudes to learning and behaviour (Reid, Hopkins and Holly, 1987). Such an environment generates tolerance and respect among students for each other's contributions.

School Culture

Effective schools, like effective organizations in other sectors, are goal-driven. They strive to achieve a consensus among all staff on core values (Peters and Waterman, 1982). These core values increasingly reflect school concerns for equity in fostering the learning of all students. Research shows that effective schools tend to achieve higher levels of learning across all ability levels than less effective schools. Principals and senior staff frequently, if not continuously, cultivate the school culture, stressing the core values and mission of the school. Establishing clear rules and guidelines for student behaviour and maintaining high expectations for all students are ways in which the goals and values of the school are translated into daily life (Mortimore, 1991). In these ways many of the core values associated with democracy, such as tolerating and respecting others, participating and expressing views, sharing and disseminating knowledge, valuing equity and equality, and the opportunity to make judgments and choices, are developed and nurtured in effective schools. These schools, above all, promote a learner- and learning-centred culture.

Building Democracy in Schools: The Role of the School Principal

If democratic values and practices are presently underrepresented in Australian schools and schooling, then more democracy can be justified on the basis of school effectiveness research. Many of the structures and processes which characterize effective schools in meeting the learning needs of their students align with democratic principles and practices. The challenge, therefore, is how to translate those aspects of school effectiveness research which relate to democracy into school-improvement practice. In particular, how does the policy context within which schools currently operate help or hinder the introduction of more democratic elements into schools? And what role does the principal play in this process?

Scholars and practitioners agree that recognizing what makes effective schools is different from making schools effective. It is the securing of school improvement, involving leadership, management and organization of schools, which presents the greatest difficulties. For schools simply to graft the school effectiveness characteristics on to present structures and processes will not guarantee effective schools. The chemistry and interplay between the key factors has also to be conducive.

In making schools more effective they become more democratic. In making them more democratic they become more effective. School effectiveness is achieved through school improvement, the essence of which is successful management of change. In building democracy and achieving school improvement the role of principals as transformational leaders (Leithwood and Jantzi, 1990) assumes high importance.

There is now a substantial body of research to prove that the traditional model of top-down change delivers poor results in implementation due to lack of staff involvement and commitment (Lezotte, 1989). Conversely, there is growing evidence that bottom-up change, especially where the whole school is seen as the unit for change, proves more effective. Where the responsibility for school and classroom improvement lies with those who work in the school rather than being imposed by outsiders, successful change is more likely (Fullan, 1985; Goodlad, 1984).

A broad policy direction of devolution and decentralization throughout all Australian states in the 1990s places emphasis on school-based management. This represents a major restructuring of Australian school systems, the like of which has never before been experienced. At the same time that schools assume more responsibilities, they are made more accountable for their performance to their school councils and central offices. Two aspects of this restructuring — parental choice of school and school-improvement planning — merit selection to highlight elements of democracy. Both of these restructuring policies provide conditions conducive to the introduction of democratic practices and ideals. They enable principals and other school-based personnel to build structures and processes which favour democracy.

Parental choice of school within government systems is increasingly allowed, if not encouraged, in most restructured systems. In some urban secondary schools, for example, up to 60 per cent of the school enrolment may come from outside the school catchment area. While the idea behind the policy is contentious — encouraging parents to send their children to the better schools will introduce competition, which will in turn force the less favoured schools to improve or face closure — parental choice and power are increased, and more democratic elements are thus introduced into the system. Furthermore, parental choice of school has a positive correlation with student achievement, and hence school effectiveness.

A second policy strand across Australian states concerns the adoption of school growth, improvement or development plans as a key feature of school-based management. Experience in North America suggests that effective schools engage in school-based management (David, 1989) and use improvement plans to implement results of school-effectiveness research. In one particularly outstanding Canadian school board, Halton, to the west of Toronto, all schools have been encouraged to adopt a school-growth planning process (Stoll and Fink, 1992). The Halton school-growth plans are similar to many school-development plans currently in their infancy in Australian schools. The development or growth plan is a small list of priorities or areas of emphasis to which the school commits itself over a period of between one and three years. This process is a systematic means of achieving development by bringing together the views and initiatives of students, parents, teachers, government, school council and community. The planning process is collaborative and therefore more sympathetically democratic. Interested parties address four stages in the development planning cycle:

- assessment — Where are we now?
- planning — Where would we like to be?
- implementation — How best can we move in that direction?
- evaluation — How do we evaluate the changes we make?

Thus parents, teachers and others increasingly have opportunities to participate in decision-making on substantive issues at whole-school level. Parental choice of school and school-development planning constitute two very important democratic processes.

The relatively recent creation of school councils in many Australian states has provided parents and other members of the school community with another avenue to participate in school decision-making. Membership of school councils must include parent, teacher, government and local-community representatives who are mainly elected, but with some appointed and co-opted. In some cases, particularly secondary schools, allowance may be made for the inclusion of student representation. They exercise important functions, including the determination of major school policies, approval of school-development plans and the school budget and they receive accountability reports from the school on its performance. School councils in some states are beginning to assume responsibility for the appointment of principal and teachers to the school staff. Members of school councils are increasingly offered training to enable them to play meaningful roles. Moyle and Andrews (1987) have identified a number of training models for school-council members.

Although these examples of contemporary restructuring policies appear to offer more democratic structures and procedures, they do not guarantee that more people will actively participate. Parents and community members, for example, may choose not to participate in school decision-making. Democratic structures and procedures may exist, but there might be a considerable lack of interest. Moreover, there may be a general reluctance on the part of principals and teachers to share school decision-making with parents and others.

While present restructuring in Australian school systems is encouraging more democracy at whole-school level, it is generally failing to penetrate through the school to the classroom level. Curriculum delivery has changed relatively little in the last 100 years. Although students are now grouped more by mixed ability, a considerable streaming effect still exists and most schools are a long way from integrating children with special educational needs into mainstream classes. The student's role is still largely passive and subordinate to the teacher. Students are rarely involved in curriculum decisions affecting their schooling and are normally denied participation in general organizational and disciplinary policies (Boomer, 1991). It is at the classroom level that perhaps the greatest challenge exists in developing democratic values and practices in the future.

Much of the foregoing highlights the critical and growing importance of school level and within-school level factors to securing the conditions conducive to democracy and school effectiveness. As Scheerens (1993) recognizes, the problem of school improvement and effectiveness exists at two levels: how to create conditions for effective instruction and learning at classroom level; and how to unite efforts in all classrooms in order to create an effective school. In shaping these school and within-school factors the part that principals play is crucial.

From the range of school-improvement strategies available to principals, four are selected here for their efficacy in promoting democratic structures, procedures and processes. They are:

- shared values and beliefs;
- student involvement and responsibility;
- teacher collegiality and development; and
- parent and community involvement and support.

Each of the four is dependent on the principal's leadership and the culture and climate established in the school and across the school community. A sense of shared values and beliefs may be developed through establishing a vision or set of goals and priorities for the school. The principal plays a major role in the encouragement of teachers', parents', and students' involvement in, commitment to, and responsibility for, the school vision. The sharing and communication of the vision is a key leadership function borne mainly, but not entirely, by the principal (Campbell-Evans, 1993).

The remaining three variables in the list centre on student, teacher and parent involvement. It is not, however, the involvement of these groups *per se* that matters as much as the culture and climate underpinning the nature of their involvement. In researching effective and less effective secondary schools in Wales over many years, Reynolds (1991) summarizes the differences using the headings 'incorporative approach' and 'coercive approach' to school organization and the ways each group of schools achieved order and fostered learning. The more effective schools utilized the incorporative strategy, involving students in the organization of the school and incorporating parents in support of the school. Students were incorporated within the classroom by encouragement to take an active and participative role in lessons, and by their verbal intervention without teachers' explicit direction. Students were also more likely to be allowed and encouraged to work in cooperative groups than their 'coerced' counterparts.

Outside the classroom, other strategies were used to incorporate the students in the effective schools. A prefect and monitor system operated, with students chosen from across the ability range. The supervision of students by students seemed to inhibit the formation of anti-school peer-group subcultures. It also had a symbolic effect of providing students with a feeling of control over their school lives.

Attempts to incorporate students were matched, according to Reynolds (1991), by attempts to enlist the support of their parents. This was achieved by establishing close, informal relations between teachers and parents, by encouraging informal visits by parents to the schools, and by frequent and full provision of information to parents on such matters as student progress and school council and staff decisions.

The same values and norms of the effective schools were reinforced through the quality of teacher–student relationships. These were more interpersonal than impersonal. Teachers forged healthy, mutually respectful relationships with students, believing that students were more likely to adopt the same value systems if they were treated fairly, and with consistency and respect. Good relationships were forged by minimal use of overt institutional control and maximal attempts to reward good behaviour rather than punish bad behaviour.

In contrast, schools using the coercive strategy were characterized by exclusion of students from the authority structures of the school, and lack of effort to incorporate the support of parents because teachers and principals believed that no parental support would be forthcoming. These schools resorted to high levels of institutional control, strict rule enforcement, and teacher distrust of students. Teachers viewed students as needing control because of their deficiency in socialization.

Embedded in the incorporative culture are many implications for principals and others in building democracy and securing school improvement. The overarching concern for principals is the cultivation of the incorporative culture in their schools. In accomplishing this it is useful to distinguish four concepts and five functional areas of leadership. The four concepts are:

- leadership and management;
- reflection, conceptualization and practice;
- modelling; and
- tight coupling.

As central figures in their schools, principals are expected to be leaders and managers and to recognize the distinctions between the two (Chapman, 1993). While management centres on the daily routines of planning, coordinating, controlling and supervising the deployment of human, financial and physical resources, leadership focuses on higher-order tasks and on people. It aims to go beyond the daily maintenance operations by concentrating on longer-term issues, including school vision, and addresses problems of motivating staff to achieve standards of performance above those normally expected. The exercise of both management and leadership is essential in building the incorporative culture essential in securing democratic schools.

It is important that principals can reflect on, and conceptualize, their schools as organizations. Assessment of the extent to which democratic ideals and practices are currently embedded in schools and need further development is crucial, as is the ability to implement plans and execute ideas in practical, workable schemes.

Developing incorporative cultures is enhanced when principals themselves model democratic behaviours and values. They then display overtly and explicitly for students, teachers, parents and others in the school community the codes of behaviour expected by the school and by themselves as leaders.

The notion of tight coupling is also important in achieving a school-wide incorporative culture (Dimmock, 1993b). Where all staff and students agree on the same democratic values and practices, which are then embedded in their daily routines pervading all levels and aspects of school work, a strong synergistic effect results through consistency and reinforcement of democratic ideals.

A more complete picture of the principal's role in securing school improvement and more democracy in schools is provided when these generic characteristics are enmeshed with the following key functional areas of leadership. The five key functional areas are:

- human resource leadership;
- educational leadership;
- moral leadership;
- organizational leadership; and
- transformational leadership.

While in reality these five areas are functionally interrelated, it is helpful to separate them for purposes of analysis. In exercising leadership in the human resource area principals clarify community-agreed values and visions for the whole school, and for individuals and teams. Although they develop different leadership styles, an essential characteristic is that the principals of democratic schools are themselves democrats. They involve others where possible, they motivate themselves and others, and gain the commitment of diverse groups and individuals to central core values. They delegate leadership to enable teachers and students to develop leadership skills. Leadership in democratic schools aims, paradoxically, to empower others to lead; it is about power sharing. The principal in a democratic school may often work from behind the scenes in encouraging others to take initiatives. Above all, while principals' leadership is about goal and task achievement, in building democratic schools it is centrally concerned with genuine care and respect for students' and teachers' interests and welfare. Caring for all individuals is a core school value that deserves modelling and tight coupling.

Principals are able to demonstrate care for students and teachers in their capacity as educational leaders. Where principals possess expert knowledge of teaching and learning principles and practices, and expertise in curricular matters, they are more able to develop close collaborative relationships and effective interpersonal communication and tight coupling with students and teachers. A capacity to evaluate the whole curriculum in terms of its breadth, balance and depth enables the principal, teachers and others to decide whether there is sufficient subject content for students to learn about democracy.

Building democratic schools in increasingly secular societies places an important onus on principals to ensure that moral leadership receives due prominence. Where principals and teachers model and justify appropriate moral behaviours in school, it is likely that students will adopt the same principles. Developing a strong sense of morality in the school community is likely to provide a firm base for nurturing democracy. Appropriate structures, procedures and processes for decision-making are central characteristics of democratic schools. Organizational leadership recognizes the importance of organizational structures and procedures in fostering democratic practices. It involves appropriate people at the right time, valuing their respective contributions and ensuring that organizational structures are in place, and sufficient resources provided to facilitate democratic procedures.

Building more democracy into the curriculum and school organization at both classroom and whole-school levels demands an ability to promote change. Principals as transformational leaders understand the change process, the fears and anxieties that accompany change, and the requirements to motivate and commit people to change.

Conclusion

It is argued that democratic values, ideals and practices permeate the structures and processes of Australian schools and schooling to a surprisingly limited extent. Equally surprising is the minimal exposure of students through curriculum subject content to the concept of democracy, including its complexity, history and importance. Given that Australian political systems are founded on democratic principles, it is hard to explain why schools reflect cultural characteristics more aligned with bureaucracy and expertise.

The justification for more democracy in schools is normally based on political, sociological or philosophical grounds. In seeking a different justification, the present argument invokes the school-effectiveness research, finding many attributes of democracy common to the practices of effective schools. Promotion of these democratic elements in schools could therefore be achieved through school-improvement programmes aimed at securing school effectiveness.

Current policies designed to restructure Australian school systems appear to increase the opportunities for the expression of democracy at school level. Strategically positioned at the centre of a complex network of relationships (Chapman, 1988), principals are key participants in building democracy in schools. Through direct personal actions and through indirect empowerment of others, principals can encourage or prevent democratic values and practices in school curricula and administrative decision-making. In restructuring schools for the twenty-first century there can be few higher ideals than to transform them into places where young people are introduced to the values and practices of democracy, and thereby enhance their learning and the school's effectiveness.

References

Boomer, G. (1991) 'Democracy, bureaucracy and the classroom', in Chapman J.D. and Dunstan, J. (Eds) *Democracy and Bureaucracy: Tensions in Public Schooling*, Basingstoke, Falmer Press, pp. 115–30.

Campbell-Evans, G. (1993) 'A values perspective on school-based management', in Dimmock, C. (Ed) *School-based Management and School Effectiveness*, London, Routledge, pp. 92–113.

Chapman, J.D. (1988) 'Teacher participation in the decision making of schools', *Journal of Educational Administration*, 26, 1, pp. 39–72.

Chapman, J.D. (1993) 'Leadership, school-based decision making and school effectiveness', in Dimmock, C. (Ed) *School-based Management and School Effectiveness*, London, Routledge, pp. 201–8.

COMER, J.P. (1980) *School Power: Implications of an Intervention Project*, New York, Free Press.

COMER, J.P. (1984) 'Home–school relationships as they affect the academic success of children', *Education and Urban Society*, 16, pp. 323–37.

COMER, J.P. (1988) 'Educating poor minority children', *Scientific American*, 259, 5, pp. 42–8.

DAVID, J.L. (1989) 'Synthesis of research on school-based management', *Educational Leadership*, 46, 8, pp. 45–53.

DIMMOCK, C. (Ed) (1993a) *School-based Management and School Effectiveness*, London, Routledge.

DIMMOCK, C. (Ed) (1993b) 'School-based management and its linkage with the curriculum', in DIMMOCK, C. (Ed) *School-based Management and School Effectiveness*, London, Routledge, pp. 1–21.

DIMMOCK, C. (1993c) 'Restructuring the school workplace: The impact on principals, teachers and school culture', *Principal Matters*, July, pp. 8–9.

FRASER, B.J., WALBERG, H.J., WELCH, W. and HATTIE, J. (1987). 'Syntheses of educational productivity research', *International Journal of Educational Research*, 11, 2, pp. 145–252.

FULLAN, M. (1985) 'Change processes and strategies at the local level', *Elementary School Journal*, 85, 5, pp. 391–420.

FULLAN, M. (1991) *What's Worth Fighting for in the Principalship? Strategies for Taking Charge in the School Principalship*, Hawthorn, Victoria, Australian Council for Educational Administration.

FULLAN, M. and HARGREAVES, A. (1991) *What's Worth Fighting for? Working together for Your School*, Hawthorn, Victoria, Australian Council for Educational Administration.

GOODLAD, J. (1984) *A Place Called School: Prospects for the Future*, New York, McGraw Hill.

HANDY, C. and AITKEN, R. (1986) *Understanding Schools as Organisations*, Harmondsworth, Pelican.

KARMEL, P. (1973) *Schools in Australia*, Report of the Interim Committee for the Australian Schools Commission, Canberra, Australian Government Publishing Service.

LEITHWOOD, K. and JANTZI, D. (1990) 'Transformational leadership: How principals can help reform school cultures', *School Effectiveness and School Improvement*, 1, 4, pp. 249–80.

LELER, H. (1983) 'Parent education and involvement in relation to schools and to parents of school-aged children', in HASKINS, R. and ADAMS, D. (Eds) *Parent Education and Public Policy*, Norwood, NJ, Ablex.

LEZOTTE, L.W. (1989) 'Base school improvement on what we know about effective schools', *American School Board Journal*, 176, 8, pp. 18–20.

LITTLE, J.W. (1987) 'Teachers as colleagues', in RICHARDSON-KOEHLER, V. (Ed) *Educators' Handbook*, White Plains, Longman, pp. 491–518.

LITTLE, J.W. (1990) 'The persistence of privacy: Autonomy and initiative in teachers' professional relations', *Teachers' College Record*, 91, 4, pp. 509–36.

MARTON, F. and NEUMAN, D. (1992) 'Constructivism and phenomenography', Invited paper at 7th International Conference on Mathematics Education, Québec, Canada, August 19–23.

MORTIMORE, P. (1991) 'The nature and findings of research on school effectiveness in the primary sector', in RIDDELL, S. and BROWN, S. (Eds) *School Effectiveness Research: Its Messages for School Improvement*, Edinburgh, The Scottish Office, HMSO, pp. 9–20.

MOYLE, C.R.J. and ANDREWS, K. (1987) 'Institute of Educational Administration, Australia', in MURPHY, J. (Ed) *Approaches to Administrative Training in Education*, New York, State University of New York.

PETERS, T.J. and WATERMAN, R.H. (1982) *In Search of Excellence*, New York, Harper & Row.

PORTER, A.C. and BROPHY, J. (1988) 'Syntheses of research on good teaching: Insights from the work of the Institute for Research on Teaching', *Educational Leadership*, May, pp. 74–85.

REID, K., HOPKINS, D. and HOLLY, P. (1987) *Towards the Effective School*, Oxford, Basil Blackwell.

REYNOLDS, D. (1991) 'School effectiveness in secondary schools: Research and its policy implications', in RIDDELL, S. and BROWN, S. (Eds) *School Effectiveness Research: Its Messages for School Improvement*, Edinburgh, The Scottish Office, HMSO, pp. 21–34.

REYNOLDS, D. (1993) 'Linking school effectiveness knowledge and school improvement practice', in DIMMOCK, C. (Ed) *School-based Management and School Effectiveness*, London, Routledge, pp. 185–200.

SCHEERENS, J. (1993) 'Basic school effectiveness research: Items for a research agenda', *School Effectiveness and School Improvement*, 4, 1, pp. 17–36.

STOLL, L. and FINK, D. (1992) 'Effecting school change: The Halton Approach', *School Effectiveness and School Improvement*, 31, pp.19–41.

TANNENBAUM, R. and SCHMIDT, W.H. (1958) 'How to choose a leadership pattern', *Harvard Business Review*, March–April, pp. 95–101.

WILDY, H. and DIMMOCK, C. (1993) 'Instructional leadership in Western Australian primary and secondary schools', *Journal of Educational Administration*, 31, 2, pp. 43–62.

Chapter 12

Democratic Values, Individual Rights and Personal Freedom in Education

Michael Herriman

Introduction

The question underlying this chapter is, 'Can education promote democratic values, and if it can, by what means can it do so?' To ask the question in such a leading way is to assume the desirability of democratic values — an assumption that few would question. It is an assumption that can be supported not only on the grounds that democratic values are advantageous to society as a whole, and to some extent are probably necessary or at least conducive to the maintenance of democratic forms of government, but also on the grounds that democratic values enhance the opportunities for participation in education, and perhaps even more importantly can lead to a form of freedom for the individual. In the desirable form, it is a value to be sought in all individual conduct. It is not just a felt ideal, but a state of awareness which should include awareness of a person's obligations as well as privileges. Yet, the easy agreement so far masks the fact that for most children, in most societies, it is unlikely that, if asked to nominate the benefits of their education, they would list the realization or attainment of democratic values. Does this mean that such values are inculcated nonetheless and are simply not recognized as such? Or does it reflect the fact that little concern is given to promoting democratic or any other values, perhaps in view of the more urgent tangibles that seem to be the main concern of education, and the school programme in particular. It seems there is even more cause for concern when it is reported by numbers of studies (Dreeben *et al.*, 1968) that the main affective outcomes of schooling are more probably a sense of powerlessness, lack of efficacy, resentment and apathy (and if there are positive effects at all, they are in the form of competitiveness and motivation to achieve rather than a sense of achievement).

If it is possible to see individual freedom and democratic values as desirable and attainable goals of education, we must ask what their status is in regard to other values. Which is most desirable? Are individual freedom and democratic values the supreme values for education? Which others might be more important? Can they ever be completely realized, or are they in the realm of the ideal, to be striven for in the way that say, equality, is — that is, with an acceptance that, in the pure sense, it is probably not achievable and, in fact, not easily recognized and that we can only hope to lessen inequality rather than remedy it? Aspin and Chapman (1994) note the 'essentially contestable' nature of these kinds of constructs, relating them to Gallie's (1956) idea that we will never agree on an exact meaning or identification for such constructs, but that does not mean we should abandon discussion of them. The meaning and interpretation we give to any social construct varies according to the wider conceptual structure we relate it to, and this no doubt changes as part of our conceptual ecosystem.

Democratic Values and Personal Freedom

It is unlikely that democratic values alone would be worthwhile if there were no opportunity to exercise them; that is, no context and conditions for the exercise of individual freedom. In fact, a person with a sense of democratic values but no sense of individual freedom would probably not desire to take part in the basic democratic processes of society. And to aim only at democratic values without providing the person with the means to exercise them freely would be quite self-defeating. Marcuse (1965) argues that liberal democracies do just that — they promote a sense of democratic values to mask the fact that there is no democracy, and that the individual has no real choice in politics or even in matters of everyday life. This idea, which he labels 'repressive tolerance', is a very challenging one, especially if, following MacPherson (1972), we examine the real world application of democracy and disabuse ourselves of the idea that western liberal democracy is the supreme form of political representation.

I therefore wish to argue that individual freedom is the value to be most sought in education, and that it is a precondition for achieving a sense of, and appreciation for, democratic values. Individual freedom may also be seen as the supreme goal of education notwithstanding the probability that it is seldom achieved. It is a freedom based not only on liberation from external compulsion, along the general lines discussed by Mill (1947), but also a freedom that manifests itself in an awareness of the challenges to a life of satisfaction or personal happiness, and the possession of a set of social and psychological attitudes that allows individuals to find contentment despite the institutional and environmental threats they face (not the least of which is the bureaucratic nature of civil administration and perhaps even the system of education as we know it). This freedom is the result of a critical and informed education, one that allows the individual to confront the contradictions and threats in post-industrial society, particularly those manifest in the influences of mass media and political sloganeering. The process of education through an emphasis on democratic means and values can probably play a role in developing this sense of freedom, but ultimately it is intellectual freedom that becomes an individual attainment. The attitudes that support it are best encapsulated in the critical temperament advocated by Karl Popper (1966), and the situations in which it flourishes are found in political arrangements conforming to his notion of an open society. It is likely that not everyone will ever achieve the level of personal freedom advocated here, but that should not be an excuse for not attempting to reach the desired state. It must also be admitted that the open society itself is an idealization and that in a way it challenges the basic assumptions of modern democracies: namely consensus and majority rule.

In accepting that individual freedom is the ultimate aim of education, however, we should also ask whether it may not be promotable by means other than inculcating democratic values. For example, would it be possible to promote individual freedom more effectively and cheaply by other than democratic means in education? Or one could take a seemingly more contrary stance and ask whether education, through its very structures and processes, is inherently undemocratic and necessarily so. Hence to expose its real nature would be to cause disillusionment, and to hide it would be hypocritical. For example, are compulsory attendance and centralized curricula by their very existence a threat to the freedom of students? Are not the methods of instruction often based on indoctrinating students (if by indoctrination we mean the presenting of material as fact or truth without admitting to students the tentative and theory-laden nature of knowledge)? We would also have to ask whether students in the earlier stages of their intellectual development have the requisite cognitive structures and conceptual sophistication to grasp not just the factual content, but also the logical structure and tentative status of what is learnt. The issue of indoctrination has received extensive treatment in the philosophical literature and it could fairly be said that most educational theorists and philosophers have accepted that there are (necessarily) indoctrinatory tendencies in pedagogy, especially in the early years of schooling. These tendencies are acceptable provided that the knowledge component is taught fairly. More will be said about this when the rights of children are discussed later in this chapter.

More recent challenges would dispute the claim of any area of knowledge to a special place. This school of thought is significant in western countries. Its adherents seek to expose what is seen as a 'conspiracy' behind not only liberal education, but education generally, which in this analysis is seen to focus on social and cultural reproduction, and even on the reproduction and reinforcement of social inequality. It is difficult to sustain the case for universal social values in the face of such a penetrating analysis, which takes as its first task the identification of the ideological assumptions underpinning all values and ideals. This type of analysis consequently leads to a regressive relativism. Rationality itself would then be subject to criticism. The best defence seems to be to argue that if a large enough community agreed to a set of conventions both for identifying and for discussing a topic (such as that of freedom and values), by that commitment they share at least some common ground and some sense of what would constitute progress in resolving the issue — if only for the present (since these kinds of topics have been debated for more than two thousand years).

But to return to the central question: are democratic values and personal freedom necessarily linked, and if not, what exactly is their relationship? Perhaps democratic values can exist without requiring freedom of the individual (in the case where the highest expression of democratic values is seen in the subjection of the individual to the corporate will, or where the prevailing ethic is in favour of preservation of the social structure even if it means subjugation of the individual will or freedom). It is doubtful, however, if individual freedom could exist in modern society without democratic values simply because of the complexity of modern society and the pressures on its members to participate, even if that only means paying taxes and having access to social benefits. On the other hand, it is often argued that the degree of control presently available to the government by means of its institutions, the media and the accessibility to massive databases provides an ideal structure for the invasion of privacy and the establishment of a totalitarian state. The possibility for freedom through true anarchy is now so remote as to be not credible, despite calls for less government (usually by those whose privateering instincts are curbed by government regulations on trade and taxation in the interest of public welfare).

The Problem of Freedom in the Modern State

The questions posed above are not easily answered, chiefly because the traditional view of freedom, which I have characterized as that derived from Mill (1947), would hold that individual freedom is not compatible with the kind of structures that support education and social welfare in a contemporary setting. Mill's view of the free individual is of one who is primarily intellectually free from the herd and from the kind of compulsions and obligations demanded by membership of the body politic, and who is morally autonomous. Mill, in advocating less governmental interference in an era that would seem to us to have been characterized by fairly minimal involvement of government in any sphere, could not of course have foreseen the nature or the bureaucratic threats of the present time though he would have been familiar enough with the oligarchical tendencies of mid-nineteenth century English governments to be able to understand well the potential threats. One wonders how he might have regarded political and social life as we know it.

For Mill, the State presents the great threat to moral autonomy. Its laws and institutions deprive persons of individual responsibility for their beliefs and actions. My argument is that the present arrangements for schooling in most systems do not allow for, or promote, the kind of individual responsibility for beliefs and actions that is conducive to developing a sense of individual freedom and democratic values in students. Schools must provide both the moral and the intellectual climate for the development of moral agency.

It is fairly certain that the State does little in later life to aid in this kind of development. The school is asked to play the role of a 'halfway house' between the home, in which the parent assumes most of the moral agency, and civil society, where the person is expected to be morally autonomous. It cannot be expected that every home has sufficient resources to ensure that all children will develop moral autonomy. If they had, then the responsibility of the school might be diminished. Of course many parents would claim the exclusive right in this respect, but I will argue later that the State has some claim on the educational development of the child, which includes promoting moral autonomy.

The traditional view of individual freedom has also been beset by the problem of the conditions for its attainment, allowing a kind of detachment and lack of participation that at best takes no regard for the welfare of others, and at worst excuses positively antisocial behaviour along Nietzschean lines. It has also allowed for so-called 'free riders', those who have participated to take advantage of the freedoms in the system for selfish benefits. Liberalism has traditionally shrugged this off as a necessary price to pay for the benefits that it brings. The traditional view also faces the problem that however much one might be made aware of morality there should be no compulsion to accept customary or a priori moral codes (i.e., one must be free to reject morality on purely intellectual grounds). If education were to attempt to enforce acceptance of certain moral views or even promote some as more desirable than others, then it could be said to be infringing on the rights of the individual to freedom in this important intellectual way.

Educating for Freedom, Rights and Democracy

Can education then do anything by way of promoting democratic values without infringing on the rights of the individual to self-determination in the realm of values? Even the most democratic of means of promoting any values seemingly confronts this dilemma (and it is clear that education has not had a history of promoting democracy within its institutions). There are some examples of schooling systems or individual schools which are run on lines that deliberately promote democracy and freedom, and some consideration of their philosophies and procedures might be informative and help solve the dilemma. Such schools usually come into existence because of the recognition by parents and certain teachers that the existing provisions do not allow for attention to individual students, and that the prevailing system is too bureaucratic to cope with individual student needs in any case.

Can there be a general form of education that results in the acceptance of democratic values and yet does not insist on them or promote them as the only option? Can existing schools move to a model which places as much emphasis on the moral and social development of students as it does on the development of cognitive and vocationally related skills? (In Australia at the present time, the last-mentioned skills, designated vaguely as competencies, appear to have become the most important goal of education.) Cognitive skills, by contrast, are not incompatible with the intellectual temperament I have espoused above. A further problem arises in modern culturally plural societies, in determining whether there is any agreement on what constitutes democratic values. It is quite conceivable, for example, that there might be a significant group in society which does not believe in equal rights for males and females, or at least would see the issue as falling under a different set of descriptions of the societal roles for males and females. This belief may be quite unexamined and deeply enshrined in political or religious beliefs. Can the State legitimately interfere here? And what if those beliefs led to the view that girls (or boys) did not need the same amount or kind of schooling? Should we avoid the issue by deciding rather that there may be only a limited set of possible democratic values? Or is the supreme democratic value a weak kind of neutrality that none could object to? Can we teach alternatives equally without somehow giving a relative sense of worth to each? Or must we decide on 'real democratic values' and reject all competitors? Thus put, it may seem that the conflict over the content of democratic values may be an issue of contention between state and parent anyway, before one even begins to examine rights in education.

We can begin by saying that, in general, to promote certain values to the exclusion of any alternatives would defeat the democratic aim. But where do we draw the line at possible alternatives? A stronger view is that democratic values and the sense of freedom that I have espoused can only really be achieved by schooling, not that it is something which is not achievable in the school. White and White (1986), using an argument of MacIntyre (1981), have put forward the claim that in order to share the 'good life', education is necessary, as it provides, in MacIntyre's view, the means by which 'children come to see . . . conformity as necessary to their own well-being as well as to that of others since the two are . . . interconnected'. The good life in this case is the life freely chosen. We might well ask how many children presently have the privilege of freely choosing a way of life (given that this would require most options be open to them)?

We should now ask how education can be arranged in order to promote individual freedom through democratic values. The first issue we face concerns the viability of all of the possible arrangements for providing education, or, more specifically, the form of agency best suited to the task. Just because democratic values are values relating to the public good there is no necessary presumption that they are best promoted by the public education system.

Therefore, one of the key issues in the debate about democratic values in education is that of deciding who has the authority and the right to educate the citizens in a society. It might be thought that with an institution as long established as education there might have been some important historical precedent, or a convincing argument in favour of one or other agency in the role of educator. In fact, the longest standing historical examples in the western tradition point to the model of a free association of scholars and students where the latter enter into a loose contract with the former, or the monastic model where scholars with a common interest group together for community and scholarship.[1] This form of education has lasted until the present day in the rare cases of truly private education. Ivan Illich (1972) also endorsed a version of it in his idea of learning webs, i.e., shopfront gatherings of individuals who reject the intervention of the State or civil authority in the process of learning. This notion of education is based on associations far removed from the compulsions of the State, though it must be acknowledged that even Plato envisaged an education that would be of benefit to the State, and a corresponding role for the State, though with quite different forms of treatment for children with differing abilities. Of course the period in question long preceded universal education as well as the complex modern corporate State with its particular democratic form. A review of prevailing worldwide practices now would reveal that states have mostly assumed the responsibility for educating their citizens, either by compulsion or with the tacit approval of those citizens, or indeed as a result of their demands. Yet, as alluded to above, there exist sufficient challenges to the State's right to do this to suggest that there are good arguments for the parents' or even the child's prerogatives in respect of education.

Claiming Educational Rights

If we accept that there may be a competing set of claims on behalf of the State and the parent, as well as a set of rights claimable by children, we must not only ask what the claims of each are, but also who is best able to represent the claims. For example, we may agree on the rights to education claimable by children, and their rights to certain treatment within a system set up to provide education, but disagree on the person or agency best suited to representing the interests of the child. If the State claims prior rights then what obligations and responsibilities does it thereby assume, and what correspondingly are the obligations and responsibilities of teachers? Specifically, to what extent is the teacher required to represent the claims of the parent and the State, or to what extent is the teacher, as primarily an agent of the State, permitted to intervene in the educational process by presenting his or her own views (or *in loco parentis*)? By contrast, in a system in which the parent chooses a private education, what prerogative, if any, does the State have in the setting of curriculum or minimum standards? We have an interesting situation in Australia in that the central government in a bipartisan move (involving all the main political parties) has agreed to fund all education — private and public. The force of this has been to solve the bitter sectarian disputes that had plagued the issue of state support, but the unintended consequence is that the government, through its requirements in relation to accountability, has gained a significant influence on all curricular matters.

Many other crucial issues depend on these more major ones. The issue of the parents' right to withdraw children from all or part of the educational process is one that is prominent in many states at present. In the USA this right is frequently asserted by minor religious sects which either reject the ethical teachings of the school system, or reject the authority of the State as a whole (seeing the secular State as a competitor with the theocratic). The move towards 'privatizing' education is often presented in the general context of giving expression to values or beliefs that parents hold to be more important than the non-sectarian or ethically relative or neutral values said to be promoted by the State (particularly in culturally plural societies). Does this threaten the viability of the social order? Related to this is the question of the right of the parent to claim support for educating children outside the State's educational provision, especially where the education requested is sectarian. Another related issue is that of vouchers — should the State provide only the financial means for parents to purchase an education of their own choosing and interfere no further in the educational process?

A further set of issues concerns such matters as the point at which the State's or the parent's duty of care for the child ought to cease, and what constitutes 'legitimate authority' in Mill's (1947) sense i.e., the right of the teacher or parent to take decisions on behalf of the student or child. These more directly relate to the issue of education for individual freedom. Attendant on these issues is that of the right to a *free* and *lifelong* education for all citizens of a state.

In analysing these issues it is important to consider the question of the development of children's rights. Specifically, what rights can be claimed by children, and at what stage of their growth, development and participation in society do the rights emerge? Certain biological rights can be identified from birth, including the right to nurturing and protection. Social welfare rights emerge early, especially those related to health and education. Other social and civil rights emerge later, but differ in some respects from the earlier ones in that they carry duties and responsibilities with them. In most states the right to free citizenship carries with it the responsibility for some participation in the body politic, including voting, paying taxes, defending the State from outside compulsion etc.[2] The focus of agency shifts from parent to state as the rights of children develop, i.e., the rights accrued by children growing into adulthood are of the kind that bring with them obligations to the State and therefore indirectly to their fellow citizens. This arrangement indirectly protects children's rights to develop their own sense of efficacy against the possibility of the parents subjecting them to unreasonable restraint. The problem is still the question of when children are able to, or should be permitted to exercise a deliberate choice in their own upbringing. This is a very unclear area. The UN Declaration on the Rights of Children, to which Australia as well as most other countries is a signatory, defines a clear and basic set of rights, but it is recognized that many countries pay them no heed.

The issues above can be seen in a fruitful perspective in the case of the former Soviet Union and Australia. It might be said that the State in the Soviet Union had assumed almost completely the right to educate its citizens, though in conjunction with local-community prerogatives particularly regarding matters such as the language of instruction. This claim on rights must be seen in its historical context, that of a nation attempting the modernization of its economy, and a massive reform of education and its provision for many who never had access to it. In Australia, the advent of universal elementary education also required a major intervention by the State, in this case the individual states rather than the Commonwealth, as the latter had no apparent constitutional responsibility for education (see Birch, this volume). The extension of universal education into the higher grades of schooling reinforced the states' role in education as the only agencies seemingly capable of providing education on the scale required.

The advent of progressive education in Australia brought about an increasing concern with the rights of children to treatment as individuals, while in the same era the massive population increase in Australia during the post-1950 period meant that the states' capacity to offer a functional education to all children was limited and hence limiting to many students. It is not my intention to examine the changes that occurred with the election of the Labor government in Australia in 1971, but it is clear that significant areas of educational disadvantage were identified in the system throughout Australia (as a result of a major inquiry into equality of provision). As a consequence of this, as well as for other, perhaps more political reasons, the intervention of the Commonwealth government in the funding and control of education in the early 1970s increased, marking a high point of both state intervention and public funding of all education in Australia. This intervention has continued with stricter accountability demands made by the Commonwealth government in areas of education it funds directly. Even more recently, the move towards a 'national curriculum', though presented as basically an attempt to standardize criteria for assessing achievement in subject areas, marks an attempt by the national government to define the actual learning goals in all major areas of the curriculum.

In both countries, changes of government and devolution of responsibility have brought arguments for a more private form of education to the fore again. The call for private education in Australia follows that in the USA, but not for the same reasons — though in neither country is there one clear reason given. In the USA, part of the pressure for private education comes from those opposed to the ideology of state education, particularly as it relates to desegregation and social-class mixing. Another part comes from those who espouse minimal state interference and welfare on principle, and from educators who see it as a possibility for reversing a decline in educational standards by giving education back to parents so that they can choose the form they think best — the hope being that if parents really feel they have control they will demand much higher standards.[3] For some proponents it is seen as a way of allowing bankrupt school districts to regain budgetary control. In Australia the call comes from classical liberals who support the minimal state, as well as from those concerned with the decline of standards, unevenness of provision and the bureaucratic inertia of public education. Some would also object to the high public expenditure on education (and the imputed lack of return in the way of improvements), the obligation for which it is thought should rest more on the parent.

A key question then concerns the form of agency which is best able and most likely to produce the desired goals of individual freedom and democratic values (as well, of course, as high standards): the State, the community or the parent? If it is decided that all have a role in education, then can that role be defined in such a way as to maximize the benefits for the individual and society? I will now examine the arguments for and against the State and the parent's involvement in education in view of the general goals of freedom and democratic values.

There are sufficient similarities in most nation states in the western world to allow one to talk about a kind of entity that might be called the modern social democratic State. This State has a constitution, is representative in structure, generally separates legislative from judicial functions, grants voting rights to its citizens, holds regular elections, promotes democracy through freedom of belief and expression and gives to the government the administration of most areas that concern social welfare and human rights of citizens, particularly that group less able to fend for themselves in this regard.[4] But this is just an idealization of a democratic state. If such states have a problem it is that they are bureaucratic and highly centralized, slow to respond to changing individual needs, and characterized by institutionalized norms. It might be argued that to this extent they are potentially, or even inherently, undemocratic and, as mentioned earlier, have the potential for oligarchy and totalitarianism. It is in this light that recent philosophical arguments for the minimal state have been put forward. The most telling arguments against the minimal state concern the potential it has to ignore the social welfare needs of its citizens, though as already suggested, many supporters of the minimal state see the bureaucratization of the modern state as more harmful to those in need of the State's welfare resources. It is also the minimal state that was envisaged by Mill and nineteenth-century writers as the agency most conducive to freedom of the individual. It is unlikely that the minimal state as conceived of in the political and philosophical literature will supplant the modern state described here, and so the ensuing discussion on rights will presume the continued existence of the social democratic state referred to above.

The State

The social democratic state perhaps is best able to ensure that all children have equality of access to education and the right to equal treatment. This is not to say that equality will always result, but rather that national provisions are more likely to identify certain needs and violation of standards that are local.[5] The State is also best able to override aberrant and ill-informed parental and communal choices or demands concerning the form or content of education (these frequently, but not necessarily intentionally, lead to restrictive and inadequate provision). It is likely that the State is the best agency for, and protector of, internationally agreed conventions which relate to fair and equal access and treatment of minority groups and children with regard to education, notwithstanding the fact that the State itself may violate these conventions. Yet it is more often the individual who mounts claims against the State's violation of such conventions — the State then being compelled to bring the claim to its judiciary.

However, the benevolence of the State is offset by its potential for acting against the interests of minorities. States have a history of majority decision-making which can count against minority interests if they are not guaranteed in a constitution. The centralized state may also be insensitive to local needs and conditions, or to individual needs of its citizens. Its party-political nature means that policy shifts can occur which are deleterious to certain interests; here again, constitutional guarantees are needed. In education, the bureaucratic tendencies of the central authority promote uniformity and lack of responsiveness or experimentation.

The Parent

Parents can function as agents of education either directly or indirectly. Their most potent argument is their direct interest in the future of the child, and their knowledge, through their guardianship role, of particular needs that the child might have. What is more uncertain is their right to compel their children to accept their system of values, especially if those values restrict the child's subsequent expression of basic freedoms or even life choices, or subject the child to lifestyles that are physically or emotionally harmful. Parents also may be ill-informed in terms of general or particular educational needs of the child based either on ignorance or on misunderstanding of their own schooling experiences. Some parents will have the option of educating their own children if that is permitted in law, but in these cases it must be asked, as the law asks, whether the child is receiving an effective education and whether it is at least of a standard achievable in the school. This is the normal test used by authorities in determining whether parents be permitted to educate their children.

Parents in most countries can exercise an option for non-public education through agency of communal or sectarian associations which run their own schools. The chief advantage of this option is that the private school usually has clear goals and principles that allow the parent at least the semblance of a choice (though it might be argued that the state school would also be capable of offering this if it were free of bureaucratic inertia). What should their prerogative be then?

Unfortunately there are no other areas of public or private concern easily related or analogous to education, from which we are able to generalize. The areas of health and community welfare appeal in some respects but they are misleading, because education is not just about a treatment, or a way of remedying a physical impairment or socially dysfunctional situation; it is fundamentally about developing the intellect in a way that is harmonious with the needs and, perhaps, desires of the person (though it is not always clear how the latter can be determined prior to participation in education). The State both compels parents to provide for education and yet leaves them little choice in subsequently obtaining it. This problem does not emerge so paradoxically in totalitarian states, where the State itself will take over the entire prerogative for education, in some cases excluding the parent for ideological reasons or reasons of convenience.[6]

The desirable relationship of parent to state is therefore not easy to define. It is a very uneasy relationship in the education system as we know it in Australia, which is probably symptomatic of the problem overall. Recently the ministries of education around Australia have followed a form of devolution which, amongst other things, espouses local control of schools somewhat along the lines of the normal pattern of school boards in the USA.[7] The moves require the formulation of a 'school policy' by each school, in the development of which parents are expected to participate. There is little evidence so far of any school in Western Australia giving parents any meaningful say in school governance, though the changes are not yet complete. The problem may be that the central authority, while wishing to sound liberal in this respect, does not trust the school itself or the principal to run critical aspects of its own affairs (such as the hiring of staff). In this case it appears to be a classic problem of bureaucratization. It may also be attributable to the fact that there has been no culture of parent participation in educational policy-making in Australia. It is often said that parents are seen as best kept beyond the school gate. It is possible that the lack of defined prerogatives for parents limits their scope for claiming any at all. The issue in Australia is also complicated by the strong position of the teachers' unions and their overriding concern with industrial matters rather than with professional issues about education itself. It is probable that no support for parents' rights could be expected from the unions unless it were done to enhance their own position of centralized power. Unions can certainly exercise more industrial leverage on one centralized authority than on the separate administration of each school.

The Child

Children are the pivot in the struggle between parent and state. Both can legitimately claim an interest in them and their educational development. In this struggle, however, little is conceded in regard to the rights claimable by the child. The natural tendency of parents to seek the best for their offspring is challenged by the State's inclination to make the child a citizen. The parents' inclinations probably tend towards protection of the child rather than inspection of the potential for his or her claiming of rights. The State has an interest in informing the child of rights in case the parent fails to do this, in just the same way as it will intervene to protect the child from other forms of parental neglect, but this interest seems not to have been extended to the rights claimable in school, despite the nation's signing of international covenants on the treatment of children.[8] Yet the institutional structure of the school for most children inhibits the chance to inspect or claim rights. The child coming to school confronts an institution far more rigid and authoritarian than most households; the prevailing ethos is one of conformity rather than individuality. This is not to reject the need for the child to be inducted into a wider community by some means; it is rather to note that the means chosen, the school, probably represents a structurally undemocratic model, reflecting an earlier view of socialization via sanctions and conformity to authority.

Talk of the child tends as well to obscure the important point that the process of education is implicated in the change from childhood to adulthood; that students by the time of leaving school are more adult than childlike. Yet a glance at the structure of high schools indicates that there has been little thought given to the adult status of students. They do not necessarily become adults as a result of schooling itself, as biological maturational processes also intervene. The important role for schools is to work in conjunction with biological change by giving students the intellectual means to cope with such change and with macrodevelopmental cognitive change. Few attempts have been made in the West to relate physical and cognitive growth to an intellectual schema for coping with the change (the nearest being that of Kohlberg); instead, the tendency has been to treat adolescence as a period to be counterposed by increasing authoritarian structures. It is of interest to note the emphasis in Soviet education on integrating the development of the child morally, socially and cognitively; indeed the theoretical basis saw these factors integrated *in development*, not only in instruction. The West has been very slow to recognize the potential interrelationship between these aspects of development, though certain theorists (e.g., Rudolf Steiner) have. Much more thought might be given to this in our system.

Problems in the Structure of Schools of Schooling

It is possible to see three aspects of school structure and function that potentially generate contradictions for the realization of democratic ideals. The first is the administrative structure of the school itself. Its hierarchical structure is based on a tradition which gave little thought to rights and democracy in its processes, emphasizing unquestioned authority. So ingrained is this structure that very few schools have seen fit to question it. Its affects can be seen in teacher attitudes also, where there is usually a rigid set of lines of command from the top–down. Many teachers feel as disaffected as students by the lack of democracy in the school. It is surprising that in discussions of school devolution the main issue is a contest over the locus of power and decision-making; the discourse seldom gets to the fundamental question of why schools have authoritarian structures. It would not be surprising, therefore, if children were to get little sense of their right to rights from the structure of the typical school.

The second aspect concerns the instructional plan and style of teaching practised in the school. This will vary from teacher to teacher and school to school. Much has been written about teaching styles and their effectiveness, so we do know that certain styles can promote learning better than others. In the quest for democratic values it is clear that the teaching style will have a significant influence on the students' internalization of values about scholarship and learning. While they may not even address value issues directly, teachers nevertheless will promote attitudes towards assessment and questioning on the part of the student that can be transferred to areas of their concern and interest which might have value components and relate to their conception of their rights. There are several areas of the curriculum that approach values directly, of course. These include history, social studies, literature, and the arts. In these areas it is desirable that the teaching style both expose and reflect the questioning and judgmental nature of ethical and aesthetic issues. A democratic teaching style alone may not guarantee that the student gains a sense of values and rights; it is also highly desirable that the class feel itself to be involved in the learning process.

The third aspect is that of the functional role of the school in directly promoting democratic values and a sense of rights and individual freedom. There are few schools or systems that would reject the notion that these ideals ought to be part of the affective outcomes of schooling, but in the public system little has been done to give explicit recognition to this implied desire. Most schools would probably hope that somehow such outcomes might in some way arise from the school ethos, as indeed they may in some cases (most probably in private rather than state schools). Many religious schools claim moral and social values as foremost in their educational aims.[9] I believe that as desirable as it is to have explicit recognition in schools of the need for moral and ethical training and in particular to promote the values chiefly in consideration here, it is unreasonable to expect that the values will result solely or even in great part from a policy which sees them being addressed mainly in this third or functional way. The claim for this emphasis is not to be denied, but it will not lead to any realization of the values unless they are implicated in, and integral to, the other structural characteristics of schools discussed above.

Changing Schools for Democracy

Specifically, schools must first question the need for their present hierarchical, authoritarian, closed and inherently undemocratic structure. This process of questioning will not stop at the top of the administrative level of the school, but must go beyond it to the system itself, particularly in the case of public education. Other authors in this volume will have covered the issue of administrative structures desirable for moving the school towards democratization. I wish only to point out the connection to the other aspects of structure and function necessary for its implementation. The first policy question for a reorganization must concern the clear setting down of ethical and democratic goals for education. These must then govern the choice not only of subject matter to be taught, but decisions on teaching style and instructional styles that are consistent with the espoused goals. This should inform the curriculum which should embody the chosen ideals in each subject. Next the question of the administrative structure of schools must be decided, but again only with the prior commitment to its resolution being determined by the identified goals and their expression in the curriculum. This would be quite a radical proposal for most, though not all, schools. It would, however, shake the foundations of the large bureaucracies which govern education and which now perhaps stand in the way of achieving democratic values. In an arrangement of the kind proposed here, the administrative role of principal would be a key one. Needless to say, the criteria for selection of that person would need to be altered from those pertaining at present, which are based still on length of service and favour males predominantly. The commitment of the person to the goals of the school must be a prime consideration in the appointment, but just as necessary would be the need for explicit training in administration which gives emphasis to the utility of democratic management structures. There is little doubt that if all schools were to undertake a reorganization along the lines proposed here, there would be need for parental involvement at all levels. The parents would not only see that their rights in respect of choice for their children were considered and respected, but it would also break down the institutional isolation of the school and force it to reflect more the model and structure of a voluntary association than that of a 'total institution' of the kind characterized by Goffman (1968).

For the reorganization to take place, it would require promulgation of a national code of rights for children generally, with an indication of the means for claiming them (which should be consistent with, but subsume the UN statement on children's rights). It would also require that each school specify a code of rights and obligations which designate the nature of the democratic values and the form of a sense of freedom to be promoted, together with a plan for its implementation in the curriculum. The child would likely come to see the school as a more benevolent institution, or at least one where his or her interests were foremost. The parents could then choose a school which might reflect their values, and as a result feel more a part of the school.

I have mentioned the necessity for democratic values to permeate the school organization and curriculum. If this were achieved there might be no need for any specific subject to be devoted to morality, ethics or even social education. A critical and democratic inquiring approach to all subjects would be much more successful. Given the ethnic and cultural diversity in most societies now it is necessary to support a broad humanism which is relativistic, and not fall into the absolutist trap (either out of despair or expedience) which characterizes the debate in the USA at present.

It is possible to identify a set of values for a modern complex multicultural democracy that would be both functional and conducive to a freedom based on respect for, and recognition of, the democratic rights of others. Personal freedom is likely to be attached to the recognition that one can only be free in today's complex society if one acknowledges an obligation to support the rights of others on the basis of these values, in particular:

- respect for a variety of democratic processes;
- tolerance of ethnic, religious, ethical, gender-identity, linguistic and political differences and guarantee of non-discrimination;
- recognition that the majority may not be right;
- freedom from unnecessary external constraint;
- recognition of, and respect for, minorities; and
- promotion of cultural pluralism.

The last point is probably equally important in both Russia and Australia. Both countries are culturally complex, but have evolved differently in that respect. Both have tried to follow the path of cultural assimilation, which, despite its intended benevolence, has led to cultural suppression. Russia has always had the experience of cultural diversity, while Australia's experience of it is quite recent and, for many persons, difficult to come to terms with. In Russia, nationality (ethnic identity) has only recently emerged as a criterion of personal identification (that is, as something more than a category on a passport), having previously been superseded by Soviet citizenship. Australia has had some forty years of gradual realization that it is not a monoculture (despite the early attempt to make 'new Australians' out of all immigrants), and some thirteen years of an explicit policy of multiculturalism. Yet in Australia the school, more than any other place, is the arena in which the cultures meet and mix. It is essential, therefore, that schools provide the means of cultural expression to each child and promote a form of democracy that is pluralistic. This must be learnt in the face of strong countervailing tendencies, not the least of which is the inclination of political parties increasingly to respond to sectional, vocal and single issue interests (or, as it is put, 'to win the ethnic vote'). That tendency is perhaps the single most serious threat to pluralistic democracy.

Conclusion

Education can possibly promote democratic values if it succeeds in giving people a sense of individual freedom. However, much of what I have said about the means of achieving democracy through education has been urged before. It underlay the whole progressivist movement in the USA and was imported to other countries as an educational philosophy. It is too difficult to assess whether it had any influence on the political arrangements in the states where it was practised, and we would have to ask whether it was ever successfully implemented in any case. What is clear is that in just asking the question about the role of democratic values in education, the essentially undemocratic structure of most schools is exposed to view. It is apparent that against the entrenched bureaucracy of education and its traditions of authoritarianism and lack of representation of student rights, any argument for democratic values which does not question the structure of schools in a major way is probably doomed to failure.

To summarize, I have argued that democratic values can only be achieved when the total structure of education is democratic. This condition includes the need for democratic methods of inquiry and teaching styles. Even then there must always be a vigilant concern for bureaucratic tendencies and the dangers of what is called 'the new managerialism', which is the conception of education as a business devolved into budgetarily determined sections ('cost centres') whose main aim is to fashion activities to conform to budget expectations. To achieve this democratic state will require a conceptual shift away from the tradition which sees the school as a shaper of behaviour. The key point in my argument is that the development of democratic values at a personal level will only be achieved as a consequence of development of a sense of personal or individual freedom. This sense is based on the person making an intelligent assessment of the benefits, demands and threats in society, having a sense of efficacy, a critical outlook, the knowledge of his or her responsibilities and a respect for the rights and freedom of all others. It also requires a high level of literacy. Needless to say, this sense and these conditions are not much in evidence in the contemporary school.

Notes

1 This arrangement also is taken (by Locke and subsequent writers) to have been the way in which representative forms of political arrangements evolved.

2 In Australia, voting is both a right and a legal responsibility, presenting a curious situation in which there is a form of compulsory democracy.

3 The case was put starkly by a US senator in the early 1970s, who said that the State might better serve its disadvantaged citizens (in this case Afro-Americans) by a policy of 'benign neglect'.

4 The increasing involvement of the State in the welfare rights of children is mirrored in the degree to which schools have become involved in the social and

psychological welfare of children. This has emerged not only out of the theoretical underpinnings of progressive education and its emphasis on the whole child but also out of a recognition that the home background affects the potential to learn. This trend has greatly altered the teacher–student relationship to the point where some teachers claim to be child-care givers rather than teachers.

5 This in view of the foregoing discussion on the improbability of attaining equality.

6 For example, in China the work unit, particularly in the case of factories with shift workers, often assumed control of the whole of the child's daily needs (as agent of the State), through the factory's creche, canteen and school.

7 The main point of difference here from the USA model is that school boards will only be involved in school-policy development, whereas in the USA they are required to frame an annual budget which is voted on by all property taxpayers in the district. They also hire the entire staff (teachers and administrators) of the district.

8 Despite my reservations about medicine as an analogy for educational process, there is an interesting comparison to be had with the issue of state intervention in the medical welfare of the children, where the courts cede to the State an *increasing* responsibility for protecting children's rights to medical care against the claims of the parent. (A notable issue concerns female circumcision where the State sees it appropriate to intervene on the child's side.)

9 At the risk of a personal anecdote I recall vividly a discussion I had with the principal of a leading Catholic school who said that his desire was that the students would develop a set of values which were prominently democratic and socially conscious and reflected a broad Christian tolerance. The values traditionally espoused by the school were much more related to traditional Catholicism in its concern with the salvation of the individual. However he felt that the majority of the parents (and the 'old boy' fathers in particular) wanted the students firstly to be good at sport, which they believed would aid the students in both their scholarship and their future lives.

References

Aspin, D.N. and Chapman, J.D. (1994) *Quality Schooling,* London, Cassells.

Dreeben, R. (1968) *On What is Learned in School*, Reading, Mass., Addison-Wesley.

Gallie, W.B. (1956) 'Essentially Contested Concepts', repr. in (1964) *Philosophy and the Histonical Understanding*, Chapter 8, London Chatto and Windus.

Goffman, E. (1968) *Asylums: Essays on the Social Situation of Mental Patients and Other Inmates*, Harmondsworth, Penguin.

Illich, I. (1972) *Deschooling Society*, London, Calder and Boyars.

MacIntyre, A. (1981) *After Virtue: A Study in Moral Theory*, London, Duckworth.

Macpherson, C.B. (1972) *The Real World of Democracy*, New York, Oxford University Press.

Marcuse, H. (1965) *One Dimensional Man*, London, Sphere.

Mill, J.S. (1947) *On Liberty*, Castell, A. (Ed) New York, Appleton-Century-Crofts.

Popper, K.R. (1966) *The Open Society and its Enemies,* 5th ed., London, Routledge and Kegan Paul.

White, J.P. and White, P.A. (1986) 'Education, liberalism and human good', in Cooper, D.E. *Education, Values and Mind: Essays for R.S. Peters*, London, Routledge and Kegan Paul.

Chapter 13

The Acquisition of the Democratic Experience by Children and Teachers

Alexander M. Tubelsky

The assimilation of democratic values by Russian students is complicated by at least two circumstances. The first impediment is the lack of deeply rooted democratic traditions in the Russian family and society as a whole. Moreover, in the past, the communal consciousness of people gave rise to judicial nihilism and the conviction that individual self-realization is possible without the observance of democratic norms. The second impediment, which is linked with the above, is the previous tendency to accept non-democratic behaviour among teachers. In their relationships with students the majority of Russian teachers neglect democratic norms and tend to be authoritarian. When conflict emerges, teachers solve it by relying on their previously formed 'common sense'.

In Russia today politicians use certain words and clichés to convey democratic ideas, yet the mechanisms for the implementation of these ideas are yet to be developed. Therefore the majority of the population has yet to be convinced that the solution to social issues is closely linked to the level of democracy. It is common knowledge that, at the moment, Russia is making its first attempts to create a law-governed state. With this in mind, it follows that the social situation of Russian children differs considerably from that of their western counterparts, who have experienced and internalized the essentials of democracy in their families and environment, and through their relationships with national institutions.

While the task of the western school is simply to guide its students toward conceptualizing the experience of democratic behaviour and linking it with historical and cultural traditions, the Russian school at this point in our history must become the major institution where such experience is generated. Within the framework of our conception of how to help children develop the ability of self-determination, our institutions are searching for pedagogical conditions under which both children and teachers can acquire and reflect on the experience of democratic behaviour. This chapter is devoted to the examination of one institution's attempt to achieve this goal and to bring about democracy in education.

The Scientific-pedagogical Unit

The Scientific-pedagogical Unit comprises a secondary school for 1100 students between 7 and 17 years of age, a kindergarten for 250 children from 3 to 6 years of age, a training department for highly qualified teachers working in innovative Russian schools (twenty trainees), and a scientific laboratory. It also conducts retraining courses for teachers and leaders of innovative schools. The Scientific-pedagogical Unit involves 120 teachers and instructors, ten researchers, and more than forty service staff members. Together with the grades 1–11 students, these personnel are all citizens of the school and enjoy equal rights under the constitution and laws of the school.

We started developing school legislation four years ago. We were especially attentive to two guiding principles:

- All students and teachers are to be personally involved in the generation and adoption of the norms and rules of school life.
- The laws of the school are to be developed gradually as the school community confronts its emerging problems. Consistent with the emerging democratic ethos, problems are to be resolved only by democratic means.

As an example, four years ago we detected an increasing number of complaints made by younger children claiming maltreatment by older students. We asked students from grades 4–8 to write notes about any cases in which they thought their dignity had been disregarded. Many such cases were revealed. Together with a group of older students we prepared for a general meeting with students and teachers. Without mentioning the names of authors, these older students read the notes out loud. Insulting nicknames, slaps on the back of the head, swearing, toys taken away by senior students — all this was openly discussed and created general emotional pressure at the meeting. Responding to the question: 'What shall we do about it?' many suggested that those who had insulted or offended others should be held accountable for their actions. Then an *ad hoc* group was elected to draft a law protecting the honour and dignity of individuals. The draft was discussed repeatedly at the general meetings and in classrooms as well. Children introduced amendments to the text and interviewed the authors. This enabled them to experience democratic behaviour first-hand. The general meeting finally adopted the law. Under this law the citizens of the school elect by secret ballot the 'Court of Honour,' which consists of seven persons with students to outnumber teachers by one. The Court of Honour is an independent body whose decisions may be reversed only by the general meeting.

In the subsequent four years, the relationship between teachers and students has changed to reflect a mutual sense of dignity rather than authoritarianism. An analysis of this change in attitude reveals that in the beginning children did not believe that conflicts among teachers and students could be resolved legally. But within a year the senior students had begun to use the law, in the first instance mostly to settle their conflicts with teachers.

Open discussion of conflicts, public announcement of decisions and apologies by teachers and students for improper behaviour increased still further the authority of the Court of Honour. Students began to appeal to the court to redress instances of disrespect for their dignity on the part of their fellow students. Teachers also appealed to the Court often with complaints against students who undermined the working atmosphere in the classroom. We noticed recently that many appeals to the Court were coming from fourth and fifth graders complaining about each other. In response, members of the Court have had to explain more than once to those children that students should appeal to the Court only if they have failed to settle a problem between themselves.

In recent times appeals to the Court have become less frequent. This, however, does not signify that its authority has decreased. We believe that both students and adults have developed a strong conviction that, when necessary, they can use the school law for protection. The number of cases involving insults and fights has been drastically reduced, whereas cases of disrespect for personal dignity have become almost non-existent. The high esteem in which the Court is held can be confirmed by the fact that annual election campaigns are intensely contested. Ballot lists contain the names of up to forty candidates — the most trusted children and teachers in the school.

The success of our first law led us to articulate a number of ideas that our students and teachers had become aware of. These now amount to the basic values of the school. We decided to state formally the unwritten rules and norms and to draw up the principal law of the school — the constitution. In order to generate and enact the constitution, we elected a parliament made up of representatives from each of grades 6–11, departments and various interest groups. The major provisions of the constitution were discussed in the classrooms. The most time-consuming task was to formulate the principal objective of the school. It was evident that, on the one hand, this objective should bolster the spirit of individual freedom, and, on the other hand, reflect the specific character of the school as an educational institution. After various definitions were discussed at length in the parliament, school council and classrooms, students eventually formulated the final version, which was entered in the constitution as follows: 'To help an individual become a free personality.'

This objective determined the content of the subsequent sections of the constitution, 'Rights of the Citizens' and 'Obligations of All Citizens of the School Council'. The constitution stipulates a separation of power into three areas. These are:

- legislative power, represented by the general meeting and school referendum;

- executive power, represented by the school council; and
- judicial power, represented by the Court of Honour.

In recent years the citizens of the school have adopted another ten laws and statutes aimed at regulating school life in accord with democratic principles. These laws cover such areas as rights and vandalism; individual curriculum; referenda; upkeep of the school; and smoking. To enshrine the democratic norms of our life in legislation is undoubtedly very important. But the greatest pedagogical significance lies in the democratic process of discussion and adoption of these norms. It is the discussion, adoption and articulation of the norms that creates the feeling of participation and enables one to perceive oneself as a co-author of school norms. This also can motivate one to apply 'one's own' law in situations in which norms are being breached.

The experience of democracy is enhanced by the special course 'The Essentials of the State and Law', which is studied in the ninth grade (teenagers aged 14 and 15 years). The course involves the close study of three extensive subjects: 'The Rights of the Individual in a Democratic State', 'Study and Upgrade of School Legislation', and 'The Essentials of Civic, Labour and Criminal Law'.

The first subject begins with the identification of students' assumptions and the comparison of these assumptions with those implicit in the texts of the World Declaration of Human Rights and the Convention of Children's Rights. Students study and discuss the draft of the Russian constitution in terms of protection of human rights. After that students voluntarily split into groups and visit various administrative and state bodies, such as the mayor's office, district authorities, municipal authorities, ministries and departments. They also interview employees of these institutions about activities related to the observance of human rights. The next day is devoted to a briefing, where the students recount functions of different state institutions, answer questions and examine the activities of these bodies from the perspective of democratic norms. On the final day students participate in a game called 'parliamentary session'. During the game, in accordance with all the requisite procedures, students discuss and enact fundamental provisions of the would-be Russian constitution.

Democratic consciousness develops to a greater extent and proves to be more effective as children immerse themselves in the second subject: 'Study and Upgrade of School Legislation'. After they have discussed the objectives of the subject as a whole and its various activities, children on an individual basis carry out a test which is intended to reveal how well the laws of the school correspond to basic human rights. Disparities that have been detected during the test then become the subject for classroom discussion. Afterwards, students draw up a draft list of amendments. The next day interested students prepare and conduct public opinion polls to assess the efficiency of their school legislation. Some students go to the junior grades to explain the school laws and answer the children's questions. On the basis of the polls, interviews and group or individual discussions, students amend and supplement different articles of the school laws. Sometimes this may result in a new version of the law, or an entirely new law may appear. After they have discussed the drafts, students on a collective basis analyse what was achieved, reflecting on any changes in their perception of democracy, and on any changes in their personal attitudes which may have manifested themselves during the work. Final marks are determined according to students' self-evaluation. If the authors wish, the drafts and supplements to the laws elaborated during the classes may be submitted to the school council, after which they are discussed by all the citizens of the school. It should be noted that one of the most important pedagogical tasks is to create situations in which students can constantly review existing laws and rules, and introduce new articles and changes to those that have become outdated. The importance of such scrutiny is not so much in the enhancement of the norms and laws as in the development in each student and teacher of a feeling that they participate directly in the creation of the legitimate and democratic atmosphere of school life.

Observation of children's behaviour as well as analyses of situations and results of surveys show that children acquire and build upon the experience of democratic participation faster and more effectively than teachers. The reason is that teachers, having spent all their life under a totalitarian system, have come to accept that they simply transmit knowledge, rather than facilitate the process of acquiring 'living' knowledge, and are more likley to assume authoritarian conduct. Therefore, we have tried to create conditions which might lead to changes in the teachers' authoritarian consciousness, and their acceptance of more democratic principles of teacher behaviour.

Two conditions in particular are important. The first is to organize work jointly between teachers and researchers in order to restructure the content of education so as to shift teaching practice from mere dissemination of knowledge and checking that knowledge has been assimilated. Instead, the emphasis will be on teaching students to develop the skill to acquire knowledge independently. This would include:

- setting and solving problems;
- setting objectives;
- structuring one's own activity and reflecting upon it;
- acquiring necessary information; and
- understanding texts of different styles (fiction, reports, scientific texts), etc.

With this pedagogical approach, the content of the subject becomes less important for its own sake. It is used by the student to acquire the above-mentioned universal skills of learning. It is the process of developing, and mastering these general means of learning that constitutes the new content of education. In such a process teachers cannot claim to possess the absolute truth, and therefore their teaching style must become more democratic.

The second condition is associated with the fact that school administrators, in a democratic institution, should waive their exclusive rights to set aims, determine directions for development and assign tasks to teachers. Teachers at our Scientific-pedagogical Unit can initiate discussions about school problems and educational issues. Teachers voluntarily join together to form problem-solving groups to deal with such issues such as:

- development of the new content of education;
- transition from a system of grades to descriptive evaluation;
- changing the nature of the work of the class teacher; and
- generation of a new organizational form for teaching junior students etc.

Such groups may operate on a regular basis for a number of years or cease their work once the problem is solved. The number of group members may vary. If they wish, teachers can discuss the results of the group work or problems they encountered at the plenary session of all the pedagogues of the school. As a rule, the plenary session does not make decisions, but it ensures joint work aimed at solving the problem.

The annual three-day council of teachers offers teachers a great opportunity to participate in identifying objectives and determining directions for the development of the school. The council is held in a country retreat prior to the beginning of each academic year. During the first day, within the framework of the subject content of education, teaching techniques and continuity of programmes are reviewed. A report from each faculty is discussed during the plenary session, where teachers of different subjects also agree on possible cooperation throughout the year.

On the second day teachers set up new working groups made up of teachers of different subjects working in the same grades, or teachers of the same grade; or teachers working on a particular problem, for instance student self-evaluation, preparing creative works, helping students to develop communicative skills, etc. Decisions and new approaches elaborated in these groups also become the subject for discussions at the plenary session. The third day of the council of teachers is for organizing the work of the school in the new academic year. Here again, if they wish, teachers may work in groups: one to draw up a timetable for the school holidays, another to generate a plan of school activities, a third to draft a curriculum for the year, etc. These groups include the school administration and senior students, who work alongside teachers. Such diverse and intensive work prior to the beginning of the academic year not only encourages teachers to work creatively after long vacations, but also enables them to experience democratic discussions with colleagues on common issues. Teachers consequently regard the decisions worked out in the groups as their own and feel personal responsibility for their enactment.

It is important that the way in which the members of the council work together — that is, working in small groups, reforming groups depending on emerging tasks, reporting the results of the group work — provides teachers with an example of how similar kinds of work should be organized with children in classrooms.

Democratic mechanisms employed by school administrators in their relationships with teachers become really effective only if they take account of the different levels of acceptance of democratic professional values and behaviours of teachers. In relation to this, all members of the pedagogical staff can be divided hypothetically into groups for individual work.

The core of the pedagogical staff consists of teachers who, regardless of their age and years in the profession, share to a large extent the aims of the school. These teachers initiate various experiments and get actively involved in developing the new content of education. This group of teachers get together on a regular basis to discuss philosophical or psychological works of general interest. Management decisions are not made at such meetings, but the results of the discussions are submitted for consideration to the entire pedagogical staff and frequently serve as the foundation for subsequent management decisions of the school administration.

The second group includes teachers who are independently searching for their own conception of teaching and are thinking about how to make their subject a means for developing a child's personality. These teachers are often invited to present their thoughts at the plenary session of the entire teaching staff or at the meeting of one of the problem-solving groups. They are frequently helped by colleagues who are also interested in discussing similar problems and ideas. They often receive recommendations of books and articles of pedagogical interest along with offers to visit other schools in order to learn about the experiences of their colleagues.

The third group, teacher novices, includes not only newly appointed teachers, but also those who for some reason do not know or have not accepted the general philosophy of the school and have not yet formed an opinion on its traditions and democratic values. Such teachers are offered a clear-cut programme designed to help them examine other colleagues' expertise and to become acquainted with various scientific-methodological approaches that have been developed within the school. They also can attend special seminars conducted by leaders of the school, researchers and other teachers.

The composition and boundaries of the groups are flexible; teachers can leave and join groups as they wish. Such differentiated work with teachers makes it possible to take into account and further develop the democratic behaviour of teachers who, as a result of past experience are at different stages in their understanding and acceptance of general democratic values and practices. Similar groups can be identified among children as well. These groups will differ from each other in the scope of their democratic behaviour and experience, and in their different attitudes toward democratic values. Our objective for the future is to establish criteria for determining groups that will be best able to meet the needs of individual students and to define the conditions for the most effective acquisition of democratic values.

Conclusion

In our school we are attempting to establish the pedagogical conditions under which both children and teachers are able to acquire and reflect on the experience of democratic behaviour. Two guiding principles underpin our operations: first, that all teachers and students are to realize that they are all equally involved in the generation and adoption of the norms and rules of school life and second that the laws of the school should be developed gradually as the school community confronts its emerging problems. In our school, problems are to be resolved only be democratic means. In this way we try to put into practical application our ideals about democratic education and the democratic school.

Chapter 14

The Child's Road to Democracy

Isak D. Froumin

Fundamental Contradictions of Education

In modern Russian society, democracy is viewed as an exceptionally positive phenomenon. However, when striving to realize democratic values in all aspects of the education system considerable problems have emerged. No doubt, in every particular reform one can find errors and shortcomings, but in Russia it could be argued that reform leaders were not fully cognizant of democratic ideas and values, or were not quite committed to them. The danger in Russia today is that reforms, if poorly implemented, might lead to disillusionment with democratic values, and a rejection of democratic reforms in education may result. Indeed, a comparative analysis of education reforms both in the West and in the East reveals a cyclic recurrence of 'democratic enthusiasm' and bitter disappointment in its results, as observed by Kirst (1984).

In my opinion the problems encountered in the course of democratic reforms in Russia are due not to any intrinsic defects in democratic ideas but in the contradictory character of the idea of mass education. Inner contradictions and tensions of education are intensified and become urgent each time they are neglected in the course of education system reform.

The factors which create these contradictions and tensions are:

- The complexity of the education process. This is due to a diversity of realities existing in it. In any teaching and learning act, besides a simple transmission of information, there is a person-to-person relationship, or in other words, an interaction of different values.
- Adding a definite place and time to this act, we come to understand that the democratic-education processes operate at several levels. Here we should also speak of the complex interaction among various elements or structural levels of the educational system: the entire mass education system, the subsystem of state-supported education, a group of schools of a certain philosophy, a single school, a group of parents and students interacting in the process of schooling, an individual student. It is obvious that democratic change should entail change at all levels, otherwise the democratic reform may prove fictitious.

However, there remains a question: Which of the levels is of greatest importance for realization of democratic values?

- The competition between formal, non-formal and informal education. Hallak (1990) points out that non-formal education is a sort of reaction to the requirement for democratization of school education. But the problem of interaction between these domains still remains insufficiently explored with regard to democratization.

These factors emphasize the complex nature of the system in which democratic values are actualized. To all appearances, complete removal of the discord between elements of the system is impossible, as it is connected with the different roles each element plays in elimination of these contradictions.

Here we deal with the fundamental contradiction between the universal character of culture and education on the one hand, and unique human life on the other hand. In other words, there is a contradiction between the cultural and the spontaneous, the traditional and situational. Speaking of contradictions manifested by culture and education Leo Tolstoy expressed it aphoristically as follows: 'In culture man obliterates himself.' Rousseau also gave much attention to this contradiction in his first work, 'Did the Rise of Science and Art Provide for Improvement of Morals?' This contradiction manifests itself today in the fact that it is impossible to develop creativity or thinking technology; in the fact that children are not prepared fully to realize their aspirations for education, in the infinity of culture to be assimilated by a finite human being, in the discrepancy between the integrity of the individual and the fragmented nature of education. This contradiction is also reflected in the disparity between collective forms of teaching in modern education and the individual character of learning, teaching and development.

From the viewpoint of democratic values this contradiction creates a number of problems and tensions; for example:

- between the social demand for uniform educational policy for all social groups and children, and the individual right to choose a school and a curriculum;
- between uniform educational standards and teaching techniques and the child's personality, and specific style of learning and development;
- between the equal right to education of every child and basic (biologically and socially conditioned) inequality of children; and
- between the two functions of education, i.e., education as a means of social and economic development, and education as an expression of the values of parents, children, and population groups.

The contradiction between culture and spontaneity concerns not only students but teachers as well. Adherent to culture, they still remain individuals and therefore they do not merely transmit information. It is therefore impossible to evaluate with any degree of precision the results of teachers' work and the causes of their dissatisfaction with rigid methods and teaching techniques. In terms of democratization this contradiction gives rise to:

- the conflict between teachers' attempts to establish a true partnership with pupils and the inequality of their status;
- the discrepancy between the social demand for uniformity of all teachers or for a school as a socially constructed institution which embodies the particular values and techniques of individual teachers; and
- the conflict between the equal rights of teachers who work with the same group of students.

All the above contradictions, conflicts and discrepancies are inherent in education in general, but they become most acute in mass school education and in the controversy between systemically imposed and free education.

Problems of Free Education

Ideas of freedom and the moral autonomy of children have been the most popular issues for the educationists of this century. Children's rights and the value of children's lives have been discussed by Dewey, Montessori, Steiner and many others. Rousseau's ideas about natural and free child raising have been revived and implemented. In his book *Emile*, Rousseau criticized authoritarian child raising and highlighted natural interest as a source of self-education. This position caused him some difficulty as he had to support some 'natural' mechanisms and methods of developing moral consciousness and achieving a level of social education in a free child's life. By such mechanisms, the child completed the task for the pedagogue. In contrast to Komensky, he recognized that the right word said to a child doesn't lead to the right thought or the right action. In this sense he didn't support a direct 'teaching freedom', but he postulated that freedom makes an individual free.

In spite of its attractiveness, Rousseau's ideal of natural pedagogy didn't become a turning point in school history in Russia. This was due to some objective tensions in its implementation. Can children be free if they need our help? Should a pedagogue refuse to help to a child who is in a predicament but doesn't ask for help? What does 'equality' mean for a weak and unskilled child? Rousseau and his followers did not answer these questions in a way that was satisfactory for Russian pedagogues seeking a way forward.

Another contribution to free pedagogy, though not quite as well known in the western world, was by the famous Russian writer Leo Tolstoy. 'Freedom is a necessary condition for any true education,' claimed Tolstoy, as he protested against any punishment and reward in education. Tolstoy organized an experimental school and had a lot of followers. But his network of schools didn't expand in Russia as they didn't coincide with the then current idea of systematic knowledge and rigid cultural norms.

After the October Revolution of 1917, Gessen, a remarkable Russian philosopher, published a voluminous work *Principles of Pedagogy* (Gessen, 1922), in which he followed the best traditions of Russian philosophy. In that work the seeming contradiction between freedom and culture was chosen as the starting point for his analysis. Criticizing the simplified opposition freedom–compulsion he wrote, 'Both Rousseau and Tolstoy considered freedom and compulsion to be facts of bringing up. Consequently they developed a negative concept of freedom being the absence of compulsion, i.e., elimination of compulsion is equivalent to a triumph of freedom. This is the point at which the alternative emerges — freedom or compulsion. For, understood as mere facts or immutabilities, they do annihilate one another and cannot coexist' (Gessen, 1922).

Historically, there are two schools of thought in the debate on free education in Russia. The first opposes the ideal of free education and the priorities of democratic change. For example, any religious educational system emphasizes, not democratic, but religious values. From the viewpoint of programmed instruction the aims of democratic education are not central. This, of course does not mean that any traditional form of instruction, say, in mathematics or biology, is basically anti-democratic or does not contribute to the formation of democratic values and aims in pupils. The so-called specialized schools with an extended curriculum in physics and mathematics which used to be popular in the Soviet period are proof of this. The entire atmosphere in such schools was much more democratic than in regular schools, and the students were more independent in their judgments. Still, the problem of a system of values (democratic values in particular) for school children has not yet been given much attention in traditional pedagogic systems, and no attempts to reveal the pedagogic mechanisms of it have been made so far. Many prominent Soviet educationalists refused to discuss the problems of democratic values in education in order to avoid conflict with the ruling totalitarian ideology; they declared that the school's aim was to provide for instruction in subjects, not to bring up the child. In this connection, a comparison of different instructional methods is possible with regard to their effects on upbringing and the acquisition of a value system. We have reason to believe that such pedagogic systems as the so-called 'developing education' by Davydov (Davydov, 1988) or 'teaching through a cultured dialogue' by Bitler have considerable potential for value-oriented education.

The second school of thought which follows from totalitarian ideology, considers democratic values to be false and unrealistic. Consequently, the school wouldn't develop them. In the Soviet system of education there was a dictatorship of communist ideology. Soviet educational leaders tried to make education value-orientated, in order to transmit the values of group authority and ideological subordination to the Communist Party through school subjects, extra-curricular activities and child organizations.

During every lesson a teacher was required, not only to convey certain information, but also to impart to children officially recognized values. Even texts of problems in physics and mathematics reflected achievements of Soviet workers and peasants. Meanwhile, traditional or democratic values were either ignored or criticized. So it was only natural that Soviet teenagers were offered, as a role model, the boy who had betrayed his own father to the hands of KGB. According to official ideology, the most serious danger was posed by the people with independent judgment. That is why one of the most important norms for child organizations which involved 100 per cent of children was 'unconditional subordination of minority to majority'. Old Soviet textbooks on pedagogy recorded direct statements that respect for an individual was of minor importance, that the interests of society were more important than those of the individual (society meant communist oligarchy). A good example of this was the special greeting of secondary-school pupils who were members of a child political organization. They held a hand above their head to symbolize that public interests are of higher importance than those of an individual. Even in recent textbooks on pedagogy there are references to 'democratic upbringing' in the sense of collectivism.

For such an educational system the ideas and experience of free education are false and useless. Nevertheless, for our purposes it would be useful to consider free and communist education as two different types of value-oriented education. The comparatively high efficiency of communist methods of upbringing proves that value-oriented education is of more limiting and regulating character than traditional scientific education, and that value-orientated education requires subtler and more integrated techniques. For this reason, many ideas and methods of communist upbringing espoused by Soviet pedagogues (for example, Makarenko) are being used in the West or by contemporary democratic pedagogues in Russia (see the chapters by Tubelsky and Gazman in this book). But it would be wrong to suppose that all those who criticize free education are supporters of communist totalitarian education.

There is one further criticism of free education made by democrats. Why do many good pedagogues who share democratic values not support the ideas of A.S. Neill or Rousseau? Experience of free schools shows that in gaining freedom we lose positive knowledge. Soviet school children normally demonstrate better results in mathematics and science than pupils from traditionally democratic school systems. It is of interest to note that in response to this criticism, the free education system in the course of its history has instituted a number of effective teaching techniques (the projects method, for example) which later on were successfully adopted by the traditional school. Still the problem of effectiveness and evaluation of success in the free school remains unsolved. This criticism is correct, as it deals with the fundamental contradiction between culture and the individual mentioned above. However, the positions of the critics and those of the criticized can be brought closer together in the discussion on the nature of knowledge conveyed through education.

Criticism of free education from an ethical standpoint is of a different character. Does the refusal to govern a child mean a refusal to take care of it? What kind of adult shall we get, a free individual or a barbarian? 'Isn't abolition of compulsion merely a substitution of one kind of compulsion for another one, and a stronger one, if freedom is understood as an individual's originality but not as tyranny of action?' (Gessen, 1922). We don't think this criticism is connected with different concepts of knowledge or democracy, but with different approaches to the child and childhood. In what way do such approaches disagree with Dewey if they share his understanding of the role of school in the upbringing of a citizen in a democratic society? Arguments that there is no systematic knowledge, or that pupils of free schools have problems with social adaptation, are arguments about the consequences. In fact, the roots of this disagreement are in the different approaches to a child. Are children members of a democratic community? Should they be treated according to democratic laws? Can a child as a free individual cooperate with adults? Are democratic values inherent? Maybe they develop gradually, and by age 7–10 a child is 'ready' to live in a 'democratic school'.

A simple and unambiguous answer to the above questions given by the followers of Rousseau and Tolstoy reflects their wish to find a pedagogical 'philosophical touchstone' valid for any situation. This is typical of modern Russian education. Freed from totalitarian ideology, it turned to another extreme — free school and anarchy in school education (Kerr, 1989). An attempt has been made to directly transfer certain positive facts of adult life into children's lives, although this results in the loss of the school's basic features as an institution where children grow up, change and mature. In fact, there is no one best way of educating. For school, as a social institution, suffers from inner antagonisms. This is the result of an artificial gap in the common natural life of children and adults. School became a place without freedom and independence for the child because of the initial unequal power relationship between teacher and students, and the limiting character of culture. The system of mass public-school education with its standard programmes and methods of teaching seems to stand against human nature. But the unlucky experience of 'more perfect' systems speaks for its stability. Highly relevant also is the stability of the goal of gradual socialization of the child.

Problems in school life and 'teaching' democracy should not be acknowledged only in an abstract way, but also in the practical sense of school types according to the age of students. The following questions arise:

- What democratic values can be assimilated in school life for different development stages, and to what degree?
- In what way does education influence the development of these values?

The dynamic and process-like character of the questions should be emphasized. A fundamental hypothesis is the assumption of a gradual change in a child's position and value mindset in the process of school education. Then the task of a pedagogue is to stimulate and enable this process to develop through special forms of teaching suitable for each stage of development, using a new content of education dependent on age. This hypothesis was formulated by Russian psychologists Vygotsky (1978), Davydov (1988), and Elkonin (1972).

In my opinion, fundamental democratic values include individual freedom and responsibility for actions. The primary focus is on the dynamic development and implementation of these values. We are to understand what a 'child's freedom' means for every development stage. What mechanisms are responsible for children's enjoying their rights as responsible individuals? How do we ensure that they develop the values of their own freedom and those of life among free individuals?

The Crisis of Childhood and Problems of the Development of an Individual

Modern development psychology considers childhood an historical phenomenon. Anthropology and social anthropology point out to its dependence on a social-cultural situation. The structure, content and the duration of childhood today differ greatly from those in traditional society. According to Mead (1928), Kon (1988), Elkonin (1984) and Gulliver (1968), in traditional society children were quite an isolated group, with no rights similar to those of adults but a certain degree of freedom inside their own group. Moral problems, human relations and social-group interrelations were solved by adults. Obtaining the status of an adult was accompanied by a special procedure of initiation.

Initiation still remains the most stable phenomenon in human history. New periods in a child's life require special new transition procedures. The transition implies a greater emancipation of a child on the one hand, and the establishment of a deeper and more responsible relationship with adults on the other. This change in the child's position is due to two factors: differences in the way of life and activities of different age groups, and the child's rejection of childhood. Any transition from one stage of development to another is related to new potentials, new degrees of freedom and new responsibilities. According to Vygotsky, the rejection of childhood was related to the appearance of ideal form — the image of future adulthood. Growing up was determined by the presence of this image of the whole human age scale. Coming of age was stimulated by special procedures along the whole age scale.

A transition procedure (initiation) marked a new school situation in a child's development; it symbolically crowned the previous stage of life and opened a new one. An important factor in the process of growing up was the community of children of the same age with which a child could identify. At every new stage this community visibly changed. Its composition, age markers, myths, and rituals changed. The key element of every transformation of a community of children of the same age was the selection accompanying each initiation. Up until the early twentieth century, selection and separation into groups in accordance with the level of maturity was done at the very beginning of schooling.

School, in a sense, was outside the process of growing up. Children came to school to learn because such was the 'ideal form' of their growing up. School reflected a 'natural' age hierarchy which developed in the family. From that came the idea that the older have more rights. It was essential that at every transition stage a selection was made with respect to the education to be received. Not all children were transferred to the next stage, and the procedure had all the characteristics of initiation. But in modern society the traditional structures and markers of coming of age have disappeared. There are a few examples of such changes (Mead, 1970). Radical changes in the family include:

- disappearance of families consisting of several generations; increase in the number of families with one parent, and in the number of working mothers;
- alienation of children from the labour of adults;
- changes in conditions of life which take place more quickly than the change of generations; and
- a long period of responsibility-free childhood (up to ages 10–12) for the majority of children.

With regard to the last point, we should emphasize that in recent decades schooling has become considerably longer. Within an 11–12 year period of schooling the social situation for a child remains unchanged. Students aren't forced to take responsibility for the choices they make. All this leads to an increase in the alienation of the generations. A number of Russian psychologists call this phenomenon 'crisis of childhood'.

One of the features of this crisis is infantilism — absence of the desire to mature, a negative attitude towards the adult world and traditional values. Research shows that most Russian senior-school students use negative, scornful terms to describe adults — parents and teachers included.

School and the Crisis of Childhood

How has the school in Russia responded to infantilism and the crisis of childhood? On the one hand, it gave children freedom, eliminating some limitations, competition and difficulties in learning, but on the other preserving the existing social unequality. Children received rights equal to adults' rights without taking additional responsibility. That is, the school ignored the problems of growing up. The 'ideal form' was not replaced by anything else, and the child lost the chance to analyse the fundamental values of the adult community, including freedom and responsibility.

It is necessary to mention here the age structure of Russian schools. Unlike most developed countries, isolated elementary and intermediate schools were practically unknown in Russia. Up to the present, almost all schools in Russia have been comprehensive, i.e., children from 7 to 17 study under one roof, often with the same teachers. During all these years, teaching styles, methods of evaluation and the teacher–pupil relationships remain unchanged. Teaching techniques hardly altered — same types of problems to be solved, same types of exercises to be done. And almost all schools in Russia were of the same sort. It meant that there was no selection, no differentiation and no need to make any choices during at least the first eight years. For this reason, most pupils aged 11 to 13 take the maturing process as something natural, something which does not require any effort on their part: 'I'll grow bigger and become an adult.' Only political children's organizations, which involved all children of a particular age, worked with age groups — from 7 to 10 (Young Octobrists), from 11 to 13 (Young Pioneers), and from 14 (Komsomolists).

This crisis of childhood is acute for Russia as it is experiencing a transitional period now. Generational antagonism is destructive. In the eyes of Russian children, the lives of the older generation have proved to be a failure, as well as useless. In many Russian families, children have a better grasp of the new social and economic situation. This means that the experience of the older generations, culture that is transmitted through education, has lost its significance for children. In this context, freedom is understood as individualism and social responsibility as totalitarianism.

Under these circumstances schools are in a difficult situation: out-of-school mechanisms providing for the development of the adult's position have disappeared. Those few mechanisms of growing up, formerly provided by the school, have also disappeared. It is obvious that school has been alienated from the process of developing values of freedom and independence. This situation is most unfavourable for learning. The old authoritarian style has become ineffective, whereas a democratic style requires children to have elementary concepts of democracy. So the school is forced to reconsider ways of developing the values of freedom and responsibility.

Attempts were made to transfer these values through special democracy classes, or courses such as 'Individual and society'. These were ineffective, as they were presented by adults who didn't incorporate democratic values in their pedagogical activity. It is of interest to note that a lot of western experts claiming to be 'teachers of democracy' have visited Russian recently. They lecture on democratic norms and distribute printed matter but the effect (especially with children) is insignificant. And this is quite understandable, as the approach is authoritarian and alien to them. Another approach is to incorporate democratic forms of social organization into the children's community: councils, parliament, court and even police.

School Contributions to Growing Up

We propose that a necessary condition for developing democratic values in school is the mechanisms of growing up. A key question is a problem of 'ideal form', and the image of adults which could be visualized by children as their future. We consider it important that democratic values — freedom and responsibility — be reflected in that image. But this means that independence and freedom, on the one hand, and responsibility and self-limitation, on the other, must be recognized as the essence of growing up.

We suggest a schooling prototype which consists of three areas: one for junior-school children, one for teenagers and one for youths. Important conditions for organizing these areas are:

- the provision of specific forms and content of education for each development stage;
- the provision of change in the conditions and content of children's lives towards more responsibility and independence; and
- the organization of meetings of school children of various ages with adults to develop a concept of adulthood and a way to achieve it.

This prototype covers all spheres of school life from school management to sports. This prototype isn't a model, but rather an approach that will enable a certain school in a certain situation to find its own way (Froumin and Elkonin, 1993).

At present, many schools in Russia are using this approach, i.e., pedagogical mechanisms of growing up. There is a variety of new pedagogical forms and ideas. The characteristics of the developmental stages determine the various forms of teaching. Traditional classes are good for primary-school pupils, laboratory classes and seminars for teenagers. With age, the forms of teaching become freer and require more independent work. A vivid example is the system of evaluation. It changes from marks in elementary school to a system of credits later. Evaluation by marks is a rigid system but it allows a pupil to 'improve' . The system of credits allows a student to plan work, but it requires more responsibility and it is more difficult to correct a mistake.

Choice is essential. Traditionally, freedom of choice is supposed to be a value. But keeping the child in mind we must ask the question: Can he or she make a choice? Does he or she possess certain intellectual capacities for this? Often the choice of subjects and levels of education by school students is formal and ineffective. What is important is the individual's attitude to choice: whether making a choice is perceived as a necessary, significant and desirable act, or not. In view of the latter we find it is doubtful whether primary students could choose subjects for learning at their schooling level.

To overcome this, an approach based on age characteristics gives a range of choice, i.e., it extends the spheres and the possibilities of choice. The pedagogue's task is to develop the skills of analysis, reflection and decision-making

— all the factors that make people aware of the choice they make, and the feeling of responsibility for it. A new domain in which to make a choice, and the process of acquiring this domain, turn into an important procedure for coming of age, and can even constitute a sort of initiation.

In elementary school, specially organized classes help children to overcome their egocentrism (described by Piaget and Kohlberg), and to develop the ability to see different viewpoints. Of special interest is the dynamic of the 'political and legislative' spheres of school life. Primary-school children are involved in decision-making concerning school life: they discuss a working plan of the school, and the main documents regulating school life are explained to them, including those about the school–parent relationship.

Teenagers may participate in social campaigns, for example, elections to the school council. But they cannot be elected. They have a course on legislature and conflict situations. They study the documents which regulate their behaviour and participate in discussions. Youths may be elected to the school council and participate in decision-making directly. But in order to enter senior school they must sign a legal document — an agreement with the school principal. And this implies personal responsibility. They are also involved in working out normative school documents.

The most important element of the above approach is the organization of inter-generation meetings. These could involve direct demonstration, when elementary-school children visit high school, or they could be some sort of cooperation, such as school theatre. One of the most original ideas is to involve teenagers and youths in pedagogical work with small children, as consultants, circle leaders, teacher assistants. All those things help school children to identify their position in the age hierarchy, to get a better view of both the nearest and remote prospects, to form their own image of adulthood.

A special pedagogical task is the organization of the transition from one stage of development to another. This includes: analysis of past experience and the changes which take place; creation of an image of a future life and preparation for it; testing to indicate whether a pupil is ready to move up the age scale.

Conclusion

The experience of Russian schools described above is aimed at the restoration of out-of-school mechanisms of growing up. It is closely related to the characteristics of the social situation in modern Russia. However, some approaches are similar to those taken by western pedagogues. These approaches aim to solve the tension between striving to give a child adult rights and freedom, and the child's lack of opportunity to exercise them. This dynamic age approach to the forms and content of education is important for the formation of a new adult generation which will adopt the values of freedom and responsibility.

References

CHAPMAN, J.D. (1990) *School-Based Decision-Making and Management*, London, Falmer Press.

DAVYDOV, V.V. (1988) 'Problems of developmental teaching: The experience of theoretical and experimental physicological research', *Soviet Education*, 30, pp. 8–10.

DEWEY, J. (1966) *Democracy and Education*, New York, The Free Press.

ELKONIN, D.B. (1972) 'Toward the problem of stages of the mental development of the child', *Soviet Psychology*, 5, 3.

ELKONIN, D.B. (1984) *Psychology of Play*, New York, London.

FROUMIN, I.D. and ELKONIN, B.D. (1993) 'Space of education as a space of maturing', *Voprosy Psychologii*, 1, pp. 16–23.

GESSEN, S.I. (1922) *Foundations of Pedagogy*, Berlin, Slovo.

GULLIVER, P.H. (1968) 'Age differentation', *International Encyclopedia of the Social Sciences*, New York.

HALLAK, J. (1990) *Investigation of Non-formal Education*, UNESCO, Paris.

KERR, S.T. (1989) 'Reform in Soviet and American Education: Parallels and Contrasts', *Phi Delta Kappan*, 71, pp. 19–28.

KIRST, M. (1984) *Who Controls Our Schools?* New York.

KON, I.S. (1988) *Rbyonok i obshestvo* (Child and Society), Moscow, Nayka Press.

MEAD, M. (1928) *Coming of Age in Samoa*, New York, Morrow.

MEAD, M. (1970) *Culture and Commitment: A Study of the General Gap*, New York, Natural History Press.

SOVIET EDUCATION (1989) *Democratization of the individual* Report of the second meeting of experimental teachers, 31, 5, pp. 80–95.

VYGOTSKY, L.S. (1978) *Mind in Society: The Development of Higher Psychological Processes*, Cambridge, Harvard University Press.

WHITTAKER, C.H. (1985) *The Origins of Modern Russian Education*, De Kalb, Northern Illinois University Press.

Appendix 1

The Russian Federation State System of Education

The state educational system of the Russian Federation includes preschool education, general secondary education, general professional education, higher education, postgraduate education and personnel training systems. There also exist the systems of federal childhood support, adult (evening) education and non-school and supplementary education.

The Preschool Education System

Network (institutions)	87,100
Number of children	9,634,700 (45%)
in town	7,376,700
in the country	2,258,000
Staff (administration included)	968,300

The General Secondary Education System

Network (institutions)	65,500
Number of children	20,000,000
in town	14,300,000
in the country	5,700,000
Staff (administration included)	1,244,300

The Adult (Evening) Education System

Network (institutions)	2,700
Number of students	500,000
Staff (administration included)	70,000

The General Professional Education System

Network (institutions)	4,350
Number of workers trained (per year)	1,700,000
Staff (administration included)	183,750

The Higher Education System (for Education only)

Network (teacher-training colleges)	97
Number of students entering (per year)	67,200

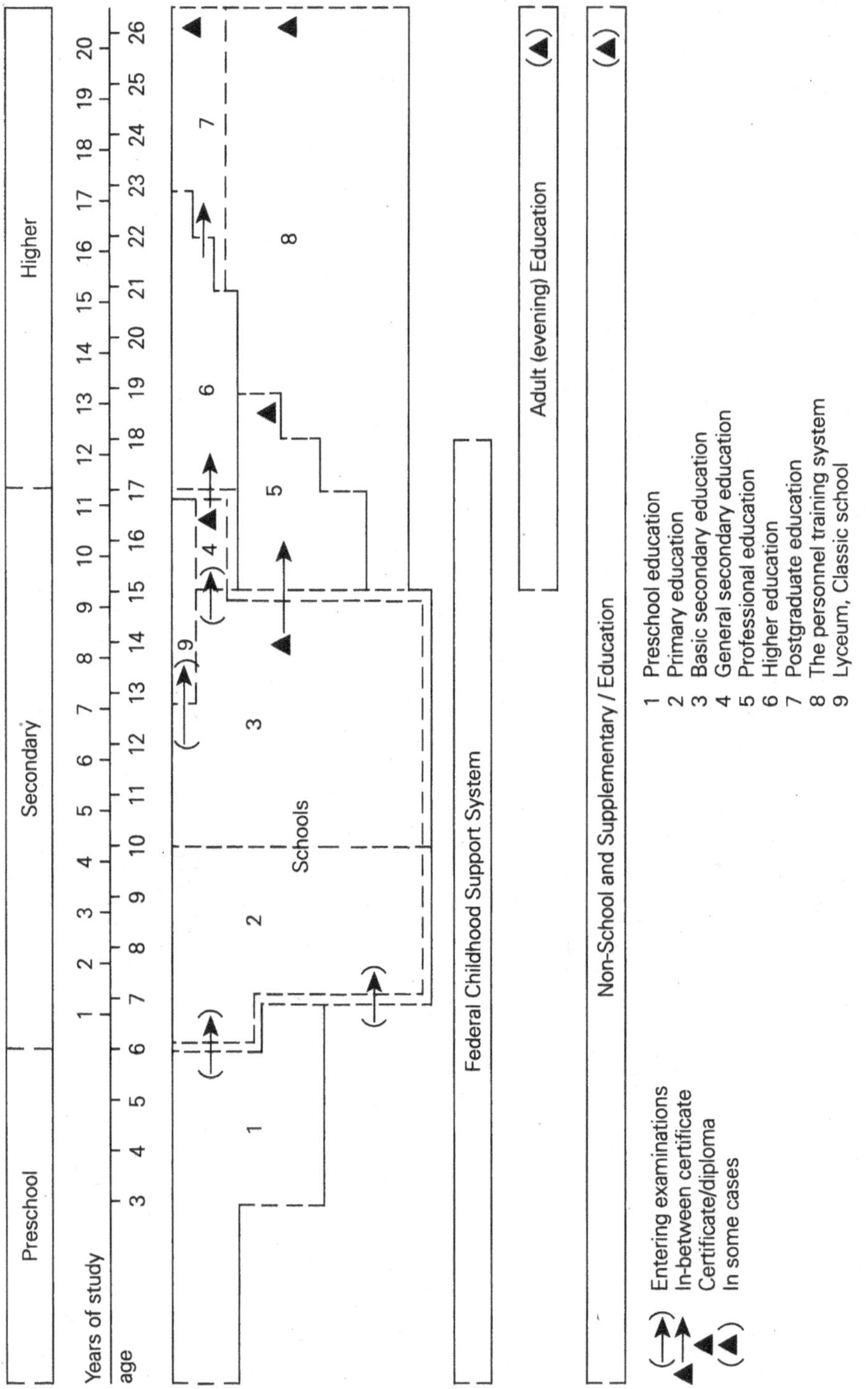

Russian Federation State System of Education

Appendix 2

The System of Education Management in Russia

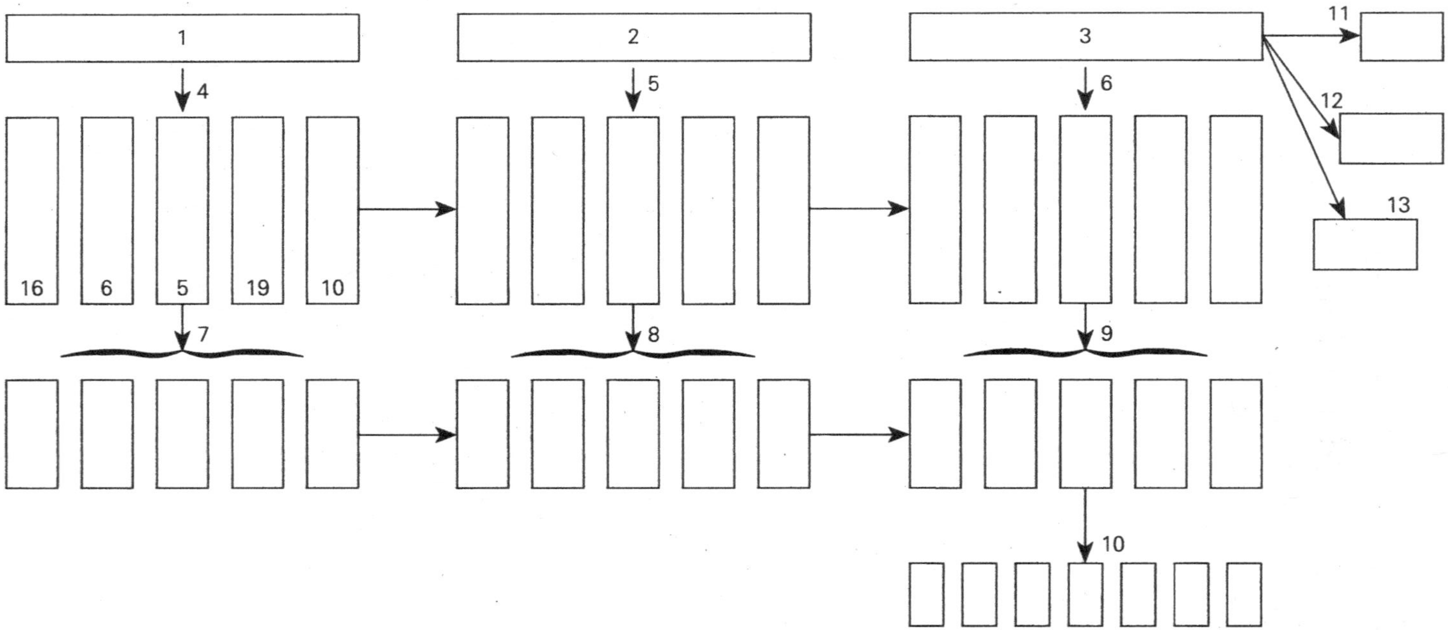

1 The Supreme Council (Parliament) of the RSFSR
2 The Council of Ministers (Government) of the RSFSR
3 The Ministry of Education of the RSFSR
4 The Council of the territory, region
5 The Executive Committee of the territory, region
7 The Council of the town, district
8 The Executive Committee of the town, district

6,9 People's Education Management Board
10 Schools
11 The Institute of Pedagogical Researchers
12 The Pedagogical Institute
13 In-service Teacher Training Institute

The System of Education Management in Russia

Appendix 3

Russian State System of Public Education

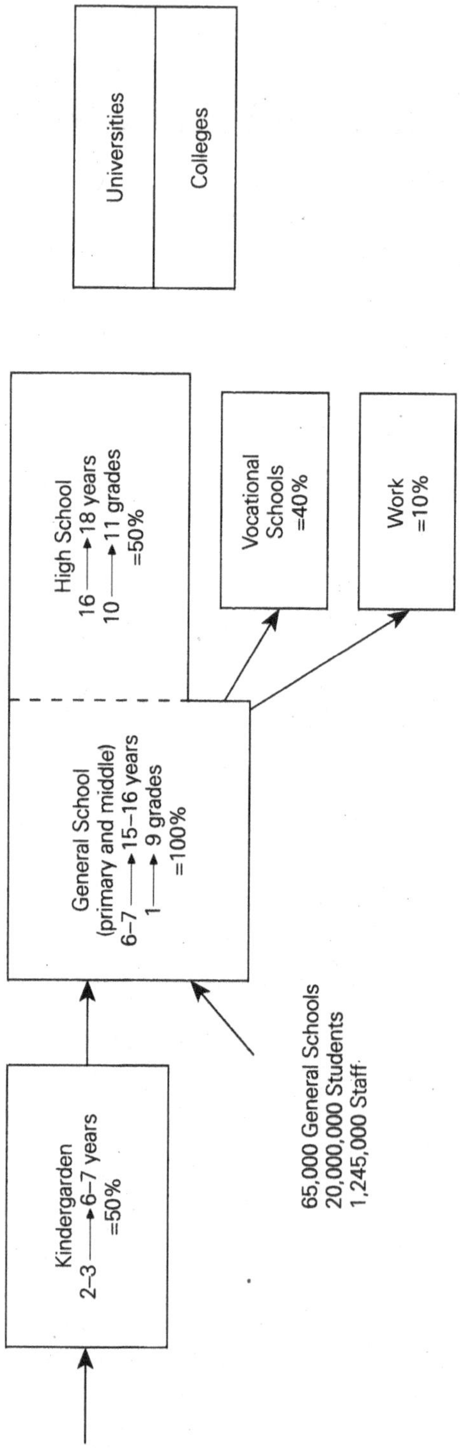

Russian State System of Public Education

List of Contributors

Alexander I. Adamsky is the head of the Centre for Social-pedagogical Planning 'Eureka' — one of the first Russian independent organizations concerned with teacher training. A well-known educational journalist, Mr Adamsky was one of the leaders of the public movement for democratization in education at the end of the 1980s.

David N. Aspin is professor in the School of Graduate Studies, Faculty of Education, Monash University. He has recently completed a five-year term as Dean of the Faculty of Education at Monash University. Before coming to Australia in 1988, Professor Aspin held for nine years the Chair of Philosophy in Education at King's College in the University of London. His interests include the theory of knowledge, ethics and the philosophy of mind.

Ian Birch is an associate professor in education at The University of Western Australia. His central research and teaching interest is in the law and education.

Judith D. Chapman is professor of education in the Graduate School of Education, The University of Western Australia. She was previously director of the School Decision Making and Management Centre in the Faculty of Education at Monash University. She has undertaken international work in the field of educational policy and administration on behalf of OECD, UNESCO and the World Bank. Her fields of interest include the effectiveness of schooling and of educational resource management, decentralization and devolution, and institutional management.

Clive Dimmock is senior lecturer in Educational Management at The University of Western Australia. His research interests focus on restructuring, school effectiveness and school improvement and principals' leadership.

Edward D. Dneprov was the Minister of Education of the Russian Federation from 1989 till 1992. He was also counsellor to the President of the Russian Federation. Now he works in the Russian Academy of Education and for a number of international agencies and foundations.

Jeffrey F. Dunstan served for forty years with the Ministry of Education in Victoria including significant periods as acting chief general manager. Subsequently he has undertaken key roles in the delivery of management programmes with Indonesia, as well as university lecturing. Dr Dunstan has been awarded the Public Service Medal and the Sir James Darling Medal for services to Victorian education.

Isak D. Froumin is the director of the Research Institute of Experimental Pedagogy of Russian Academy of Education with the University Laboratory School 'Univers'. He is associate professor of the Department of Education of Krasnoyarsk State University.

Oleg Gazman was counsellor to the Russian Minister of Education in 1991. He is a specialist in values education and the author of a number of books and many papers. He is now head of the research division on education and values of the Russian Academy of Education.

Michael Herriman is senior lecturer in education and director of the Centre for English as a Second Language at the University of Western Australia. He has had several fellowships in Russia and has published widely in the areas of literacy, language awareness and English language testing.

Yelena A. Lenskaya is the head of the Department of International Co-operation of the Ministry of Education of Russian Federation. She is also head of the Russian Research Laboratory on Comparative Education.

Brian Spicer is senior lecturer in the School of Graduate Studies in the Faculty of Education at Monash University. He is a specialist in resource management, management of curriculum, and geography in education. He is currently working as a consultant in Pakistan and has previously undertaken work in Indonesia on behalf of IDP and the World Bank.

Yevgenii V. Tkachenko is a professor of chemistry and was previously rektor of the Pedagogical University of Yecaterinburg. He is also well-known in the field of vocational education. He moved to Moscow in 1992 to assume the position of first deputy of the Ministry of Education. He was appointed Minister of Education of the Russian Federation in 1993.

Alexander M. Tubelsky is the principal of the Centre of Experimental Pedagogics 'School of Self-Identity' (Moscow Experimental School 734) which is a well-known Russian school and research laboratory. He is a specialist in moral education and the area of children's group activity. He is the president of the Russian Association for Innovative Schools.

Index